The Role of the Reader

Advances in Semiotics

General Editor, Thomas A. Sebeok

The Role of the Reader

Explorations in the Semiotics of Texts

UMBERTO ECO

INDIANA UNIVERSITY PRESS
Bloomington

First Midland Book Edition 1984

Copyright © 1979 by Umberto Eco

Manufactured in the United States of America

Library of Congress Cataloging in Publication Data

Eco, Umberto.
    The role of the reader.

    (Advances in semiotics)
    Bibliography: p.
    Includes index.
    1.   Semiotics—Addresses, essays, lectures.
    2.   Discourse analysis—Addresses, essays, lectures.
    I.   Title.   II.   Series.
    P99.E28   801'.95   78–18299
    ISBN 0–253–11139–0   5 6 8 7

Contents

Preface

Six of the nine essays published in this book were written between 1959 and 1971. "The Poetics of the Open Work" (Chapter 1) and "The Myth of Superman" (Chapter 4)—written respectively in 1959 and in 1962, before I fully developed my semiotic approach—represent two opposing aspects of my interest in the dialectic between 'open' and 'closed' texts. The introductory essay of this book makes clear what I mean *today* by such a categorial polarity and how I see it as a special case of a more general semiotic phenomenon: the cooperative role of the addressee in interpreting messages.

"The Poetics of the Open Work" deals with various sorts of texts, but all the other essays collected here concern verbal texts. "The Semantics of Metaphor" (Chapter 2) and "On the Possibility of Generating Aesthetic Messages in an Edenic Language" (Chapter 3)—both of 1971—examine how the procedures of aesthetic manipulation of language produce the interpretive cooperation of the addressee. The two essays on the popular novel, "Rhetoric and Ideology in Sue's *Les Mystères de Paris*" (Chapter 5) and "Narrative Structures in Fleming" (Chapter 6)—both of 1965—deal, as does the essay on Superman, with texts which aim at producing univocal effects and which *seem* not to call for cooperative activity on the part of the reader. However, I realize today, after having developed a general semiotic framework in my book *A Theory of Semiotics* (1976), that even these essays are dominated by the problem of the role of the reader in interpreting texts.

From such a perspective the essay in Peirce and contemporary semantics (Chapter 7), written in 1976, offers many clues for establishing a richer theoretical background for the concept of interpretative cooperation.

In *"Lector in Fabula*: Pragmatic Strategy in a Metanarrative Text" (Chapter 8), written at the end of 1977 for this book, I try to connect the modalities of textual interpretation with the problem of possible worlds.

To make clear (to myself as well as to my readers) the constancy of the theme of interpretative cooperation in the essays collected here, I have written the introductory essay, "The Role of the Reader." Here the textual problems approached in the course of the earlier essays are viewed in connection with the present state of the art—which is taken fully into account only in *"Lector in Fabula."* It might be argued that the analyses made between 1959 and 1971 should be rewritten in a more up-to-date jargon. But afterwit is everybody's wit; it is better that the earlier essays remain as witnesses to a constant exploration into textuality made during twenty years of prehistorical attempts. The few

[vii]

cuts and the slight changes in technical terminology these essays have undergone are only cosmetics applied to achieve homogeneous translation and do not affect their original structures.

Perhaps "The Role of the Reader" raises a number of questions which the previous research does not answer satisfactorily. But the state of the art (text semiotics, having grown up incredibly during the last decade, has reached a dreadful level of sophistication) obliges me not to conceal a number of problems—even as they remain unresolved. Many of the present text theories are still heuristic networks full of components represented by mere 'black boxes'. In "The Role of the Reader" I also deal with some black boxes. The earlier analyses deal only with boxes I was able to fill up—even though without appealing formalizations. It goes without saying that the role of the reader of this book is to open and to overfill (by further research) all the boxes that my essays have necessarily left inviolate.

The Role of the Reader

INTRODUCTION

The Role of the Reader

0.1. How to produce texts by reading them

0.1.1. The text and its interpreter

The very existence of texts that can not only be freely interpreted but also cooperatively generated by the addressee (the 'original' text constituting a flexible *type* of which many *tokens* can be legitimately realized) posits the problem of a rather peculiar strategy of communication based upon a flexible system of signification. "The Poetics of the Open Work" (1959)[1] was already haunted by the idea of unlimited semiosis that I later borrowed from Peirce and that constitutes the philosophical scaffolding of *A Theory of Semiotics* (1976) (hereafter *Theory*). But at the same time, "The Poetics of the Open Work" was presupposing a problem of pragmatics.[2] An 'open' text cannot be described as a communicative strategy if the role of its addressee (the reader, in the case of verbal texts) has not been envisaged at the moment of its generation *qua* text. An open text is a paramount instance of a syntactic-semantico-pragmatic device whose foreseen interpretation is a part of its generative process.

When "The Poetics of the Open Work" appeared in 1965 in French as the first chapter of my book *L'oeuvre ouverte*,[3] in a structuralistically oriented milieu, the idea of taking into account the role of the addressee looked like a disturbing intrusion, disquietingly jeopardizing the notion of a semiotic texture to be analyzed in itself and for the sake of itself. In 1967, discussing structuralism and literary criticism with an Italian interviewer, Claude Lévi-Strauss said that he could not accept the perspective of *L'oeuvre ouverte* because a work of art "is an object endowed with precise properties, that must be analytically isolated, and this work can be entirely defined on the grounds of such properties. When Jakobson

[3]

and myself tried to make a structural analysis of a Baudelaire sonnet, we did not approach it as an 'open work' in which we could find everything that has been filled in by the following epochs; we approached it as an object which, once created, had the stiffness—so to speak—of a crystal; we confined ourselves to bringing into evidence these properties."[4]

It is not necessary to quote Jakobson (1958) and his well-known theory of the functions of language to remind ourselves that, even from a structuralistic point of view, such categories as sender, addressee, and context are indispensable to the understanding of every act of communication. It is enough to consider two points (picked almost at random) from the analysis of Baudelaire's "Les Chats" to understand the role of the reader in the poetic strategy of that sonnet: "Les chats . . . ne figurent en nom dans le texte qu'une seule fois . . . dès le troisième vers, les chats deviennent un sujet sous-entendu . . . remplacé par les pronoms anaphoriques *ils, les, leurs* . . . etc."[5] Now, it is absolutely impossible to speak apropos of the anaphorical role of an expression without invoking, if not a precise and empirical reader, at least the 'addressee' as an abstract and constitutive element in the process of actualization of a text.

In the same essay, two pages later, it is said that there is a semantic affinity between the *Erèbe* and the *horreur des ténèbres*. This semantic affinity does not lie in the text as an explicit linear linguistic manifestation; it is the result of a rather complex operation of textual inference based upon an intertextual competence. If this is the kind of semantic association that the poet wanted to arouse, to forecast and to activate such a cooperation from the part of the reader was part of the generative strategy employed by the author. Moreover, it seems that this strategy was aiming at an imprecise or undetermined response. Through the above semantic affinity the text associated the cats to the *coursiers funèbres*. Jakobson and Lévi-Strauss ask: "S'agit-il d'un désir frustré, ou d'une fausse reconnaissance? La signification de ce passage, sur la quelle les critiques se sont interrogés, reste à dessein ambigue."

That is enough, at least for me, to assume that "Les Chats" is a text that not only calls for the cooperation of its own reader, but also wants this reader to make a series of interpretive choices which even though not infinite are, however, more than one. Why not, then, call "Les Chats" an 'open' text? To postulate the cooperation of the reader does not mean to pollute the structural analysis with extratextual elements. The reader as an active principal of interpretation is a part of the picture of the generative process of the text.

There is only one tenable objection to my objection to the objection of Lévi-Strauss: if one considers even anaphorical activations as cases of cooperation on the part of the reader, there is no text escaping such a rule. I agree. So-called open texts are only the extreme and most provocative exploitation—for poetic purposes—of a principle which rules both the generation and the interpretation of texts in general.

0.1.2. Some problems of the pragmatics of communication

As is clearly maintained in *Theory* (2.15), the standard communication model proposed by information theorists (Sender, Message, Addressee— in which the message is decoded on the basis of a Code shared by both the virtual poles of the chain) does not describe the actual functioning of communicative intercourses. The existence of various codes and sub- codes, the variety of sociocultural circumstances in which a message is emitted (where the codes of the addressee can be different from those of the sender), and the rate of initiative displayed by the addressee in mak- ing presuppositions and abductions—all result in making a message (insofar as it is received and transformed into the *content* of an *expres- sion*) an empty form to which various possible senses can be attributed. Moreover, what one calls 'message' is usually a *text,* that is, a network of different messages depending on different codes and working at different levels of signification. Therefore the usual communication model should be rewritten (even though to a still extremely simplified extent) as in Figure 0.1.

A more reasonable picture of the whole semantico-pragmatic process would take the form (Figure 0.2) already proposed in *Theory,* where, even disregarding both the rightmost quarter of the square (all the 'aberrant' presuppositions) and the lower components (circumstances orienting or deviating the presuppositions), the notion of a crystal-like textual object is abundantly cast in doubt.

It should be clear that Figure 0.2 is not depicting any specially 'open' process of interpretation. It represents a semantico-pragmatic process in general. It is just by playing upon the prerequisites of such a general process that a text can succeed in being more or less open or closed. As for aberrant presuppositions and deviating circumstances, they are not realizing any openness but, instead, producing mere states of indeter-

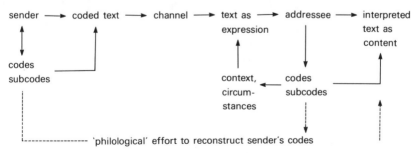

Figure 0.1

6]

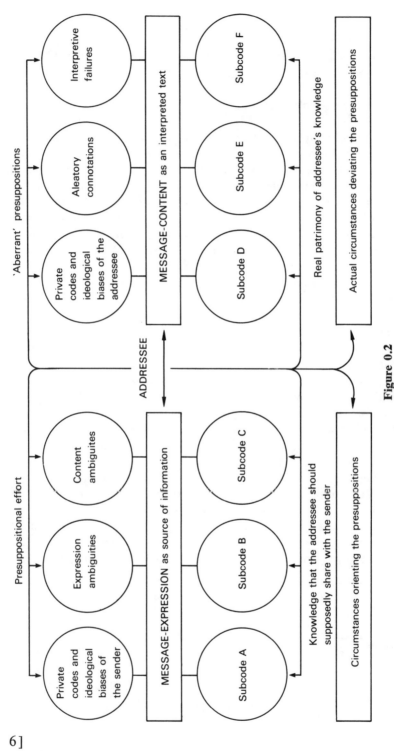

Figure 0.2

Reprinted from *A Theory of Semiotics*, p.142.

minacy. What I call open texts are, rather, reducing such as indeterminacy, whereas closed texts, even though aiming at eliciting a sort of 'obedient' cooperation, are in the last analysis randomly open to every pragmatic accident.

0.2.   The Model Reader

0.2.1.   Producing the Model Readers

To organize a text, its author has to rely upon a series of codes that assign given contents to the expressions he uses. To make his text communicative, the author has to assume that the ensemble of codes he relies upon is the same as that shared by his possible reader. The author has thus to foresee a model of the possible reader (hereafter Model Reader) supposedly able to deal interpretatively with the expressions in the same way as the author deals generatively with them.

At the minimal level, every type of text explicitly selects a very general model of possible reader through the choice (i) of a specific linguistic code, (ii) of a certain literary style, and (iii) of specific specialization-indices (a text beginning with /According to the last developments of the TeSWeST . . ./ immediately excludes any reader who does not know the technical jargon of text semiotics). Other texts give explicit information about the sort of readers they presuppose (for example, children's books, not only by typographical signals, but also by direct appeals; in other cases a specific category of addressee is named: /Friends, Romans, Countrymen . . ./). Many texts make evident their Model Readers by implicitly presupposing a specific encyclopedic competence. For instance, the author of *Waverley* opens his story by clearly calling for a very specialized kind of reader, nourished on a whole chapter of intertextual encyclopedia:

(1)   *What could my readers have expected from the chivalrous epithets*
       of Howard, Mordaunt, Mortimer or Stanley, or from the softer and
       more sentimental sounds of Belmore, Belville, Belfield and Belgrave,
       but pages of inanity, similar to those which have been so christened
       for half a century past?

But at the same time text (1) *creates* the competence of its Model Reader. After having read this passage, whoever approaches *Waverley* (even one century later and even—if the book has been translated into another language—from the point of view of a different intertextual competence) is asked to *assume* that certain epithets are meaning «chivalry» and that there is a whole tradition of chivalric romances displaying certain deprecatory stylistic and narrative properties.

Thus it seems that a well-organized text on the one hand presupposes a model of competence coming, so to speak, from outside the text, but on the other hand works to build up, by merely textual means, such a competence (see Riffaterre, 1973).

0.2.2. Model Readers for closed texts

We have seen that, pragmatically speaking, this situation is a very abstract and optimal one. In the process of communication, a text is frequently interpreted against the background of codes different from those intended by the author. Some authors do not take into account such a possibility. They have in mind an average addressee referred to a given social context. Nobody can say what happens when the actual reader is different from the 'average' one. Those texts that obsessively aim at arousing a precise response on the part of more or less precise empirical readers (be they children, soap-opera addicts, doctors, law-abiding citizens, swingers, Presbyterians, farmers, middle-class women, scuba divers, effete snobs, or any other imaginable sociopsychological category) are in fact open to any possible 'aberrant' decoding. A text so immoderately 'open' to every possible interpretation will be called a *closed* one.

Superman comic strips or Sue's and Fleming's novels belong to this category. They apparently aim at pulling the reader along a predetermined path, carefully displaying their effects so as to arouse pity or fear, excitement or depression at the due place and at the right moment. Every step of the 'story' elicits just the expectation that its further course will satisfy. They seem to be structured according to an inflexible project. Unfortunately, the only one not to have been 'inflexibly' planned is the reader. These texts are potentially speaking to everyone. Better, they presuppose an average reader resulting from a merely intuitive sociological speculation—in the same way in which an advertisement chooses its possible audience. It is enough for these texts to be interpreted by readers referring to other conventions or oriented by other presuppositions, and the result is incredibly disappointing (or exciting—it depends on the point of view). This was the case of Sue's *Les Mystères de Paris,* which, written initially in a dandyish mood to please cultivated readers, aroused as a result a passionate process of identification on the part of an illiterate audience; when, on the contrary, it was written to educate such a "dangerous" audience to a moderate vision of social harmony, it produced as a side effect a revolutionary uprising.

For the saga of Superman and for the *acta sanctorum* of James Bond, we lack comparable sociopsychological evidence, but it is clear that they can give rise to the most unforeseeable interpretations, at least at the ideological level. My ideological reading was only one among the possible: the most feasible for a smart semiotician who knows very well the 'codes' of the heavy industry of dreams in a capitalistic society. But why not read Superman stories only as a new form of romance that is free from any pedagogical intention? Doing so would not betray the nature of the saga. Superman comic strips are *also* this. And much more. They can be read in various ways, each way being independent from the others.

0.2.3. Model Readers for open texts

This cannot happen with those I call 'open' texts: they work at their peak revolutions per minute only when each interpretation is reechoed by the others, and vice versa.

Consider, in the essay on the semantics of metaphor (Chapter 2), the interplay of possible interpretations foreseen by Joyce apropos of the trial of Shaun. Consider, even at the reduced scale of a laboratory model of poetic language (in Chapter 3, on Edenic language) the way in which a productively ambiguous message leaves Adam and Eve free to reconsider the whole of their semantic universe, but, at the same time, makes them bound to the indecomposable unity of their alternative interpretations.

An author can foresee an 'ideal reader affected by an ideal insomnia' (as happens with *Finnegans Wake*), able to master different codes and eager to deal with the text as with a maze of many issues. But in the last analysis what matters is not the various issues in themselves but the maze-like structure of the text. You cannot use the text as you want, but only as the text wants you to use it. An open text, however 'open' it be, cannot afford whatever interpretation.

An open text outlines a 'closed' project of its Model Reader as a component of its structural strategy.

When reading a Fleming novel or a Superman comic strip, one can at most guess what kind of reader their authors had in mind, not which requirements a 'good' reader should meet. I was not the kind of reader foreseen by the authors of Superman, but I presume to have been a 'good' one (I would be more prudent apropos of the intentions of Fleming). On the contrary, when reading *Ulysses* one can extrapolate the profile of a 'good *Ulysses* reader' from the text itself, because the pragmatic process of interpretation is not an empirical accident independent of the text *qua* text, but is a structural element of its generative process.[6] As referred to an unsuitable reader (to a negative Model Reader unable to do the job he has just been postulated to do), *Ulysses qua Ulysses* could not stand up. At most it becomes another text.

It is possible to be smart enough to interpret the relationship between Nero Wolfe and Archie Goodwin as the umpteenth variation of the Oedipus myth without destroying Rex Stout's narrative universe. It is possible to be stupid enough to read Kafka's *Trial* as a trivial criminal novel, but at this point the text collapses—it has been burned out, just as a 'joint' is burned out to produce a private euphoric state.

The 'ideal reader' of *Finnegans Wake* cannot be a Greek reader of the second century B.C. or an illiterate man of Aran. The reader is strictly defined by the lexical and the syntactical organization of the text: the text is nothing else but the semantic-pragmatic production of its own Model Reader.

We shall see in the last essay of this book (Chapter 8) how a story by Alphonse Allais, *Un drame bien parisien,* can be read in two different ways, a naive way and a critical way, but both types of readers are inscribed within the textual strategy. The naive reader will be unable to enjoy the story (he will suffer a final uneasiness), but the critical reader will succeed only by enjoying the defeat of the former. In both cases—anyway—it will be only the text itself—such as it is made—that tells us which kind of reader it postulates. The exactness of the textual project makes for the freedom of its Model Reader. If there is a "jouissance du texte" (Barthes, 1973), it cannot be aroused and implemented except by a text producing all the paths of its 'good' reading (no matter how many, no matter how much determined in advance).

0.2.4. Author and reader as textual strategies

In a communicative process there are a sender, a message, and an addressee. Frequently, both sender and addressee are grammatically manifested by the message: "*I* tell *you* that. . . ."

Dealing with messages with a specific indexical purpose, the addressee is supposed to use the grammatical clues as referential indices (/I/ must designate the empirical subject of that precise instance of utterance, and so on). The same can happen even with very long texts, such as a letter or a private diary, read to get information about the writer.

But as far as a text is focused *qua* text, and especially in cases of texts conceived for a general audience (such as novels, political speeches, scientific instructions, and so on), the sender and the addressee are present in the text, not as mentioned poles of the utterance, but as 'actantial roles' of the sentence (not as *sujet de l'énonciation,* but as *sujet de l'énoncé*) (see Jakobson, 1957).

In these cases the author is textually manifested only (i) as a recognizable *style* or textual *idiolect*—this idiolect frequently distinguishing not an individual but a genre, a social group, a historical period (*Theory,* 3.7.6); (ii) as mere actantial roles (/I/ = «the subject of the present sentence»); (iii) as an illocutionary signal (/I swear that/) or as a perlocutionary operator (/suddenly something *horrible* happened . . ./). Usually this conjuring up of the 'ghost' of the sender is ordered to a symmetrical conjuring up of the 'ghost' of the addressee (Kristeva, 1970).

Consider the following expressions from Wittgenstein's *Philosophical Investigations*, 66:

(2) *Consider for example the proceedings that we call "games." I mean board-games, card-games, ball-games.* . . . Look and see *whether there is anything common to all. For if you look at them you will not see something that is common to* all, *but similarities, relationships, and a whole series of them at that.*

All the personal pronouns (whether explicit or implicit) are not indicating a person called Wittgenstein or any empirical reader: they are textual strategies. The intervention of a speaking subject is complementary to the activation of a Model Reader whose intellectual profile is determined only by the sort of interpretive operations he is supposed to perform (to detect similarities, to consider certain games . . .). Likewise the 'author' is nothing else but a textual strategy establishing semantic correlations and activating the Model Reader: /I mean board-games/ and so on, means that, within the framework of that text, the word /game/ will assume a given semantic value and will become able to encompass board-games, card-games, and so on.

According to this text Wittgenstein is nothing else but *a philosophical style,* and his Model Reader is nothing else but his capability to cooperate in order to reactualize that philosophical style.

In the following paragraphs I shall renounce the use of the term /author/ if not as a mere metaphor for «textual strategy», and I shall use the term Model Reader in the terms stipulated above.

In other words, the Model Reader is a textually established set of felicity conditions (Austin, 1962) to be met in order to have a macro-speech act (such as a text is) fully actualized.

0.3. Textual levels

0.3.1. Narrative and nonnarrative texts

To say that every text is a syntactic-semantico-pragmatic device whose foreseen interpretation is part of its generative process is still a generality. The solution would be to represent an 'ideal' text as a system of nodes or joints and to establish at which of them the cooperation of the Model Reader is expected and elicited.

Probably such an analytical representation escapes the present possibilities of a semiotic theory: this has been attempted only apropos of concrete texts (even though the categories provided *ad hoc* were aiming at a more universal application). The most successful examples are, I think, Barthes' (1970) analysis of *Sarrazine* and Greimas' (1976) of Maupassant's *Deux amis*. More detailed analyses of shorter textual fragments (such as Petőfi's, 1975, on *Le petit prince*) are clearly conceived more as experiments on the applicability of the theory than as approaches to a deeper comprehension of a given text.

When trying to propose a model for an ideal text, current theories tend to represent its structure in terms of *levels*—variously conceived as ideal steps of a process of generation or of a process of interpretation (or both). So shall I proceed.

In order to represent as 'ideal' a text endowed with the highest number of levels, I shall consider mainly *a model for fictional narrative texts.*[7] This decision is due to the fact that most of the essays collected in this book deal with narrativity. However, a fictional narrative text encompasses most of the problems posited by other types of texts. In a fictional narrative text, one can find examples of conversational texts (questions, orders, descriptions, and so on) as well as instances of every kind of speech act.

Van Dijk (1974) distinguishes between *natural* and *artificial* narrative. Both are instances of action description, but, while the former is relating events supposedly experienced by human or human-like subjects living in the "real" world and traveling from an initial state of affairs to a final one, the latter concerns individuals and actions belonging to an imaginary or 'possible' world. Obviously, artificial narrative does not respect a number of pragmatic conditions to which natural narrative is, on the contrary, submitted (in fiction, for instance, the speaker is not strictly supposed to tell the truth), but even this difference is irrelevant to my present purpose. So-called artificial narrativity simply encompasses a more complex range of extensional problems (see the discussion on possible worlds in Chapter 8).

Therefore my model will concern *narrative texts in general* (be they artificial or natural). I presume that an idealization of textual phenomena at a higher rate of complexity will serve also for more elementary textual specimens.

Undoubtedly, a fictional text is more complex than a conversational counterfactual conditional, even though both are dealing with possible states of affairs or possible courses of events. There is a clear difference between telling a girl what might happen to her if she naively were to accept the courtship of a libertine and telling someone (possibly undifferentiated) what in eighteenth-century London *definitely* happened to a girl named Clarissa when she naively accepted the courtship of a libertine named Lovelace.

In this second case we are witnessing certain precise features characterizing a fictional text: (i) through a special introductory formula (implicit or explicit), the reader is invited not to wonder whether the reported facts are true (at most one is interested in recognizing them as more or less 'verisimilar', a condition in turn suspended in romance or in fairy tales); (ii) some individuals are selected and introduced through a series of descriptions hung to their proper names and endowing them with certain properties; (iii) the sequence of actions is more or less localized in space and time; (iv) the sequence of actions is considered finite—there is a beginning and an end; (v) in order to tell what definitely happened to Clarissa, the text is supposed to start from an initial state of affairs concerning Clarissa and to follow her through certain changes of state, offering to the addressee the possibility of wondering about what could happen to Clarissa in the next step of the narration; (vi) the whole course of events described by the novel can be summarized and reduced to a set of macropropositions, to the skeleton of a story (or *fabula*), thus establishing a further level of the text which should not be identified with the so-called linear text manifestation.

Nevertheless, a counterfactual conditional differs from a piece of fiction only insofar as in the first case the addressee is requested to cooperate more actively in the realization of the text he receives—to make on his own the story that the text has simply suggested.

In the course of the following paragraphs, I shall also examine some cases in which a nonnarrative text seems not to fit my model. We shall see that we can either reduce the model or expand certain virtualities of the text. It is usually possible to transform a nonnarrative text into a narrative one.

Certainly, narrative texts—especially fictional ones—are more complicated than are many others and make the task of the semiotician harder. But they also make it more rewarding. That is why, probably, today one learns about textual machinery more from the researchers who dared to approach complex narrative texts than from those who limited themselves to analyzing short portions of everyday textuality. Maybe the latter have reached a higher degree of formalization, but the former have provided us with a higher degree of understanding.

0.3.2.   Textual levels: A theoretical abstraction

The notion of textual level is a very embarrassing one. Such as it appears, in its linear manifestation, a text has no levels at all. According to Segre (1974:5) 'level' and 'generation' are two metaphors: the author is not 'speaking', he 'has spoken'. What we are faced with is a textual surface, or the *expression plane* of the text. It is not proved that the way we adopt to actualize this expression as *content* mirrors (upside down) that adopted by the author to produce such a final result. Therefore the notion of textual level is merely theoretical; it belongs to semiotic metalanguage.

In Figure 0.3 the hierarchy of operations performed to interpret a text is *posited* as such for the sake of comprehensibility. I have borrowed many suggestions from the model of Petőfi's TeSWeST (*Text-Struktur*

Welt-Struktur-Theorie)[8] even though I try to introduce into my picture many items from different theoretical frameworks (such as Greimas' actantial structures). What seems to me interesting in Petőfi's model is the double consideration of both an intensional and an extensional approach.

Petőfi's model establishes rigidly the direction of the analysis, whereas my diagram (Figure 0.3) does not necessarily reflect the real steps empirically made by the interpreter. In the actual process of interpreta-

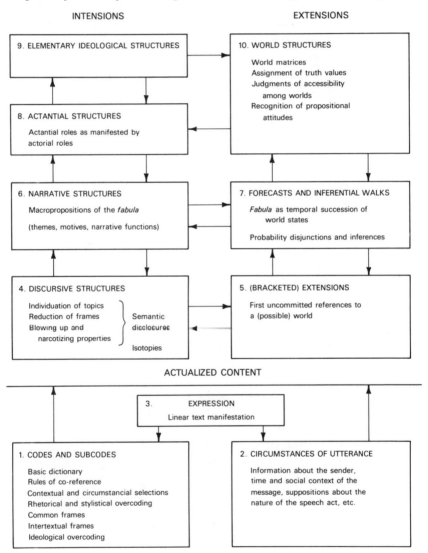

INTENSIONS   EXTENSIONS

9. ELEMENTARY IDEOLOGICAL STRUCTURES

10. WORLD STRUCTURES

World matrices
Assignment of truth values
Judgments of accessibility
   among worlds
Recognition of propositional
   attitudes

8. ACTANTIAL STRUCTURES

Actantial roles as manifested by
actorial roles

6. NARRATIVE STRUCTURES

Macropropositions of the *fabula*

(themes, motives, narrative functions)

7. FORECASTS AND INFERENTIAL WALKS

Fabula as temporal succession of
world states

Probability disjunctions and inferences

4. DISCURSIVE STRUCTURES

Individuation of topics
Reduction of frames   Semantic
Blowing up and   disclosures
   narcotizing properties
                           Isotopies

5. (BRACKETED) EXTENSIONS

First uncommitted references to
a (possible) world

ACTUALIZED CONTENT

3.   EXPRESSION
     Linear text manifestation

1. CODES AND SUBCODES

Basic dictionary
Rules of co-reference
Contextual and circumstancial selections
Rhetorical and stylistical overcoding
Common frames
Intertextual frames
Ideological overcoding

2. CIRCUMSTANCES OF UTTERANCE

Information about the sender,
time and social context of the
message, suppositions about the
nature of the speech act, etc.

Figure 0.3

tion, all the levels and sublevels of my diagram (which are in fact mere metatextual 'boxes') are interconnected in a continuous coming and going. The cooperation of the interpreter at the lower levels can succeed only because some hypotheses which concern upper levels (and vice versa) are hazarded. The same happens also for a generative process: frequently an author makes decisions concerning the deep semantic structure of his story only at the moment in which he chooses at the lexical level, for merely stylistic reasons, a given expression. Likewise the arrows do not mark any idealized temporal and logical process of interpretation, but rather show the interdependences among 'boxes'.

Figure 0.3 thus considers (metalinguistically) levels of possible abstraction at which the cooperative activity can take place. Therefore, in order to avoid any misunderstanding, instead of speaking of textual 'levels' (a metaphor which inevitably risks suggesting a hierarchy of concrete operations), I shall speak of 'boxes', so referring only to specific points of my visualized theoretical postulation.

The only way in which Figure 0.3 presumably portrays a concrete case of textual interpretation is in the fact that it necessarily starts from box 3 (linear text manifestation) and that one cannot jump from box 3 to the others without relying at least on box 1 (the system of codes and subcodes indispensable to transforming the expression plane into the content plane).

0.4. Linear text manifestation and circumstances of utterance

0.4.1. I call linear text manifestation the text such as it appears verbally with its lexematic surface. The reader applies to these *expressions* a given code or system of codes and subcodes, to transform them into the first levels of content.

Text (3) is an excerpt from *Der grosse Lalula* by Christian Morgenstern:

(3) Kroklowafgi? Semememi!
Seikronto prafriplo.
Bifzi, bafzi; hulalomi . . .
quasti besti bo . . .

This text has a linear manifestation (expression) to which no content can be ordered, since the author did not refer to any existing code (I am excluding for the sake of simplicity phonic connotations as well as the halo of 'literariness' acquired by this pre-Dada experiment).

Text (4) is an excerpt from *Toto-Vaca* by Tristan Tzara:

(4) ka tangi te kivi
kivi

ka rangi te mobo
moho . . .

This text has a linear manifestation to which I cannot order any content, although some of my readers probably would since it seems it was originally a Maori poem.

At this level there takes place the phonetic interpretation, particularly important for texts such as (3) and (4), but to be disregarded during the following analysis, where, dealing with narrative texts, I am obviously more interested in 'higher' boxes. See, however, *Theory* (3.7.4) for a discussion on the "further segmentation of the expression plane" taking place in aesthetic texts. See also in *Theory* the sections on *ratio difficilis* and *invention* (3.4.9, 3.6.7, 3.6.8) concerning those cases in which the manipulation of the expression plane radically involves the very nature of codes. The essay on Edenic language (Chapter 3) indirectly deals with these problems.

0.4.2. Figure 0.3 considers an immediate connection between the text linear manifestation and the *act of utterance* (which in Figure 0.2 is included among the circumstances orienting presuppositions).

In this connection between sentence and utterance (*énoncé* and *énonciation*), the addressee of any text immediately detects whether the sender wants to perform a propositional act or another kind of speech act. If the text is structurally simple and if it explicitly aims at indicating, ordering, questioning, and so on, probably the addressee switches alternately from box 2 to box 10, therefore deciding both what the sender is meaning and—in terms of mentioning something—whether he is lying or telling the truth, whether he is asking or ordering something possible or impossible, and so on. Other boxes can be further activated according to the complexity of the text and to the subtlety of the addressee (hidden ideological structures can be presupposed even by a text such as /Come here, bastard!/).

When a fictional text is read, the reference to the act of utterance has instead other functions. This reference can take two forms. The more elementary results in establishing a sort of metatextual proposition such as «there is (was) a human individual who utters (uttered) the text I am presently reading and who asks for an act of suspension of disbelief since he is (was) speaking about a possible course of events». (Note that the same metatextual proposition works also for a scientific text, except for the suspension of disbelief—the reader is on the contrary invited to especially trust the speaker.) More elaborate operations can be implemented when the reader tries to reconstruct for philological reasons the original circumstances of the utterance (historical period, ethnic or cultural profile of the speaker, and so on). In this case, as soon as these external circumstances are detected, they are inserted into box 1, to be transformed into pieces of encyclopedic knowledge (contextual and circumstantial selections, frames, and any other type of overcoding).

0.5. Bracketed extensions

As far as the reader recognizes the existence of certain individuals (be they animate or not) furnished with certain properties (among which the possible properties of performing certain actions), he probably makes some indexical presuppositions, that is, he assigns those subjects to a possible world. In order to apply the information provided by the lexicon, he assumes a transitory identity between this world and the world of his experience (reflected by the lexicon).

If, by chance, in the course of his decoding, the reader discovers some discrepancy between the world as pictured by the social lexicon and the world as pictured by the idiolectal lexicon of the text (for instance, a stone—inanimate—has the property of speaking), he practically 'jumps' at box 10 or puts the extension into brackets, that is, he suspends his disbelief, waiting for more semantic information, to be actualized at box 4 (discursive structures).

0.6. Discursive structures

0.6.1. Codes, overcoding, frames

At box 4 the reader confronts the text linear manifestation with the system of codes and subcodes provided by the language in which the text is written (box 1). Such a system is presupposed by the present research in the format of an encyclopedia, structured as the Model Q proposed in *Theory* (2.12).

This begins the transformation of the expression into content, word by word, phrase by phrase. In a frenzy of lexicological optimism, one could say that the virtual context of every verbal expression is already established by the lexicon and that the reader has nothing to do but pick up there what must be correlated to the expressions. Everyone knows that things are not that simple (see *Theory,* 2.15): even a comprehensive theory of the 'amalgamation' between sememes meets with the problem of 'contextual meaning'.

I do not believe, however—as many text theorists maintain—that there is an incurable gap between lexical meaning and textual meaning. I do not believe, since semantic compositional analysis proved to be unsuccessful in explaining complex processes of textual amalgamation, that it should be completely substituted by an autonomous set of textual rules providing the final interpretation of lexical meanings. I believe, on the contrary, that, if a text can be generated and interpreted, this ought to happen for the same semiotic reasons for which lexical meanings are graspable and for which a sentence can be both generated and interpreted. The only problem is to insert into semantic compositional spectrums also contextual and circumstantial selections (*Theory*, 2.11), to add over-coded rules (*Theory*, 2.14), and to consider within the sememic representation also *textual operators* (see 0.6.2). The essay on Peircean semantics (Chapter 7) should encourage such a perspective.

In 0.6.2 we shall see that even a textual category such as 'frame' is based upon the model of a sememic representation in terms of case grammar. We shall also see, in 0.7.4, that there is a strong structural similarity between this type of sememic representation and the more abstract structures. Therefore, we can assume that *a sememe is in itself an inchoative text whereas a text is an expanded sememe*.[9]

That is why it is not so realistic to consider the boxes of Figure 0.3 as 'real' steps in text interpretation: they are virtual poles of an interpretative movement which is far and away more continuous and whose timing is rather unpredictable.

Having said this, we can proceed with examining the various codes and subcodes of box 1.

0.6.1.1. *Basic dictionary.* At this sublevel the reader resorts to a lexicon with the format of a basic dictionary and immediately detects the most basic semantic properties of the sememes involved, so as to make a first tentative amalgamation. If the text says that /once upon a time there was a young princess called Snow White. She was very pretty/, the reader detects by a first semantic analysis of «princess» that Snow White is surely a «woman». The sememe «princess» is virtually much more complex (for instance, «woman» entails «human female», and a human female should be represented by many properties such as having certain body organs, and so on). At this point the reader does not know as yet which of these *virtual* properties must be *actualized*. This decision will be helped only by further amalgamation and by textual operators. At this sublevel the reader also actualizes the syntactic properties of the lexemes (singular, feminine, noun, and so on) and can begin to establish co-references.

0.6.1.2. *Rules of co-reference.* On the basis of the first semantic analysis and of the detection of syntactical properties, the reader disambiguates anaphorical and deictic expressions (various shifters). Thus he is able to decide that the /she/ of the text quoted above must be referred to the princess. We shall see in 0.6.2 that one cannot disambiguate most of these co-references without resorting to textual operators. The reader in any case outlines here the first tentative *co-textual* relations. At this level the reader operates every transformation from surface to deep structure of the *single* sentences. In cases of ambiguities he awaits for textual clues (see 0.6.3).

0.6.1.3. *Contextual and circumstantial selections.* While co-textual relations are all the links displayed through expressed lexemes by the linear text manifestation, contextual selections are previously established by a semantic representation with the format of an encyclopedia (see *Theory,* 2.11) and are only virtually present in a given text. It is one of the tasks of the reader to actualize them (by disregarding any alternative selection). Contextual selections are coded abstract possibilities of meeting a given term in connection with other terms belonging to the same semiotic systems (in this case, a given language). Thus a good encyclopedic representation of /whale/ should record at least two contextual selections: in a context dominated by the sememe «ancient», a whale is a fish; in the context dominated by the sememe «modern», a whale is a mammal.

Circumstantial selections code the possible co-occurrence of a given term with external circumstances. (See in *Theory,* 2.11, how also these circumstances, insofar as they are conventionally recorded by the encyclopedia, are registered as semiotic items of another semiotic system, for instance, a social or a gestural one.) Thus /aye/ means «I vote yes» in the framework of certain types of formal meetings and «I will obey» in the framework of the Navy.

As a matter of fact, circumstantial selections act as such only when the addressee connects the received expression with the act of utterance and with the extraverbal environment. In a narrative text even these data are verbally expressed and even external circumstances are linguistically described. Thus circumstantial selections become contextual.

Context and (coded) circumstances depend on the fact that the encyclopedia also encompasses an *intertextual competence* (see Kristeva, 1970): every text refers back to previous texts.

0.6.1.4. *Rhetorical and stylistic overcoding.* Overcoded rules (see *Theory,* 2.14) tell the reader whether a given expression (be it a single term, a sentence, or an entire textual sequence) is used rhetorically. At this level the reader inserts the competence, allowing recognition of a metaphor or any other trope and avoiding naive denotative interpretation of figures of speech. /Once upon a time/ is an overcoded expression establishing (i) that the events take place in an indefinite nonhistorical epoch, (ii) that the reported events are not 'real', (iii) that the speaker wants to tell a fictional story.

Among overcoded rules also rank *genre rules* (that will function more explicitly at box 7) and other literary conventions. For instance, in the story analyzed in Chapter 8 of this book (*Un drame bien parisien* by

Alphonse Allais), the title of the first chapter introduces a /Monsieur/ and a /Dame/. In the first lines of the text a given Raoul and a given Marguerite are introduced. Resorting to an onomastic dictionary, the reader interprets them as two human beings, respectively male and female. An overcoded rule tells him that (irony or other figure excepted) the title of a chapter usually announces the content of it. The reader thus co-refers /Monsieur/ to Raoul and /Dame/ to Marguerite and detects that they are adult and presumably belong to a bourgeois milieu.

The text continues by saying that Raoul and Marguerite are /married/. The text does not say that they are married to each other, but the Model Reader has no doubt about this. He is in fact resorting to overcoded stylistic rules. Allais knows that his Model Reader does not need more information about this marriage. When a speaker wants to trick us with such a sort of overcoding, he makes it explicit. To quote a joke of Woody Allen's: "I desperately wish to return to the womb. Anybody's."

0.6.1.5. *Inferences by common frames.* In *Un drame bien parisien*, chapter 2, Raoul and Marguerite, very jealous of each other, are quarreling. At a certain point Raoul pursues Marguerite, and the French text says as follows:

(5) *La main levée, l'oeil dur, la moustache telle celle des chats furibonds, Raoul marcha sur Marguerite. . . .*

The reader understands that Raoul raises his hand to strike, even though the linear text manifestation shows neither the fact nor the intention. In fact, the English translator of the story (see Appendix 2) translates "hand raised to strike." It is a correct interpretation. However, were Raoul a senator at a legislative session, a raised hand would mean a request to speak. Since he is a husband quarreling with his wife, we make the only possible inference (supported also by the other characteristics of Raoul manifested by the text: remorseless gaze, bristling moustache . . .). But the inference was possible only because the reader was resorting to the conventional *frame* «violent altercation».

According to current research both in Artificial Intelligence and in text theories, a *frame* looks like something half-way between a very comprehensive encyclopedic sememic representation expressed in terms of a case grammar (see *Theory*, 2.11.1) and an instance of *overcoding*. Probably this notion is still an empirical one (and as such it is used in Artificial Intelligence) to be better defined within the framework of a semiotic theory (by distinguishing between coded and overcoded frames). But for the present purposes it can be used without further technicalities. A frame is "a data-structure for representing a stereotyped situation like being in a certain kind of living room or going to a child's birthday party" (Winston, 1977:180) and frames are "(cognitive) knowledge representations about the 'world' which enable us to perform such basic cognitive acts as perception, language comprehension and actions" (van Dijk, 1976b:31). In this sense the frame for supermarket determines "units or chunks of concepts . . . denoting certain courses of events or courses of actions involving several objects, persons, properties, relations or facts" (van Dijk, 1976b:36; see for a previous attempt Petőfi, 1976b). Thus the supermarket frame would involve virtually the notion of a place where people enter to buy items of different types, pick them up without mediation of any vendor, pay for them all together at a terminal counter, and so on. Probably a good frame of this sort involves also the list of all the commodities one can find in a supermarket (brooms: *yes;* cars: *no*). In this sense a frame is already an inchoative text or a condensed story— but also an encyclopedic representation of a sememe can be such; see the essay on Peirce (Chapter 7) and the example of the encyclopedic representation of lithium: I am presently uncertain whether this text represents an enlarged case-grammar-like encyclopedic analysis or the frame «producing lithium».[10]

0.6.1.6. *Inferences by intertextual frames.* No text is read independently of the reader's experience of other texts. Intertextual knowledge (see especially Kristeva, 1970) can be considered a special case of overcoding and establishes its own intertextual frames (frequently to be identified with genre rules). The reader of (5) is convinced that Raoul raises his hand to strike because a lot of narrative situations have definitely overcoded the situation «comic quarrel between husband and wife». Even iconographical frames (thousand of hands raised to strike in thousands of pictures) help the reader to make his inference: intertextual knowledge (the extreme periphery of a semantic encyclopedia) encompasses all the semiotic systems with which the reader is familiar. The case (Joyce's Minucius Mandrake) studied in Chapter 2, on metaphor, is a good instance of a textual riddle that can be disambiguated only by means of intertextual information. (In my interpretation both the common frame «trial» and the textual frame «Mandrake hypnotizes» enter into play.) In Sue's *Les Mystères de Paris,* the first introduction of Fleur-de-Marie immediately reechoes the literary topos of *'la vierge souillée'.* Every character (or situation) of a novel is immediately endowed with properties that the text does not directly manifest and that the reader has been "programmed" to borrow from the treasury of intertextuality.

Common frames come to the reader from his storage of encyclopedic knowledge and are mainly rules for practical life (Charniak, 1975). Intertextual frames, on the contrary, are already literary 'topoi', narrative schemes (see Riffaterre, 1973; 1976).

Frequently, the reader, instead of resorting to a common frame, picks up from the storage of his intertextual competence already reduced intertextual frames (such as typical situations: the Oedipean triangle as proposed by Freud is one among these); genre rules produce textual frames more reduced than common frames. The intertextual frame «the great train robbery» made popular by a number of early western movies encompasses fewer actions, individuals, and other properties than does the common frame «train robbery» as referred to by professional outlaws.

0.6.1.7. *Ideological overcoding.* In *Theory* (3.9) I have described ideological systems as cases of overcoding. Let me say, for the present purpose, that the reader approaches a text from a personal ideological perspective, even when he is not aware of this, even when his ideological bias is only a highly simplified system of axiological oppositions. Since the reader is supposed to single out (in box 9) the elementary ideological structures of the *text,* this operation is overdetermined by his ideological *subcodes.*

This means that not only the outline of textual ideological structures is governed by the ideological bias of the reader but also that a given ideological background can help one to discover or to ignore textual ideological structures. A reader of Fleming's stories who shares the ideological judgments expressed by the text at the level of discursive structures is probably not eager to look for an underlying ideological scaffolding at a more abstract level; on the contrary, a reader who challenges many of the author's explicit value judgments is to go further with an ideological analysis so as to 'unmask' the hidden catechization performed at more profound levels.

But ideological biases can also work as code-switchers, leading one to read a given text in the light of 'aberrant' codes (where 'aberrant' means only different from the ones envisaged by the sender). Typical examples are the medieval interpretation of Virgil and the proletarian interpretation of *Les Mystères de Paris.* In both cases the code-switching took place in spite of the explicit ideological commitment of the author.

Finally, an ideological bias can lead a critical reader to make a given text say more than it apparently says, that is, to find out what in that text is ideologically presupposed, untold. In this movement from the ideological subcodes of the interpreter to the ideological subcodes tentatively attributed to the author (the encyclopedia of his social group or historical period being verified in singling out the ideological structures of the text), even the most closed texts are surgically 'opened': fiction is transformed into document and the innocence of fancy is translated into the disturbing evidence of a philosophical statement.

Sometimes a text asks for ideological cooperation on the part of the reader (Brecht); at other times the text seems to refuse any ideological commitment, although its ideological message consists just in this refusal.

Such is the case of *Finnegans Wake,* where the vanishing of everything into the mist of a linguistic dream does not represent an escape from ideology but, rather, the reiteration of a *Weltanschauung* transparently expressed by the whole linguistic strategy of the book.

0.6.2. Semantic disclosures

When faced with a lexeme, the reader does not know which of its virtual properties (or semes, or semantic markers) has to be actualized so as to allow further amalgamations.

Should every virtual property be taken into account in the further course of the text, the reader would be obliged to outline, as in a sort of vivid mental picture, the whole network of interrelated properties that the encyclopedia assigns to the corresponding sememe. Nevertheless (and fortunately), we do not proceed like that, except in rare cases of so-called eidetic imagination. All these properties are not to be *actually* present to the mind of the reader. They are *virtually* present in the encyclopedia, that is, they are socially *stored,* and the reader picks them up from the semantic store only when required by the text.[11] In doing so the reader implements *semantic disclosures* or, in other words, actualizes nonmanifested properties (as well as merely suggested sememes).

Semantic disclosures have a double role: they *blow up* certain properties (making them textually relevant or pertinent) and *narcotize* some others.

For instance, in *Un drame bien parisien* it is said that Raoul is a /Monsieur/ and therefore a male human adult. Ought it to be actualized that a human adult has two arms, two legs, two eyes, a warm-blooded circulatory system, two lungs, and a pancreas? Since many overcoded expressions (such as the title) tell the reader that he is not dealing with an anatomical treatise, he keeps these properties narcotized until chapter 2, where (see above, text (5)) Raoul raises his hand. At this point the virtual property of having hands must be actualized or blown up. Raoul can very well survive (textually) without lungs, but, were we reading the story of Hans Castorp falling ill in Mann's *Zauberberg,* the question about lungs would not sound so preposterous.

However, to remain narcotized does not mean to be abolished. Virtual properties can always be actualized by the course of the text. In any case they remain perhaps unessential, but by no means obliterated. It is unessential to the course of the text that Raoul has a warm-blooded circulatory system, but were this property denied the reader would have to refocus his cooperative attention by looking for other intertextual frames, since the story would shift from comedy to Gothic.

To realize all the needed semantic disclosures, a mere comparison between manifested sememes is not enough. Discoursive structures need a textual operator: the *topic.*

0.6.3. Topics and isotopies

Frames and sememic representations are both based on processes of unlimited semiosis, and as such they call for the responsibility of the addressee. Since the semantic encyclopedia is in itself potentially infinite, semiosis is unlimited, and, from the extreme periphery of a given sememe, the center of any other could be reached, and vice versa (see also the Model Q in *Theory*, 2.12). Since every proposition contains every other proposition (as shown in Chapter 7, on Peirce), a text could generate, by further semantic disclosures, every other text. (By the way, this is exactly what happens in intertextual circulation: the history of literature is a living proof of this hypothesis.)

We have thus to decide how a text, in itself potentially infinite, can generate only those interpretations it can foresee (it is not true that, as Valéry claims, "il n'y a pas de vrai sens d'un texte": we have seen that even the more 'open' among experimental texts direct their own free interpretation and preestablish the movement of their Model Reader). In fact, "a frame may contain a great many details whose supposition is not specifically warranted by the situation" (Winston, 1977:180), and "it seems obvious that when I organize a party, or when I read a story about such a party, I need not actualize the whole supermarket by the simple fact that I briefly go to the supermarket to get some peanuts for my guests. . . . In a situation in which 'getting peanuts for my guests' is *topic* . . . the only aspect which is relevant is the successfulness of the act realizing my purpose" (van Dijk, 1976b:38).

Many of the codes and subcodes listed in 0.6.1 do not strictly concern text interpretation. They may also concern single lexemes or sentences (except perhaps for the operations of co-reference). But even at the level of simple sentences, each of these operations risks proving unsuccessful, as many exercises on grammatical ambiguities are still demonstrating: outside a textual framework, green colorless ideas can neither exist nor sleep furiously, and we cannot understand who (or what) are flying planes.

When we find an ambiguous sentence or a small textual portion isolated from any co-text or circumstance of utterance, we cannot disambiguate it without resorting to a presupposed 'aboutness' of the co-text, usually labeled as the *textual topic* (of which the expressed text is the *comment*). It is usually detected by formulating a *question*.

Consider, for instance, the following famous vicious example:

(6) *Charles makes love with his wife twice a week. So does John.*

This short text allows a malicious reader to make embarrassing inference about the morality of this friendly 'triangle', while a more virtuous one can interpret it as a statistical statement about the sexual rhythms of two different couples.

Nevertheless, let us try to see (6) as the proper answer to each of the following questions:

(7) *How many times a week do Charles and John make love with their own wives?* (Topic: sexual rhythm of two couples.)

(8) *I do not really understand the relationship between those three. What's going on—I mean, sexually?* (Topic: relation between a woman and two men.)

At this point (6) can be easily disambiguated.[12]

The topic as a textual operator is not, however, merely a matter of the reader's initiative. A satisfactory semantic representation should consider the relation with the textual topic as one of its compositional features. This appears very clear in the compositional analysis of a 'syncategore-matic' such as /so/.

Returning to (6) and to the questions (7) and (8) that disambiguate it, we should consider (as stored within the encyclopedia) a composi-tional analysis of /so/ according to which a first semantic marker sound-ing more or less like «in the same way as» should be supported by the selection «referring to the topic». In this way the sememe presupposes the co-text and the text is nothing else but a normal expansion of the sememe.

Consider now an expression like /on the other hand/ in the following texts:

(9) *Mary loves apples. John, on the other hand, hates them.*
(10) *Mary loves apples. On the other hand, she hates bananas.*
(11) *Mary loves apples. John, on the other hand, is fond of bananas.*
(12) *Mary is playing her cello. John, on the other hand, is eating bananas.*

According to the expressions under examination, one could think that /on the other hand/ marks an alternative to the subject and her action in (9), the action and the object in (10), the subject and the object in (11) and everything in (12).

The problem becomes clear when (9)–(12) are seen as the proper answer to four different questions:

(13) *Do Mary and John love apples?* (Topic: people who love apples.)
(14) *What kind of fruit does Mary love?* (Topic: fruit Mary loves.)
(15) *What kind of fruit does John love?* (Topic: fruit John loves.)
(16) *What the hell are those kids doing? They were supposed to have their music lesson!* (Topic: John and Mary's music lesson.)

Text (12) is particularly convincing about the co-text-sensitive nature of /on the other hand/: there is no reason to think that eating bananas is alternative to making music until the precise question (16) has established a textual opposition.

One must therefore rely upon a semantic representation of the ready-made syntagm /on the other hand/ which takes into account the semantic marker «alternativity to» and the selection «referring to the topic».

It is imprudent to speak of *one* textual topic. In fact, a text can function on the basis of various embedded topics. There are first of all *sentence* topics; *discursive* topics at the level of short sequences can rule the understanding of microstructural elements, while *narrative* topics can rule the comprehension of the text at higher levels. Topics are not always explicit. Sometimes these questions are manifested at the first level, and the reader simply cooperates by reducing the frames and by blowing up the semantic properties he needs. Sometimes there are topic-markers such as titles.[13] But many other times the reader has to guess where the real topic is hidden.

Frequently a text establishes its topic by reiterating blatantly a series of sememes belonging to the same semantic field (*key words*).[14] In this case these sememes are obsessively reiterated throughout the text. At other times, on the contrary, these sememes cannot be statistically detected because, rather than being abundantly distributed, they are *strategically located*. In these cases the sensitive reader, feeling something unusual in the *dispositio,* tries to make abductions (that is, to single out a hidden rule or regularity) and to test them in the course of his further reading. That is why in reading literary texts one is obliged to look backward many times, and, in general, the more complex the text, the more it has to be read twice, and the second time from the end.

In Chapter 8 we shall see that Allais' story displays as a matter of fact two topics, one for the naive reader and one for the critical one. The former topic is rather evident, based as it is upon a blatant reiteration of key words. The latter is more carefully concealed—or, like the purloined letter, is made visible only to a critical reader able to 'smell' where the relevant key words are strategically located.

Thus, according to which topic he has identified, the reader can read the text either as the story of an adultery or as the story of a misunderstanding. Such a double reading takes place at the higher level of narrative macropropositions (box 6), but the key words are disseminated in the linear text manifestations.

In either case the topic directs the right amalgamations and the organization of a single level of sense, or *isotopy*. Greimas (1970) calls isotopy "a redundant set of semantic categories which make possible the uniform reading of the story" (p. 188). There is a strong relation between topic and isotopy (as denounced by the same etymological root); nevertheless, there is a difference between the two concepts for at least two reasons. The topic as question governs the semantic disclosures, that is, the selection of the semantic properties that can or must be taken into account during the reading of a given text; as such, topics are means to produce isotopies. Since the relevant semantic categories (upon which to establish an isotopy) are not necessarily manifested, the topic as question is an abductive schema that helps the reader to decide which semantic properties have to be actualized, whereas isotopies are the actual textual verification of that tentative hypothesis.[15]

Thus the abduction of the textual topic helps the reader to select the right frames, to reduce them to a manageable format, to blow up and to narcotize given semantic properties of the lexemes to be amalgamated, and to establish the isotopy according to which he decides to interpret the linear text manifestation so as to actualize the discoursive structure of a text. But there is a hierarchy of isotopies, and we shall find that this category also works at the next level.

0.7. Narrative structures

0.7.1. From plot to *fabula*

0.7.1.1.   Once he has actualized the discursive level, the reader knows what 'happens' in a given text. He is now able to summarize it, therefore reaching a series of levels of abstraction by expressing one or more macropropositions (see van Dijk, 1975).

In order to understand this progressive abstractive process, let us retain an old opposition, still valid as a first approach to the question: the difference proposed by Russian formalists between *fabula* (story) and *sjuzet* (plot or discourse).[16]

The *fabula* is the basic story stuff, the logic of actions or the syntax of characters, the time-oriented course of events. It need not necessarily be a sequence of human actions (physical or not), but can also concern a temporal transformation of ideas or a series of events concerning inanimate objects.

The plot is the story as actually told, along with all its deviations, digressions, flashbacks, and the whole of the verbal devices.

According to these definitions the plot should correspond to the discursive structure. One may also consider the plot as a first tentative synthesis made by the reader once all the operations of actualization of the discursive structures are accomplished. Perhaps, in this more restricted sense, in this first synthesis of the actualized intensions, some lexical elements as well as minor or (apparently) irrelevant microsequences get dropped out. Let us suppose that certain sentences can also be reformulated by a very analytical paraphrasis. Because of all these uncertainties, I have not recorded the phase of actualization of plot by a special 'box'.

What is certain is that, through an imprecise series of mediatory abstractions, the reader comes to elaborate a more precise series of macropropositions that constitute a *possible fabula.*

It is a common naiveté of many current text theories to believe that these macropropositions must constitute a *synthesis* of micropropositions expressed at the level of discursive structures. This is true in many cases (the whole of *Oedipus Rex* can be summarized as «find out the guilty!»), but there are a number of narrative situations where the macropropositions must *expand* the discursive structures. To give only a few examples, what is the *fabula* carried on by the first two verses of Dante's *Divine Comedy?* According to the medieval theory of four senses, there are at least four *fabulae,* each of them expanded beyond the first surface level. The narrative structure of /*Dieu invisible crea le monde visible*/ is—as every linguist knows very well—«There is a God. God is invisible. God created the world. The world is visible». Take also Corneille's /qu'il mourût!/ and try to *expand* the *fabula* expressed by this short speech act.

I referred to "a possible" *fabula* since this concept (at least in the form traditionally accepted) is a problematic one. According to the power of abstraction that the reader is able to manage, the *fabula* can be established and recognized at different levels. *Fabulae* are narrative isotopies. *Ivanhoe* can be both the story of what happens to Cedric, Rowena, Rebecca, and so on, and the story of the clash between Normans and Anglo-Saxons. It depends upon whether one has to reduce the novel for a screenplay, to write book-jacket copy, or to find three lines for an appealing advertisement to be placed in a quarterly of Marxist studies.

Is *Oedipus Rex* the story of detection, incest, or parricide? I think that (while there is a traditional story concerning parricide and incest) Sophocles' tragedy is the story of a detection concerning another story, namely, the traditional story of parricide and incest. However, one can decide that the basic 'stuff' one is interested in is the traditional story that the plot reveals step by step through the various phases of the detection. Therefore *Oedipus Rex* has a first-level story (detection) and a second-level one. Obviously, as far as the process of further abstraction goes, the reader is approaching the deepest intensional levels (box 8). A first intermediate level before entry to box 8 is the reduction of the *fabula* into a series of narrative structures à la Propp. A shallower level is the assimilation of the *fabula* to the binary disjunctions proposed by Bremond (1973) or a first reduction to standard *themes* or *motives.*

0.7.1.2. It seems that there are texts without a narrative level, such as questions, commands, minimal conversation pieces. In fact, if one is ordering me /come here/, I can summarize the content of the expression as «There is someone wanting me to go there» or something like that. Once again, the macroproposition is longer than the microproposition manifesting it.

As for conversational texts, consider the following:

(17) *Paul: Where is Peter?*
      Mary: Out.
      Paul: I see. I thought he was still sleeping.

From text (17) one can extrapolate a story telling that (i) in the world of Paul's and Mary's knowledge (probably identifiable with the 'real' one), there is a certain Peter; (ii) Paul believed p (= Peter is still sleeping) while Mary assumed she knew that q (= Peter is out); (iii) Mary informed Paul about q and Paul did not believe any longer that p was the case and presumed to know that q was the case.

Once this has been ascertained, all the other problems concerning this dialogue (presuppositions about the fact that Peter is a male human being, that he is known both to Mary and to Paul, that the conversation takes place within a house or any other closed space, that Paul wants to know something about Peter, and that the time of the conversation is probably late morning) are a matter of semantic disclosure.

In text (17) the *fabula* can be the one I have tried to extrapolate, but a more abstract macroproposition may be «Paul is looking for Peter», «Paul is asking Mary about Peter», or «Mary gives Paul unexpected information». Later it will become evident that each of these three summaries involves other boxes (the third summary, for instance, involves box 10).

In the same way all the examples of conversational implicature given by Grice (1967) carry on a virtual story. The pragmatic value of implicatures consists only in that they oblige the addressee to outline a story where there apparently was the accidental or malicious flouting of a conversational maxim:

(18) *A: I am out of petrol.*
      B: There is a garage round the corner.

(Story: A needs petrol and B wants to help him. B knows that A knows that usually garages sell petrol, knows that there is a garage round the corner, and knows (or hopes) that this garage is open and has petrol to sell. So he informs A about the location of the garage. Will or will not A follow successfully the suggestion of B?) As you see, this story has also a potential rate of narrative suspense.

0.7.1.3.   One should accept either a large or a more restricted definition of *fabula*. A restricted definition of a narrative structure as a description of actions requires, for instance, for any action an *intention,* a *person* (agent), a *state* or possible world, a *change,* its *cause,* and a *purpose*—to which one can also add *mental states, emotions,* and *circumstances.* A description of an action should then be *complete* and *relevant* while the actions described should be *difficult,* the agent should *not have an obvious choice* of which course of actions to take in order to change the state which is inconsistent with his wishes, the following events should be *unexpected,* and some of them should be *unusual* or strange (van Dijk, 1974).

Many other requirements could be added. But this strict definition concerns only cases of so-called natural narrative ("I'll tell you what happened yesterday to my husband . . .") and, among artificial or fictional narratives, the classical forms of novel and romance. The requirements of unexpectedness or relevance seem not to hold for cases of contemporary experimental novels, whereas the Book of Genesis from the beginning to the creation of Adam undoubtedly tells a relevant story (with an agent, a purpose, changes, and causes), but none of the reported events is unexpected either to the agent or to the reader.

Therefore we can assume a more flexible notion of story (not so dissimilar from the one proposed by Aristotle's *Poetics*) in which it is enough to isolate an agent (no matter whether human or not), an initial state, a series of time-oriented changes with their causes, a final (even if transitorily so) result. In this sense there is a story even in the chemical description given by Peirce (see Chapter 7) about the production of lithium.

Thus one can recognize one or more *fabulae* even in those avant-garde narrative texts in which it seems that there is no story at all: at most it is difficult to ascertain who the agents are, what causes what, and where a relevant change takes place.[17] It is even possible to assign a *fabula* to a metaphysical treatise such as Spinoza's *Ethica more geometrico demonstrata.* Consider its opening sentences:

(19) *Per causam sui intelligo id cujus essentia involvit existentiam; sive id cujus natura non potest concipi nisi existens.*

There is at least a presupposed agent (Ego) who makes an action (*intelligo*) concerning an object (*id*) who becomes in turn the agent of an embedded story (God is *causa sui*). As a matter of fact, in this story there is no change: the *Ethica* tells of a universe in which nothing 'new' happens (since the order and the connection of things is the same as the order and the connection of ideas). There is an agent *which* causes its own absolute permanence through any lapse of time (before time existed). It is not true, however, that change and time order are denied: they are at a zero degree. The *fabula* can be an *antifabula.* It is also true that at such an elementary level the *fabula* becomes a matter for box 8, a pure opposition of roles; or for box 10, a world structure.

But, if the text does not tell a consistent *fabula,* there is another way to approach it from a narrative point of view: the text narrates the various steps of its own construction. It is possible to read a scientific essay this way, as does Greimas (1975), where he analyzes a *"discours non figuratif"* such as Dumezil's introduction to *Naissance d'Archange.* Greimas discovers in this scientific text not only an *"organisation discursive"* (corresponding to box 4) but also an *"organisation narrative,"* corresponding to a part of box 6 (as far as narrative functions as loss or victory are identified) and to boxes 9 and 10. The text thus appears as the story of a research, with its temporal steps, the modification imposed on the starting situation by an acting subject (the researcher—or Science in person).

0.7.2. Forecasts and inferential walks

0.7.2.1. However, the role of the reader does not consist only in choosing the level of abstraction at which to produce the macropropositions of the *fabula.* The *fabula* is not produced once the text has been definitely read: the *fabula* is the result of a continuous series of abductions made during the course of the reading. Therefore the *fabula* is always experienced step by step.

Since every step usually involves a change of state and a lapse of time, the reader is led to make an intermediate *extensional* operation: he considers the various macropropositions as statements about events taking place in a still-bracketed possible world. Each of these statements concerns the way in which a given individual determines or undergoes a certain change of state, and the reader is induced to wonder what could happen at the next step of the story.

To wonder about the next step of a given story means to face a state of disjunction of probabilities.

In fact, such disjunctions occur at every sentence of a narrative step, even within the boundaries of a single sentence: *"La Marquise sortit à cinq heures . . ."*—to do what, to go where? But the condition of a neurotic reader compelled to ask Whom? What? at every occurrence of a transitive verb (even though witnessing a profound affinity between sememic structures and narrative ones) is usually neutralized by the normal reading speed.

The 'relevant' disjunction of probability ought then to take place at the junction of those macropropositions the reader has identified as relevant components of the *fabula.*

In many cases the right clues to establishing these junctions are given either at the text linear manifestation level (subdivision in chapters and paragraphs and other graphic devices; in the *roman-feuilleton,* the temporal distribution by instalments) or at the surface intensional level (explicit warnings or connotative hints, innuendos, allusions preparing states of suspense). It is, in other words, the plot to display all the devices able to elicit expectations at the level of the *fabula.*

To expect means to forecast: the reader collaborates in the course of the *fabula,* making forecasts about the forthcoming state of affairs. The further states must prove or disprove his hypotheses (see Vaina, 1976; 1977).

The end of the text not only confirms or contradicts the last forecasts, but also authenticates or inauthenticates the whole system of long-distance hypotheses hazarded by the reader about the final state of the *fabula.*

In Figure 0.3 this dialectic of forecasts and proofs is scored at box 7, half-way between boxes 5 and 10, which concern extensions. This dialectic is in fact unpredictably distributed all along the interpretative journey, but it definitely concerns the world structure of the text, that is, the deep extensional level, and only at that level can it be rigorously analyzed.

0.7.2.2. In order to make forecasts which can be approved by the further course of the *fabula,* the Model Reader resorts to intertextual frames. Consider text (5) (see 0.6.1.5). As Raoul raises his hand, the reader understands that Raoul wants to beat Marguerite (semantic disclosure) and expects that he will actually beat Marguerite. This second interpretative movement has nothing to do with the actualization of discursive structures: it represents a forecast activated at the level of *fabula* (by the way, it will be disproved by the course of the story: Raoul will not actually beat Marguerite).

The reader was encouraged to activate this hypothesis by a lot of already recorded narrative situations (intertextual frames). To identify these frames the reader had to 'walk', so to speak, outside the text, in order to gather intertextual support (a quest for analogous 'topoi', themes, or motives).[18]

I call these interpretative moves *inferential walks:* they are not mere whimsical initiatives on the part of the reader, but are elicited by discursive structures and foreseen by the whole textual strategy as indispensable components of the construction of the *fabula.*

Frequently, the *fabula* is made *also* of presupposed macropropositions already actualized by other texts, which the reader is invited to insert into the story so that they can be taken for granted in its following steps. It is a common styleme in many traditional novels for a text to say "Our reader has surely already understood that . . ." while untold phrases constitute important components of modern stories. Sometimes, even when the expected step is made explicit, the fact that it was expected by inferential walks is part of the textual strategy: we enjoy the final identification of Oliver Twist just because we were supposed to yearn passionately for it during the intermediate steps of the story.

In *Les Mystères de Paris* are infinite points, from beginning to end, in which the Model Reader is allowed to take inferential walks so as to suppose that Fleur-de-Marie is the daughter of Rodolphe. From the Greek comedy on, he has at his disposal an intertextual frame which fits the situation perfectly. Sue is so convinced that his reader has taken such an inferential walk that at a certain point he is unable to defend his position, and he candidly confesses that he knows that the readers know the truth (which should be revealed only at the end of his immense novel). The fact that he anticipates such a solution before the middle of the novel is a curious case of narrative impotence, due to extratextual determinations (the commercial and technical constraints of the *feuilleton* genre that he was experiencing for the first time in human history). Thus *Les Mystères de Paris* has a good *fabula* but a bad plot. But Sue's unfortunate accident tells us to what extent foreseen inferential walks are encompassed by the generative project (see Chapter 6 of this book). Chapter 8 deals expressly with this problem.

0.7.3. Open and closed *fabulae*
Not every choice made by the reader at the various disjunctions of probability has the same value. In a novel such as Sue's, the more advanced choices are less equiprobable than are the first ones (the narration being a Markovian chain like the tonal musical process). In a novel such as Fleming's, the contrary happens: it is easy to hazard what Bond will do as a first move and hard to guess how he will succeed in getting out of a scrape. This difficulty is, however, reduced by the constancy of the same narrative scheme throughout the various novels. So the probabilities are different for the naive reader and for the 'smart' one, whose competence encompasses the intertextual frames established by Fleming. The analysis of the iterative scheme made in the essay (Chapter 4) on Superman (a genre rule governing most popular stories) suggests that probably the Model Reader such popular texts require is a 'smart' one.

On the contrary, there are texts aiming at giving the Model Reader the solutions he does not expect, challenging every overcoded intertextual frame as well as the reader's predictive indolence.

The type of cooperation requested of the reader, the flexibility of the text in validating (or at least in not contradicting) the widest possible range of interpretative proposals—all this characterizes narrative structures as more or less 'open'.

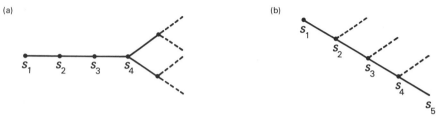

Figure 0.4

I shall try to represent two kinds of liberality in openness by the two diagrams of Figure 0.4 (where the nodes *s* represent states of the *fabula* at which a forecast is in some way elicited). In case (a) the sender leads the addressee step by step to a state of pluriprobability (many courses of events are given as equiprobable). The end of the text is not its final state, since the reader is invited to make his own free choices and to re-evaluate the entire text from the point of view of his final decision. Such a situation is typical of many avant-garde texts (fictional and nonfictional) and of post-Webernian music.

A typical instance of such a diagram is the episode of Minucius Mandrake analyzed in Chapter 2: the episode does not end, or may end in various ways. Likewise the reader can imagine various possible outcomes after the end of the text linear manifestation of *Gordon Pym* (the final note of the author does not reduce, but even enhances, the openness).

In case (b) the sender offers his addressee continual occasions for forecasting, but at each further step he reasserts, so to speak, the rights of his own text, saying without ambiguity what has to be taken as 'true' in his fictional world. Typical from this point of view are detective novels.[19]

Obviously, the diagrams in Figure 0.4 represent two abstract types of cooperation, a sort of straight opposition between *open* and *closed* narrative structures. In reality the practice of generating and interpreting texts represents a graded continuum of possible interaction α . . . . ω, where α is the offer of a maximal freedom, and ω the most repressive request of conformity. A text can rank at a given position γ (as far as the intentions of its author are concerned) and obtain a result δ or μ according either to a failure in its strategy or to the cultural and psychological background of the addressee.

0.7.4.   The sememe and the *fabula*
This dialectic of proposals and expectations rules *also* nonfictional texts. Consider this minimal textual stimulus:

(20) *Robin is a bachelor, as . . .*

which can arouse at least four possible choices (only one will be obviously authenticated by the further textual course):

(21) *he is serving under the standard of Batman.*
(22) *he has a homosexual relation with Batman.*
(23) *he got a B.A. at the Gotham City College.*
(24) *it is a seal* (this choice being verisimilar only for a lexicalist).

I realize that there is a difference between the expectations displayed vis-à-vis a *fabula* and those aroused by the manifestation of the lexeme /bachelor/. In this second case the interpreter only expects to ascertain which of the already *coded* senses of /bachelor/ (young knight, unmarried, B.A., unmated seal) will be textually actualized. But are we sure that in the course of a story something different happens? A story actualizes pre-overcoded narrative functions, that is, intertextual frames.

The way in which semantic disclosures and narrative forecasts are strictly interdependent, and co-dependent on the same storage of encyclopedic knowledge, is demonstrated very well by the following (rather elementary) example.

In Cyrus S. Sulzberger's *The Tooth Merchant,* the narrator begins by saying that he was sleeping in Istanbul in a brothel with a prostitute, Iffet,

(25) *when suddenly there was a scream at the door followed by a thump on the stairs. "Aaaaaaiiiiieee, the American Fleet," moaned Iffet, hauling the flyblown sheet about her head as the police burst in.*

We have the chance to have also at our disposal the Italian translation of this text. A translation is an actualized and manifested interpretation—therefore an important witness for our purposes. The Italian translation reads as follows:

(26) *quando fummo risvegliati di soprassalto da strilli giù in basso, seguiti da uno scalpiccio su per le scale. "Ahiahiai, la flotta americana!" gemette Iffet coprendosi la testa col lenzuolo. Irruppe invece la polizia.*

The translator (hereafter our Model Reader) has made the following first inference: that the narrator is speaking in the first person, that he was sleeping, and that he is able to report about the scream means that he has been awakened by the scream. From a short surface microproposition, the Model Reader has extrapolated a more analytical macroproposition: x was sleeping, then there was a scream, then x woke up, then x heard the scream. The reference was to the common frame «to be suddenly awakened by a noise» (involving a very subtle time order, with relations of contemporaneity). In fact, why at the manifestation level was the scream 'sudden'? Sudden with respect to whom? This /suddenly/ is a hypallage; it is not the scream which is sudden, it is the experience of it undergone by the narrator (*rhetorical overcoding*).

The English text says that there was a scream at the door. Which door? The one of the room where the narrator was sleeping[20] or the one downstairs on the street (this difference being suggested by another *common frame*)? The Model Reader decomposes this 'sudden' action into more analytical propositions: if there was first a scream and then a thump on the stair, this means that the scream took place downstairs. Therefore the translation *discloses* the fact that there was a scream *downstairs*.

Notice that /scream/ is translated as «strilli». This is correct, but I smell, as an Italian native speaker, that /strillo/ is more 'feminine' than is /scream/ (*stylistic overcoding*). The Model Reader, resorting to a given *common frame,* has decided that downstairs there was a 'madame'.

Let me avoid any discussion about the presupposed ability of the reader (other than the translator) to understand why Iffet moans and why she makes the (false) forecast concerning the American Fleet. In short, if there is a violent and noisy arrival of somebody, then *they* must be a consistent crowd; a crowd in a brothel, in a city with a port, means sailors (unexpected) and probably ones not native to the city; in the Mediterranean area, under the agreements of the North Atlantic Treaty Organization, they cannot be but the American Fleet (number of *synecdoches*); the entire American Fleet is too much even for a professional such as Iffet; and so on: to understand this rather sophomoric wit, the reader is supposed to take a lot of inferential walks.

Iffet /hauls/ (*rhetorical overcoding*—anyway, see Chapter 8, on metaphor) the flyblown sheet (*rhetorical hyperbole,* connoting the regretful status of the brothel—disregarded by the translator, also because the brothel in question was previously scored as one among the "foulest in Europe"). Where the hell does this sheet come from? Suppose this text is submitted to a computer. If the computer is fed only with a lexicon, it understands /sheet/, but does not understand why there are sheets in a brothel and which one is that hauled by Iffet. Fortunately, the computer (as well as the Model Reader) is furnished with a *common frame:* in brothels there are rooms, these rooms have beds, these beds have sheets. According to the previous frame «sleeping in a brothel», whoever sleeps in such places sleeps on a bed, and so on. I am not playing a Byzantine game. That is exactly what a reader *is supposed* to do in order to actualize the surface intensional level. I could add, Why does this frightened woman cover her head with a sheet when in danger? Other frames are put in play.

Despite Iffet's forecasts (and probably despite the naive reader's), it is not the American Fleet which enters; it is the police.

Iffet believed it was the American Fleet because she was resorting to a wrong *common frame* (while the reader relied upon the wrong *intertextual frame*). The *fabula* obliges the reader (and Iffet) to correct their forecasts. Another frame is activated. Rightly enough, the translator introduces the new event by an /invece/ («on the other hand»: contrary to Iffet's topic).

At this point the semantic disclosures are irreparably mixed with inferences at the narrative level. And both send the reader back to box 10 (world structures and different propositional attitudes creating possible worlds).

A text is not a 'crystal'. If it were a crystal, the cooperation of the reader would be part of its molecular structure.

0.8. Deeper levels

0.8.1. At this point Figure 3 becomes very stiff vis-à-vis the flexibility of movements presumably accomplished by the reader.

In box 8 I am considering Greimas' *actants* and *actantial roles*. Similar structures (at slightly different levels of abstraction) are envisaged by Burke (1969) (agent, counteragent, and so on), Pike (1964) (situational roles), Fillmore (1970), and others. At this level the *fabula* and every other narrative structure are by a further abstraction reduced to pure formal positions (subject, object, sender, and addressee) which produce actantial roles. These roles are manifested at the inferior levels by *actorial* structures (the actantial roles are filled up by concrete actors, elements of the *fabula*—but already manifested at the surface intensional level of discursive structures).

0.8.2. At this point the reader has many tasks to perform. He must verify his forecasts apropos of the *fabula,* so facing the world structures of the text. He must recognize what the text accepts and mentions as 'actual' and what has to be recognized as a mere matter of propositional attitudes on the parts both of the reader and of the characters of the story (a character believes *p* while *p* is false; the reader believes that *q* is the case, while the next state of the *fabula* disproves his expectation). Thus the reader must compare these world structures with each other and must, so to speak, accept the textual truth.

But at the same time the reader has to compare (if he has not yet done so) the world such as is presented by the text with his own 'real' world, that is, the world of his (presumed) concrete experience, at least such as it is framed by his own encyclopedia. In other words, should the reader have put into brackets the problems aroused by box 5, now he has to deparenthesize his suspension of disbelief. Even if the text is a fictional one, the comparison with the 'real' world is indispensable in order to acknowledge the 'verisimilitude' of the *fabula*.

All the operations encompassed by box 10 are so complex, involving as they do problems of modal logic, that they cannot be dealt with within the framework of the present overview. Chapter 8 is devoted to this matter.

0.8.3. As for box 9, it encompasses another complex series of intensional operations and—along with box 8—represents the intensional counterpart of box 10. Since the theory of possible worlds has been proposed just in order to solve intensional problems by translating them into extensional terms, I suspect that the two horns of my dilemmatic diagram are in the last analysis reducible to one another.

I record in box 9 'ideological' (or axiological) structures, such as Good vs. Bad, Positive vs. Negative, True vs. False, or even (à la Greimas) Life vs. Death and Nature vs. Culture. I wonder whether the extensional world structures can be reduced to such elementary oppositions or not: undoubtedly in certain texts one is dealing with possible textual worlds where the involved properties are exclusively of this type.

0.8.4. Notice that, within Greimas' intensional framework, actantial structures are influenced (overdetermined) by so-called modalities and imputed truth values (*veridiction*) (see, for instance, Greimas, 1973:165; 1976:80). These operations are the intensional reverberation of the assignment of truth values in box 10: given relations at the actantial level are considered insofar as they are textually *predicated* as true or false, and depending on propositional attitudes of the characters, equally predicated by the text.

At this point intensional approaches (mainly performed by the semiotics of narrativity) and extensional (modal) approaches (mainly adopted from the logic of natural languages) seem to overlap each other. What differs is the type of formalization these problems undergo in different theories, and, at the present state of the art, every attempt to merge these diverse approaches risks giving rise to misleading contaminations.

The only thing which is clear is that these deeper levels are not a mere terminological figment, since every reader is moving within box 9 when making interpretative decisions about the ideology of a given text, and within box 10 when making decisions about the credibility of the reported events and of the beliefs, lies, or wishes of the characters. Chronologically prior to the development of such efforts in formalization, my essays on Superman (Chapter 4) and Bond (Chapter 6) are dealing only with the ideological oppositions to be detected at the deepest intensional levels, although in the case of Superman there is also the problem of mutual accessibility among possible worlds.

0.8.5. As far as the problem of the textual levels is concerned, one could say that there are more things in a text than are dreamt of in our text theories. But there are also *fewer* things than are dreamt of. The structure of the compositional spectrum of a given *sememe* is the same as the structure of a *frame* and of the *actantial structure*. The world structures are dominated by the opposition of presence and absence, necessity or accidentality of properties. Ideological structure oppositions can be translated into truth assignments (True vs. False)—and vice versa, as logicians hardly suspect. There are ideological structures also in logical *fabulae*.

0.9. Conclusion for an introduction

At the end of this survey, and taking into account the results of the following essays, I am now able to restate my preliminary statements.

The aesthetic dialectics between openness and closedness of texts depends on the basic structure of the process of text interpretation in general.

This structure is made possible by the nature of the system of codes and subcodes constituting the world of the encyclopedia: contradictory in its very format (see *Theory,* 2.13) and ruled by a constitutive mechanism of unlimited semiosis, the semantic space can be reduced only through the cooperative activity performed by the reader in actualizing a given text.

The reader finds his freedom (i) in deciding how to activate one or another of the textual levels and (ii) in choosing which codes to apply.

At this point one can wonder at which specific level certain aesthetic texts, which give the impression of being particularly open, call for the decisive collaboration on the part of the reader. Undoubtedly, texts (as well as literary genres) can be characterized according to their privileged level of openness. Can one say that in poetry the most happens at the level of semantic disclosures and at that of deepest intensional structures? That in Kafka's novels the place of the most blatantly elicited choices is the one of the narrative structures? That a play of Pirandello works mainly at the level of world structures focusing on propositional attitudes?

My final approach to *Un drame bien parisien* (a 'minor' work of literature, indeed, if such a high-brow distinction still makes sense) should demonstrate that, in a 'well-made' literary work (as well as in every work of art), there is no openness at a given level which is not sustained and improved by analogous operations at all other levels.

This does not happen with *closed* works. I can read James Bond's story at the level of the *fabula* (and maybe of ideological structures) as a manifestation of a transversal *désir,* every surface image being the figure of a more profound and irreducible pulsion (nothing is impossible for a brilliantly perverse mind), but the text linear manifestation and the discursive structures remain what they are: a museum of *déjà vu,* a recital of overcoded literary commonplaces.

On the contrary, those texts that according to Barthes (1973) are able to produce the 'jouissance' of the unexhausted virtuality of their expressive plane succeed in this effect just because they have been planned to invite their Model Readers to reproduce their own processes of deconstruction by a plurality of free interpretive choices.

Naturally, a text can also be read as an uncommitted stimulus for a personal hallucinatory experience, cutting out levels of meaning, placing upon the expression 'aberrant' codes. As Borges once suggested, why not read the Odyssey as written after the *Aeneid* or the *Imitation of Christ* as written by Céline?

A semiotic theory offers the proper categories to explain also this sort of experience (*Theory*, 3.7.8). Everything can become open as well as closed in the universe of unlimited semiosis.[21]

I think, however, that it is possible to distinguish between the free interpretative choices elicited by a purposeful strategy of openness and the freedom taken by a reader with a text assumed as a mere stimulus. The essays collected in this book deal with a shaded gamut of different attitudes toward different types of text. Kristeva (1970:185ff) speaks of a traditional 'closed' text as of a cube, or an Italian stage where the author disguises his own productive activity and tries to convince the spectator that he and him are the same. It is not by chance that Allais' *Un drame bien parisien* concludes my analyses: not only does this text reestablish in the open air the gap between sender and addressee, but it also portrays its own productive process.

To conclude a book of textual explorations with a metanarrative text that speaks ambiguously and with tongue in cheek of its own ambiguity and of its own derisory nature seems to me an honest decision. After having let semiotics speak abundantly about texts, it is correct to let a text speak by itself about its semiotic strategy.

NOTES

1. This article was published later as the first chapter of *Opera Aperta— Forma e indeterminazione nelle poetiche contemporanee* (Milan: Bompiani, 1962).

2. I take the term 'pragmatics' in its current sense. Thus pragmatics concerns itself not only with the interpretation of indexical expressions but with the "essential dependence of communication in natural languages on speaker and hearer, on linguistic context and extralinguistic context . . . on the availability of background knowledge, on readiness to obtain this background knowledge and on the good will of the participants in a communication act" (Bar-Hillel, 1968:271; see also Montague, 1968, Petőfi, 1974).

3. *L'oeuvre ouverte* (Paris: Seuil, 1966).

4. Interview by Paolo Caruso in *Paese sera-Libri* (January 20, 1967). Reprinted in *Conversazioni con Lévi-Strauss, Foucault, Lacan,* ed. Paolo Caruso (Milan: Mursia, 1969).

5. Roman Jakobson and Claude Lévi-Strauss, " 'Le Chats' de Charles Baudelaire," *L'Homme* (January 1962).

6. This notion of the Model Reader can be extrapolated also from other text theories. See, for example, Barthes (1966), Riffaterre (1971), Schmidt (1973, 1976), and van Dijk (1976c). This 'dialogical' nature of texts has already been advocated by Baxtin.

7. On a definition of fictionality, see Barthes (1966), van Dijk (1976a, 1976c), and Schmidt (1976). For a critical overview of the traditional notions, see Scholes and Kellogg (1966).

8. See Petőfi (1976b, 1976c). See also, for another subdivision between *deep structures, superficial structures,* and *structures of manifestation,* Greimas and Rastier (1968).

9. See Barthes (1966) on the story as a 'grande phrase'. See also Todorov (1969) and van Dijk (1972b). According to Greimas (1973), a given semantic unit (for example, «fisher») is in its very sememic structure a potential narrative program: "Le *pêcheur* porte en lui, évidemment, toutes les possibilités de son faire, tout ce que l'on peut s'attendre de lui en fait de comportement; sa mise en isotopie discursive en fait un rôle thématique utilisable pour le récit. Le personnage de roman . . . ne deploie sa figure complète qu'a la dernière page, grâce à la mémorisation operée par le lecteur" (p. 174).

10. Another frame in Peirce is the situation "how to make an apple pie" (CP, I.341). I am not sure that the notion of 'frame' has the same value as in Bateson (1955) and in Goffman (1974). The answer seems to be positive when Goffman says that "there is a sense in which what is play for the golfer is work for the caddy" (1974:8); but frames as suggested by Bateson are rather a metatextual framing of textual situations in order to make them comprehensible. In this sense they are more similar to *genre rules* ("pay attention, this is a joke" or "this situation is structured according to a double bind . . .").

11. "Le lexème est, par consequent, une organisation sémique virtuelle qui, à des rares exceptions près . . . n'est jamais réalisé tel quel dans le discours manifesté. Tout discours, du moment du'il pose sa propre isotopie sémantique, n'est qu'une exploitation très partielle des virtualités considerables que lui offre le thesaurus lexématique: s'il poursuit son chemin, c'est en le laissant parsemé de figures du monde qu'il a rejetées, mais qui continuent à vivre leur existence virtuelle, prêtes à ressusciter au moindre effort de memorisation" (Greimas, 1973:170).

12. Christine Brooke-Rose (personal communication) suggests that no ambiguity would arise were the sentence /Charles walks his dog twice a day. So does John/. It means that in (6) one of the first moves of the interpreter is to evoke the intertextual frame «adulterine triangle», since thousands of texts record such a situation. On the contrary, no text (as far as one remembers) records the story of a morbid passion of two men for the same dog, and it is

enough to activate the common frame «walking *his own* pet». Thus no ambiguity arises.

13. See van Dijk (1976b:50) for a description of tentative attributions of topics. There is a *probabilistic* strategy with *provisional topics*. Sometimes, on the contrary, the topic is made explicit by expressions such as /The crucial point is . . ./, and so on (*topic markers*). For genres as topics see Culler (1975, ch. 7).

14. See Greimas (1973:170) and his notion of *'parcours figuratif'*. See also Grupe d'Entrevernes (1977:24) and van Dijk (1975) on 'key words'.

15. The concept of isotopy goes far beyond the level of discoursive structures. It is possible to establish isotopies at every textual level. See Kerbrat-Orecchioni (1976) for a classification of semantic, phonetic, prosodic, stylistic, *'énonciative'*, rhetorical, presuppositional, syntactic, narrative isotopies.

16. For a first survey of the question, see Erlich (1954).

17. See, for example, the analysis of Roussel's *Nouvelles Impressions d'Afrique* given by Kristeva (1970:73ff).

18. See Kristeva (1969, 1970). See also the notion of *proairetic code* in Barthes (1970).

19. Besides, there is a third *false* request for cooperation. In this third situation the sender gives false clues to the addressee so as to excite his will for cooperation, pulling (or pushing) him along the wrong way and leaving him to go on until he reaches a point of no return. Here none of the reader's expectations happens to be validated by the final state of the story, but the reader has gone too far to obliterate his excess of cooperation and the other story he has developed. But at this point, instead of limiting himself to disproving the reader's choices, the author titillates the reader's false story even more, as though there were something true in it, notwithstanding the straight refusal that the text has opposed to the reader's forecasts. Such a story would have a pragmatic unhappy end, but it would represent a text about the pragmatic procedures in text generation and interpretation. Such is *Un drame bien parisien,* analyzed in Chapter 8.

20. That he was sleeping in a room (the previous sequences say only that he was sleeping in a brothel) is made clear by the *common frame* «sleeping in a brothel». The suspicion that he was the janitor and not a customer is already excluded by another *common frame,* since it has been previously said that the action takes place in the *late* morning.

21. In *Theory* (3.6) I developed a typology of modes of sign production. Since to interpret a text means to actualize its content starting from its expression, it would be interesting to ascertain which modes of production are implemented at the various boxes of Figure 0.3. Such a question goes beyond the boundaries of the present discussion, but one can say that in actualizing the various interpretative levels all the modes listed in Table 39 of *Theory* are, in principle, encompassed. Dealing with a verbal text, one is mainly concerned with *replicas* of *combinational units,* but in box 3, at the linear manifestation, many *programmed stimuli* and *pseudocombinational units* can be found, both at the grammatological level and at the level of its phonetic actualization. When looking for key words so as tentatively to outline textual topics, the reader deals

with words taken as *symptoms* and *clues.* Intertextual frames are a matter of *stylization,* whereas explicit intertextual quotations are cases of *ostension.* The temporal succession of macropropositions at the level of narrative structures, since its concerns time-oriented sequences, involves phenomena of *vectorialization.* In modern novels in which the structure of the story portrays ideological attitudes or suggests a possible form of the world, there are phenomena of *projections* and *graphs,* ruled by *ratio difficilis*—both at the level of narrative structures and at the level of discursive structures, when temporal or causal displacements in the organization of the manifested course of events mirror more profound contradictions in the organization of world structures. These tentative suggestions aim at orienting a possible critical interpretation of concrete texts.

Part One   Open

CHAPTER ONE

The Poetics of the Open Work

1.1.   A number of recent pieces of instrumental music are linked by a common feature: the considerable autonomy left to the individual performer in the way he chooses to play the work. Thus he is not merely free to interpret the composer's instructions following his own discretion (which in fact happens in traditional music), but he must impose his judgment on the form of the piece, as when he decides how long to hold a note or in what order to group the sounds: all this amounts to an act of improvised creation. Here are some of the best known examples of the process.

(1)   In *Klavierstück XI,* by Karlheinz Stockhausen, the composer presents the performer a single large sheet of music paper with a series of note groupings. The performer then has to choose among these groupings, first for the one to start the piece and, next, for the successive units in the order in which he elects to weld them together. In this type of performance, the instrumentalist's freedom is a function of the "combinative" structure of the piece, which allows him to "mount" the sequence of musical units in the order he chooses.

(2)   In Luciano Berio's *Sequence for solo flute,* the composer presents the performer a text which predetermines the sequence and intensity of the sounds to be played. But the performer is free to choose how long to hold a note inside the fixed framework imposed on him, which in turn is established by the fixed pattern of the metronome's beat.

(3)   Henri Pousseur has offered the following description of his piece *Scambi:*

"L'opera in movimento e la coscienza dell'epoca," *Incontri Musicali* 3 (1959). Bruce Merry, trans., "The Poetics of the Open Work," *Twentieth Century Studies* (December 1974). This chapter is a revised version of the translation.

[47]

Scambi is not so much a musical composition as a *field of possibilities,* an explicit invitation to exercise choice. It is made up of sixteen sections. Each of these can be linked to any two others, without weakening the logical continuity of the musical process. Two of its sections, for example, are introduced by similar motifs (after which they evolve in divergent patterns); another pair of sections, on the contrary, tends to develop towards the same climax. Since the performer can start or finish with any one section, a considerable number of sequential permutations are made available to him. Furthermore, the two sections which begin on the same motif can be played simultaneously, so as to present a more complex structural polyphony. It is not out of the question that we conceive these formal notations as a marketable product: if they were tape-recorded and the purchaser had a sufficiently sophisticated reception apparatus, then the general public would be in a position to develop a private musical construct of its own and a new collective sensibility in matters of musical presentation and duration could emerge.

(4) In Pierre Boulez' *Third Sonata for piano,* the first section (*Antiphonie, Formant 1*) is made up of ten different pieces on ten corresponding sheets of music paper. These can be arranged in different sequences like a stack of filing cards, though not all possible permutations are permissible. The second part (*Formant 2, Thrope*) is made up of four parts with an internal circularity, so that the performer can commence with any one of them, linking it successively to the others until he comes round full circle. No major interpretative variants are permitted inside the various sections, but one of them, *Parenthèse,* opens with a prescribed time beat, which is followed by extensive pauses in which the beat is left to the player's discretion. A further prescriptive note is evinced by the composer's instructions on the manner of linking one piece to the next (for example, *sans retenir, enchaîner sans interruption,* and so on).

What is immediately striking in such cases is the macroscopic divergence between these forms of musical communication and the time-honored tradition of the classics. This difference can be formulated in elementary terms as follows: a classical composition, whether it be a Bach fugue, Verdi's *Aïda,* or Stravinsky's *Rite of Spring,* posits an assemblage of sound units which the composer arranged in a closed, well-defined manner before presenting it to the listener. He converted his idea into conventional symbols which more or less oblige the eventual performer to reproduce the format devised by the composer himself. Whereas the new musical works referred to above reject the definitive, concluded message and multiply the formal possibilities of the distribution of their elements. They appeal to the initiative of the individual performer, and hence they offer themselves, not as finite works which prescribe specific repetition along given structural coordinates, but as 'open' works, which are brought to their conclusion by the performer at the same time as he experiences them on an aesthetic plane.[1]

To avoid any confusion in terminology, it is important to specify that here the definition of the 'open work', despite its relevance in formulating a fresh dialectics between the work of art and its performer, still requires to be separated from other conventional applications of this term. Aesthetic theorists, for example, often have recourse to the notions of 'completeness' and 'openness' in connection with a given work of art. These two expressions refer to a standard situation of which we are all aware in our reception of a work of art: we see it as the end product of an author's effort to arrange a sequence of communicative effects in such a way that each individual addressee can refashion the original composition devised by the author. The addressee is bound to enter into an interplay of stimulus and response which depends on his unique capacity for sensitive reception of the piece. In this sense the author presents a finished product with the intention that this particular composition should be appreciated and received in the same form as he devised it. As he reacts to the play of stimuli and his own response to their patterning, the individual addressee is bound to supply his own existential credentials, the sense conditioning which is peculiarly his own, a defined culture, a set of tastes, personal inclinations, and prejudices. Thus his comprehension of the original artifact is always modified by his particular and individual perspective. In fact, the form of the work of art gains its aesthetic validity precisely in proportion to the number of different perspectives from which it can be viewed and understood. These give it a wealth of different resonances and echoes without impairing its original essence; a road traffic sign, on the other hand, can only be viewed in one sense, and, if it is transfigured into some fantastic meaning by an imaginative driver, it merely ceases to be *that* particular traffic sign with that particular meaning. A work of art, therefore, is a complete and *closed* form in its uniqueness as a balanced organic whole, while at the same time constituting an *open* product on account of its susceptibility to countless different interpretations which do not impinge on its unadulterable specificity. Hence every reception of a work of art is both an *interpretation* and a *performance* of it, because in every reception the work takes on a fresh perspective for itself.

Nonetheless, it is obvious that works like those of Berio and Stockhausen are 'open' in a far more tangible sense. In primitive terms we can say that they are quite literally 'unfinished': the author seems to hand them on to the performer more or less like the components of a construction kit. He seems to be unconcerned about the manner of their eventual deployment. This is a loose and paradoxical interpretation of the phenomenon, but the most immediately striking aspect of these musical forms can lead to this kind of uncertainty, although the very fact of our uncertainty is itself a positive feature: it invites us to consider *why* the contemporary artist feels the need to work in this kind of direction, to try to work out what historical evolution of aesthetic sensibility led up to it and which factors in modern culture reinforced it. We are then in a position to surmise how these experiences should be viewed in the spectrum of a theoretical aesthetics.

1.2. Pousseur has observed that the poetics of the 'open' work tends to encourage 'acts of conscious freedom' on the part of the performer and place him at the focal point of a network of limitless interrelations, among which he chooses to set up his own form without being influenced by an external *necessity* which definitively prescribes the organization of the work in hand.[2] At this point one could object (with reference to the wider meaning of 'openness' already introduced in this essay) that any work of art, even if it is not passed on to the addressee in an unfinished state, demands a free, inventive response, if only because it cannot really be appreciated unless the performer somehow reinvents it in psychological collaboration with the author himself. Yet this remark represents the theoretical perception of contemporary aesthetics, achieved only after painstaking consideration of the function of artistic performance; certainly an artist of a few centuries ago was far from being aware of these issues. Instead nowadays it is primarily the artist who is aware of its implications. In fact, rather than submit to the 'openness' as an inescapable element of artistic interpretation, he subsumes it into a positive aspect of his production, recasting the work so as to expose it to the maximum possible 'opening'.

The force of the subjective element in the interpretation of a work of art (any interpretation implies an interplay between the addressee and the work as an objective fact) was noticed by classical writers, especially when they set themselves to consider the figurative arts. In the *Sophist* Plato observes that painters suggest proportions, not by following some objective canon, but by judging them in relation to the angle from which they are seen by the observer. Vitruvius makes a distinction between 'symmetry' and 'eurhythmy', meaning by this latter term an adjustment of objective proportions to the requirements of a subjective vision. The scientific and practical development of the technique of perspective bears witness to the gradual maturation of this awareness of an interpretative subjectivity pitted against the work of art. Yet it is equally certain that this awareness has led to a tendency to operate against the 'openness' of the work, to favor its 'closing out'. The various devices of perspective were just so many different concessions to the actual location of the observer in order to ensure that he looked at the figure in *the only possible right way,* that is, the way the author of the work had devised various visual devices to oblige the observer's attention to converge on.

Let us consider another example. In the Middle Ages there grew up a theory of allegory which posited the possibility of reading the Scriptures (and eventually poetry, figurative arts), not just in the literal sense, but also in three other senses: the moral, the allegorical, and the anagogical. This theory is well known from a passage in Dante, but its roots go back to St. Paul ("videmus nunc per speculum in aenigmate, tunc autem facie ad faciem"), and it was developed by St. Jerome, Augustine, Bede, Scotus Erigena, Hugh and Richard of St. Victor, Alain of Lille, Bonaventure, Aquinas, and others in such a way as to represent a cardinal point of medieval poetics. A work in this sense is undoubtedly endowed with a measure of 'openness'. The reader of the text knows that every sentence and every trope is 'open' to a multiplicity of meanings which he must hunt for and find. Indeed, according to how he feels at one particular moment, the reader might choose a possible interpretative key which strikes him as exemplary of this spiritual state. He will *use* the work according to the desired meaning (causing it to come alive again, somehow different from the way he viewed it at an earlier reading). However, in this type of operation, 'openness' is far removed from meaning 'indefiniteness' of communication, 'infinite' possibilities of form, and complete freedom of reception. What in fact is made available is a range of rigidly preestablished and ordained interpretative solutions, and these never allow the reader to move outside the strict control of the author. Dante sums up the issue in his thirteenth Letter:

> We shall consider the following lines in order to make this type of treatment clearer: *In exitu Israel de Egypto, domus Jacob de populo barbaro, facta est Judea sanctificatio eius, Israel potestas eius.* Now if we just consider the literal meaning, what is meant here is the departure of the children of Israel from Egypt at the time of Moses. If we consider the allegory, what is meant is our human redemption through Christ. If we consider the moral sense, what is meant is the conversion of the soul from the torment and agony of sin to a state of grace. Finally, if we consider the anagogical sense, what is meant is the release of the spirit from the bondage of this corruption to the freedom of eternal glory.

It is obvious at this point that all available possibilities of interpretation have been exhausted. The reader can concentrate his attention on one sense rather than on another, in the limited space of this four-tiered sentence, but he must always follow rules that entail a rigid univocality. The meaning of allegorical figures and emblems which the medieval reader is likely to encounter is already prescribed by his encyclopedias, bestiaries, and lapidaries. Any symbolism is objectively defined and organized into a system. Underpinning this poetics of the necessary and the univocal is an ordered cosmos, a hierarchy of essences and laws which poetic discourse can clarify at several levels, but which each individual must understand in the only possible way, the one determined by the creative *logos*. The order of a work of art in this period is a mirror of imperial and theocratic society. The laws governing textual interpretation are the laws of an authoritarian regime which guide the individual in his every action, prescribing the ends for him and offering him the means to attain them.

It is not that the *four* solutions of the allegorical passage are quantitatively more limited than the *many* possible solutions of a contemporary 'open' work. As I shall try to show, it is a different vision of the world which lies under these different aesthetic experiences.

If we limit ourselves to a number of cursory historical glimpses, we can find one striking aspect of 'openness' in the 'open form' of Baroque. Here it is precisely the static and unquestionable definitiveness of the classical Renaissance form which is denied: the canons of space extended round a central axis, closed in by symmetrical lines and shut angles which cajole the eye toward the center in such a way as to suggest an idea of 'essential' eternity rather than movement. Baroque form is dynamic; it tends to an indeterminacy of effect (in its play of solid and void, light and darkness, with its curvature, its broken surfaces, its widely diversified angles of inclination); it conveys the idea of space being progressively dilated. Its search for kinetic excitement and illusory effect leads to a situation where the plastic mass in the Baroque work of art never allows a privileged, definitive, frontal view; rather, it induces the spectator to shift his position continuously in order to see the work in constantly new aspects, as if it were in a state of perpetual transformation. Now if Baroque spirituality is to be seen as the first clear manifestation of modern culture and sensitivity, it is because here, for the first time, man opts out of the canon of authorized responses and finds that he is faced (both in art and in science) by a world in a fluid state which requires corresponding creativity on his part. The poetic treatises concerning *'maraviglia'*, 'wit', *'agudezas'*, and so on, really strain to go further than their apparently Byzantine appearance: they seek to establish the new man's inventive role. He is no longer to see the work of art as an object which draws on given links with experience and which demands to be enjoyed; now he sees it as a potential mystery to be solved, a role to fulfill, a stimulus to quicken his imagination. Nonetheless, even these conclusions have been codified by modern criticism and organized into aesthetic canons. In fact, it would be rash to interpret Baroque poetics as a conscious theory of the 'open work'.

Between classicism and the Enlightenment, there developed a further concept which is of interest to us in the present context. The concept of 'pure poetry' gained currency for the very reason that general notions and abstract canons fell out of fashion, while the tradition of English empiricism increasingly argued in favor of the 'freedom' of the poet and set the stage for the coming theories of creativity. From Burke's declarations about the emotional power of words, it was a short step to Novalis' view of the pure evocative power of poetry as an art of blurred sense and vague outlines. An idea is now held to be all the more original and stimulating insofar as it ". . . allows for a greater inter-play and mutual convergence of concepts, life-views and attitudes. When a work offers a multitude of intentions, a plurality of meaning and above all a wide variety of different ways of being understood and appreciated, then under these conditions we can only conclude that it is of vital interest and that it is a pure expression of personality."[3]

To close our consideration of the Romantic period, it will be useful to refer to the first occasion when a conscious poetics of the 'open' work appears. The moment is late-nineteenth-century Symbolism; the text is Verlaine's *Art Poétique:*

> De la musique avant toute chose,
> et pour cela préfère l'impair
> plus vague et plus soluble dans l'air
> sans rien en lui qui pèse et qui pose.

Mallarmé's programmatic statement is even more explicit and pronounced in this context: "Nommer un objet c'est supprimer les trois quarts de la jouissance du poème, qui est faite du bonheur de deviner peu à peu: le suggérer . . . voilà le rêve . . . ." The important thing is to prevent a single sense from imposing itself at the very outset of the receptive process. Blank space surrounding a word, typographical adjustments, and spatial composition in the page setting of the poetic text—all contribute to create a halo of indefiniteness and to make the text pregnant with infinite suggestive possibilities.

This search for *suggestiveness* is a deliberate move to 'open' the work to the free response of the addressee. An artistic work which 'suggests' is also one which can be performed with the full emotional and imaginative resources of the interpreter. Whenever we read poetry there is a process by which we try to adapt our personal world to the emotional world proposed by the text. This is all the more true of poetic works that are deliberately based on suggestiveness, since the text sets out to stimulate the private world of the addressee in order that he can draw from inside himself some deeper response that mirrors the subtler resonances underlying the text.

A strong current in contemporary literature follows this use of symbol as a communicative channel for the indefinite, open to constantly shifting responses and interpretative stances. It is easy to think of Kafka's work as 'open': trial, castle, waiting, passing sentence, sickness, metamorphosis, and torture—none of these narrative situations is to be understood in the immediate literal sense. But, unlike the constructions of medieval allegory, where the superimposed layers of meaning are rigidly prescribed, in Kafka there is no confirmation in an encyclopedia, no matching paradigm in the cosmos, to provide a key to the symbolism. The various existentialist, theological, clinical, and psychoanalytic interpretations of Kafka's symbols cannot exhaust all the possibilities of his works. The work remains inexhaustible insofar as it is 'open', because in it an ordered world based on universally acknowledged laws is being replaced by a world based on ambiguity, both in the negative sense that directional centers are missing and in a positive sense, because values and dogma are constantly being placed in question.

Even when it is difficult to determine whether a given author had symbolist intentions or was aiming at effects of ambivalence or indeterminacy, there is a school of criticism nowadays which tends to view all modern literature as built upon symbolic patterns. W. Y. Tindall, in his book on the literary symbol, offers an analysis of some of the greatest modern literary works in order to test Valéry's declaration that ". . . il n'y a pas de vrai sens d'un texte." Tindall eventually concludes that a work of art is a construct which anyone at all, including its author, can put to any use whatsoever, as he chooses. This type of criticism views the literary work as a continuous potentiality of 'openness', in other words, an indefinite reserve of meanings. This is the scope of the wave of American studies on the structure of metaphor, or of modern work on 'types of ambiguity' offered by poetic discourse.[4]

Clearly, the work of James Joyce is a major example of an 'open' mode, since it deliberately seeks to offer an image of the ontological and existential situation of the contemporary world. The "Wandering Rocks" chapter in *Ulysses* amounts to a tiny universe that can be viewed from different points of perspective: the last residue of Aristotelian categories has now disappeared. Joyce is unconcerned with a consistent unfolding of time or a plausible spatial continuum in which to stage his characters' movements. Edmund Wilson has observed that, like Proust's or Whitehead's or Einstein's world, "Joyce's world is always changing as it is perceived by different observers and by them at different times."[5]

In *Finnegans Wake* we are faced with an even more startling process of 'openness': the book is molded into a curve that bends back on itself, like the Einsteinian universe. The opening word of the first page is the same as the closing word of the last page of the novel. Thus the work is *finite* in one sense, but in another sense it is *unlimited*. Each occurrence, each word stands in a series of possible relations with all the others in the text. According to the semantic choice which we make in the case of one unit so goes the way we interpret all the other units in the text. This does not mean that the book lacks specific sense. If Joyce does introduce some keys into the text, it is precisely because he wants the work to be read in a certain sense. But this particular 'sense' has all the richness of the cosmos itself. Ambitiously, the author intends his book to imply the totality of space and time, of all spaces and all times that are possible. The principal tool for this all-pervading ambiguity is the pun, the *calembour,* by which two, three, or even ten different etymological roots are combined in such a way that a single word can set up a knot of different submeanings, each of which in turn coincides and interrelates with other local allusions, which are themselves 'open' to new configurations and probabilities of interpretation. The reader of *Finnegans Wake* is in a position similar to that of the person listening to postdodecaphonic serial composition as he appears in a striking definition by Pousseur:

> Since the phenomena are no longer tied to one another by a term-to-term determination, it is up to the listener to place himself deliberately in the midst of an inexhaustible network of relationships and to choose for himself, so to speak, his own modes of approach, his reference points and his scale, and to endeavour to use as many dimensions as he possibly can at the same time and thus dynamize, multiply and extend to the utmost degree his perceptual faculties.[6]

Nor should we imagine that the tendency toward openness operates only at the level of indefinite suggestion and stimulation of emotional response. In Brecht's theoretical work on drama, we shall see that dramatic action is conceived as the problematic exposition of specific points of tension. Having presented these tension points (by following the well-known technique of epic recitation, which does not seek to influence the audience, but rather to offer a series of facts to be observed, employing the device of 'defamiliarization'), Brecht's plays do not, in the strict sense, devise solutions at all. It is up to the audience to draw its own conclusions from what it has seen on stage. Brecht's plays also end in a situation of ambiguity (typically, and more than any other, his *Galileo*), although it is no longer the morbid ambiguousness of a half-perceived infinitude or an anguish-laden mystery, but the specific concreteness of an ambiguity in social intercourse, a conflict of unresolved problems taxing the ingenuity of playwright, actors, and audience alike. Here the work is 'open' in the same sense that a debate is 'open'. A solution is seen as desirable and is actually anticipated, but it must come from the collective enterprise of the audience. In this case the 'openness' is converted into an instrument of revolutionary pedagogics.

1.3. In all the phenomena we have so far examined, I have employed the category of 'openness' to define widely differing situations, but on the whole the sorts of works taken into consideration are substantially different from the post-Webernian musical composers whom I considered at the opening of this essay. From the Baroque to modern Symbolist poetics there has been an ever-sharpening awareness of the concept of the work susceptible to many different interpretations. However, the examples considered in the preceding section propose an 'openness' based on the *theoretical, mental* collaboration of the consumer, who must freely interpret an artistic *datum,* a product which has already been organized in its structural entirety (even if this structure allows for an indefinite plurality of interpretations). On the other hand, a composition like *Scambi,* by Pousseur, represents a fresh advance. Somebody listening to a work by Webern freely reorganizes and enjoys a series of interrelations inside the context of the sound system offered to him in that particular (already fully produced) composition. But in listening to *Scambi* the auditor is required to do some of this organizing and structuring of the musical discourse. He collaborates with the composer in *making* the composition.

None of this argument should be conceived as passing an aesthetic judgment on the relative validity of the various types of works under consideration. However, it is clear that a composition such as *Scambi* poses a completely new problem. It invites us to identify inside the category of 'open' works a further, more restricted classification of works which can be defined as 'works in movement', because they characteristically consist of unplanned or physically incomplete structural units.

In the present cultural context, the phenomenon of the "work in movement" is certainly not limited to music. There are, for example, artistic products which display an intrinsic mobility, a kaleidoscopic capacity to suggest themselves in constantly renewed aspects to the consumer. A simple example is provided by Calder's "Mobiles" or by mobile compositions by other artists: elementary structures which possess the quality of moving in the air and assuming different spatial dispositions. They continuously create their own space and dimensions to fill it with.

If we turn to literary production to try to isolate an example of a "work in movement," we are immediately obliged to take into consideration Mallarmé's *Livre,* a colossal and far-reaching work, the quintessence of the poet's production. He conceived it as the work which would constitute not only the goal of his activities but also the end goal of the world: "Le monde existe pour aboutir à un livre." Mallarmé never finished the book, although he worked on it at different periods throughout his life. But there are sketches for the ending which have recently been brought to light by the acute philological research of Jacques Schérer.[7]

The metaphysical premises for Mallarmé's *Livre* are enormous and possibly questionable. I would prefer to leave them aside in order to concentrate on the dynamic structure of this artistic object which deliberately set out to validate a specific poetic principle: "Un livre ni commence ni ne finit; tout au plus fait-il semblant." The *Livre* was conceived as a mobile apparatus, not just in the mobile and 'open' sense of a composition such as *Coup de dès,* where grammar, syntax, and typesetting introduced a plurality of elements, polymorphous in their indeterminate relation to each other.

However, Mallarmé's immense enterprise was Utopian: it was embroidered with evermore disconcerting aspirations and ingenuities, and it is not surprising that it was never brought to completion. We do not know whether, had the work been completed, the whole project would have had any real value. It might well have turned out to be a dubious mystic and esoteric incarnation of a decadent sensitivity that had reached the extreme point of its creative parabola. I am inclined to this second view, but it is certainly interesting to find at the very threshold of the modern period such a vigorous program for a *work in movement,* and this is a sign that certain intellectual currents circulate imperceptibly until they are adopted and justified as cultural data which have to be organically integrated into the panorama of a whole period.

1.4.   In every century the way that artistic forms are structured reflects the way in which science or contemporary culture views reality. The closed, single conception in a work by a medieval artist reflected the conception of the cosmos as a hierarchy of fixed, preordained orders. The work as a pedagogical vehicle, as a monocentric and necessary apparatus (incorporating a rigid internal pattern of meter and rhymes) simply reflects the syllogistic system, a logic of necessity, a deductive consciousness by way of which reality could be made manifest step by step without unforeseen interruptions, moving forward in a single direction, proceeding from first principles of science which were seen as one and the same with the first principles of reality. The openness and dynamism of the Baroque mark, in fact, the advent of a new scientific awareness: the substitution of the *tactile* by the *visual* means that the subjective element comes to prevail and attention is shifted from the *essence* to the *appearance* of architectural and pictorial products. It reflects the rising interest in a psychology of impression and sensation, in short—an empiricism which converts the Aristotelian concept of real substance into a series of subjective perceptions by the viewer. On the other hand, by giving up the essential focusing center of the composition and the prescribed point of view for its viewer, aesthetic innovations were in fact mirroring the Copernican vision of the Universe. This definitively eliminated the notion of geocentricity and its allied metaphysical constructs. In the modern scientific universe, as in architecture and in Baroque pictorial production, the various component parts are all endowed with equal value and dignity, and the whole construct expands towards a totality which is near to the infinite. It refuses to be hemmed in by any ideal normative conception of the world. It shares in a general urge toward discovery and constantly renewed contact with reality.

In its own way the 'openness' that we meet in the decadent strain of Symbolism reflects a cultural striving to unfold new vistas. For example, one of Mallarmé's projects for a pluridimensional deconstructible book envisaged the breaking down of the initial unit into sections which could be reformulated and which could express new perspectives by being deconstructed into correspondingly smaller units which were also mobile and reducible. This project obviously suggests the universe as it is conceived by modern, non-Euclidean geometries.

Hence it is not overambitious to detect in the poetics of the 'open' work —and even less so in the 'work in movement'—more or less specific overtones of trends in contemporary scientific thought. For example, it is a critical commonplace to refer to the spatiotemporal continuum in order to account for the structure of the universe in Joyce's works. Pousseur has offered a tentative definition of his musical work which involves the term 'field of possibilities'. In fact, this shows that he is prepared to borrow two extremely revealing technical terms from contemporary culture. The notion of 'field' is provided by physics and implies a revised vision of the classic relationship posited between cause and effect as a rigid, one-directional system: now a complex interplay of motive forces is envisaged, a configuration of possible events, a complete dynamism of structure. The notion of 'possibility' is a philosophical canon which reflects a widespread tendency in contemporary science: the discarding of a static, syllogistic view of order, a corresponding devolution of intellectual authority to personal decision, choice, and social context.

If a musical pattern no longer necessarily determines the immediately following one, if there is no tonal basis which allows the listener to infer the next steps in the arrangement of the musical discourse from what has physically preceded them, this is just part of a general breakdown in the concept of causation. The two-value truth logic which follows the classical *aut-aut,* the disjunctive dilemma between *true* and *false,* a fact and its contradictory, is no longer the only instrument of philosophical experiment. Multivalue logics are now gaining currency, and these are quite capable of incorporating *indeterminacy* as a valid stepping-stone in the cognitive process. In this general intellectual atmosphere, the poetics of the open work is peculiarly relevant: it posits the work of art stripped of necessary and foreseeable conclusions, works in which the performer's freedom functions as part of the *discontinuity* which contemporary physics recognizes, not as an element of disorientation, but as an essential stage in all scientific verification procedures and also as the verifiable pattern of events in the subatomic world.

From Mallarmé's *Livre* to the musical compositions which we have considered, there is a tendency to see every execution of the work of art as divorced from its ultimate definition. Every performance *explains* the composition, but does not *exhaust* it. Every performance makes the work an actuality, but is itself only complementary to all possible other performances of the work. In short, we can say that every performance offers us a complete and satisfying version of the work, but at the same time makes it incomplete for us, because it cannot simultaneously give all the other artistic solutions which the work may admit.

Perhaps it is no accident that these poetic systems emerge at the same period as the physicists' principle of *complementarity,* which rules that it is not possible to indicate the different behavior patterns of an elementary particle simultaneously. To describe these different behavior patterns, different *models,* which Heisenberg has defined as adequate when properly utilized, are put to use, but, since they contradict one another, they are therefore also complementary.[8] Perhaps we are in a position to state that for these works of art an incomplete knowledge of the system is in fact an essential feature in its formulation. Hence one could argue, with Bohr, that the data collected in the course of experimental situations cannot be gathered in one image, but should be considered as complementary, since only the sum of all the phenomena could exhaust the possibilities of information.[9]

Above I discussed the principle of ambiguity as moral disposition and dilemmatic construct. Again, modern psychology and phenomenology use the term 'perceptive ambiguities', which indicates the availability of new cognitive positions which fall short of conventional epistemological stances and which allow the observer to conceive the world in a fresh dynamics of potentiality before the fixative process of habit and familiarity comes into play. Husserl observed that

> . . . each state of consciousness implies the existence of a horizon which varies with the modification of its connections together with other states, and also with its own phases of duration (. . .). In each external perception, for instance, the sides of the objects which are *actually perceived* suggest to the viewer's attention the unperceived sides which, at the present, are viewed only in a nonintuitive manner and are expected to become elements of the succeeding perception. This process is similar to a continuous *projection* which takes on a new meaning with each phase of the perceptive process. Moreover, perception itself includes horizons which encompass other perceptive possibilities, such as one might experience by changing deliberately the direction of his perception, by turning his eyes one way instead of another, or by taking a step forward or sideways, and so forth.[10]

Sartre notes that the existent object can never be reduced to a given series of manifestations, because each of these is bound to stand in relationship with a continuously altering subject. Not only does an object present different *Abschattungen* (or profiles), but also different points of view are available by way of the same *Abschattung*. In order to be defined, the object must be related back to the total series of which, by virtue of being one possible apparition, it is a member. In this way the traditional dualism between being and appearance is replaced by a straight polarity of finite and infinite, which locates the infinite at the very core of the finite. This sort of 'openness' is at the heart of every act of perception. It characterizes every moment of our cognitive experience. It means that each phenomenon seems to be 'inhabited' by a certain *power,* in other words, 'the ability to manifest itself by a series of real or likely manifestations'. The problem of the relationship of a phenomenon to its ontological basis is altered by the perspective of perceptive 'openness' to the problem of its relationship to the multiplicity of different order perceptions which we can derive from it.[11]

This intellectual position is further accentuated in Merleau-Ponty:

> How can anything ever *present itself* truly to us since its synthesis is never completed? How could I gain the experience of the world, as I would of an individual actuating his own existence, since none of the views or perceptions I have of it can exhaust it and the horizons remain forever *open?* . . . The belief in things and in the world can only express the assumption of a complete synthesis. Its completion, however, is made impossible by the very nature of the perspectives to be connected, since each of them sends back to other perspectives through its own horizons. . . . The contradiction which we feel exists between the world's reality and its incompleteness is identical to the one that exists between the ubiquity of consciousness and its commitment to a field of presence. This ambiguousness does not represent an imperfection in the nature of existence or in that of consciousness, it is its very definition. . . . Consciousness, which is commonly taken as an extremely enlightened region, is, on the contrary, the very region of indetermination.[12]

These are the sorts of problems which phenomenology picks out at the very heart of our existential situation. It proposes to the artist, as well as to the philosopher and the psychologist, a series of declarations which are bound to act as a stimulus to his creative activity in the world of forms:

> It is therefore essential for an object and also for the world to present themselves to us as 'open' . . . and as always promising future perceptions.[13]

It would be quite natural for us to think that this flight away from the old, solid concept of necessity and the tendency toward the ambiguous and the indeterminate reflect a crisis of contemporary civilization. Or, on the other hand, we might see these poetical systems, in harmony with modern science, as expressing the positive possibility of thought and action made available to an individual who is open to the continuous renewal of his life patterns and cognitive processes. Such an individual is productively committed to the development of his own mental faculties and experiential horizons. This contrast is too facile and Manichean. Our main intent has been to pick out a number of analogies which reveal a reciprocal play of problems in the most disparate areas of contemporary culture and which point to the common elements in a new way of looking at the world.

What is at stake is a convergence of new canons and requirements which the forms of art reflect by way of what we could term *structural homologies*. This need not commit us to assembling a rigorous parallelism —it is simply a case of phenomena like the 'work in movement' simultaneously reflecting mutually contrasted epistemological situations, as yet contradictory and not satisfactorily reconciled. Thus the concepts of 'openness' and dynamism may recall the terminology of quantum physics: indeterminacy and discontinuity. But at the same time they also exemplify a number of situations in Einsteinian physics.

The multiple polarity of a serial composition in music, where the listener is not faced by an absolute conditioning center of reference, requires him to constitute his own system of auditory relationships.[14] He must allow such a center to emerge from the sound continuum. Here are no privileged points of view, and all available perspectives are equally valid and rich in potential. Now, this multiple polarity is extremely close to the spatiotemporal conception of the universe which we owe to Einstein. The thing which distinguishes the Einsteinian concept of the universe from quantum epistemology is precisely this faith in the totality of the universe, a universe in which discontinuity and indeterminacy can admittedly upset us with their surprise apparitions, but in fact, to use Einstein's words, do not presuppose a God playing random games with dice but the Divinity of Spinoza, who rules the world according to perfectly regulated laws. In this kind of universe, relativity means the infinite variability of experience as well as the infinite multiplication of possible ways of measuring things and viewing their position. But the objective side of the whole system can be found in the invariance of the simple formal descriptions (of the differential equations) which establish once and for all the relativity of empirical measurement.

1.5. This is not the place to pass judgment on the scientific validity of the metaphysical construct implied by Einstein's system. But there is a striking analogy between his universe and the universe of the work in movement. The God in Spinoza, who is made into an untestable hypothesis by Einsteinian metaphysics, becomes a cogent reality for the work of art and matches the organizing impulse of its creator.

The *possibilities* which the work's openness makes available always work within a given *field of relations*. As in the Einsteinian universe, in the 'work in movement' we may well deny that there is a single prescribed point of view. But this does not mean complete chaos in its internal relations. What it does imply is an organizing rule which governs these relations. Therefore, to sum up, we can say that the *work in movement* is the possibility of numerous different personal interventions, but it is not an amorphous invitation to indiscriminate participation. The invitation offers the performer the chance of an oriented insertion into something which always remains the world intended by the author.

In other words, the author offers the interpreter, the performer, the addressee a work *to be completed*. He does not know the exact fashion in which his work will be concluded, but he is aware that once completed the work in question will still be his own. It will not be a different work, and, at the end of the interpretative dialogue, a form which is *his* form, will have been organized, even though it may have been assembled by an outside party in a particular way that he could not have foreseen. The author is the one who proposed a number of possibilities which had already been rationally organized, oriented, and endowed with specifications for proper development.

Berio's *Sequence,* which is played by different flutists, Stockhausen's *Klavierstück XI,* or Pousseur's *Mobiles,* which are played by different pianists (or performed twice over by the same pianists), will never be quite the same on different occasions. Yet they will never be gratuitously different. They are to be seen as the actualization of a series of consequences whose premises are firmly rooted in the original data provided by the author.

This happens in the musical works which we have already examined, and it happens also in the plastic artifacts we considered. The common factor is a mutability which is always deployed within the specific limits of a given taste, or of predetermined formal tendencies, and is authorized by the concrete pliability of the material offered for the performer's manipulation. Brecht's plays appear to elicit free and arbitrary response on the part of the audience. Yet they are also rhetorically constructed in such a way as to elicit a reaction oriented toward, and ultimately anticipating, a Marxist dialectic logic as the basis for the whole field of possible responses.

All these examples of 'open' works and *works in movement* have this latent characteristic which guarantees that they will always be seen as 'works' and not just as a conglomeration of random components ready to emerge from the chaos in which they previously stood and permitted to assume any form whatsoever.

Now, a dictionary clearly presents us with thousands upon thousands of words which we could freely use to compose poetry, essays on physics, anonymous letters, or grocery lists. In this sense the dictionary is clearly open to the reconstitution of its raw material in any way that the manipulator wishes. But this does not make it a 'work'. The 'openness' and dynamism of an artistic work consist in factors which make it susceptible to a whole range of integrations. They provide it with organic complements which they graft into the structural vitality which the work already possesses, even if it is incomplete. This structural vitality is still seen as a positive property of the work, even though it admits of all kinds of different conclusions and solutions for it.

1.6.   The preceding observations are necessary because, when we speak of a work of art, our Western aesthetic tradition forces us to take 'work' in the sense of a personal production which may well vary in the ways it can be received but which always maintains a coherent identity of its own and which displays the personal imprint that makes it a specific, vital, and significant act of communication. Aesthetic theory is quite content to conceive of a variety of different poetics, but ultimately it aspires to general definitions, not necessarily dogmatic or *sub specie aeternitatis,* which are capable of applying the category of the 'work of art' broadly speaking to a whole variety of experiences, which can range from the *Divine Comedy* to, say, electronic composition based on the different permutations of sonic components.

We have, therefore, seen that (i) 'open' works, insofar as they are *in movement,* are characterized by the invitation to *make the work* together with the author and that (ii) on a wider level (as a sub*genus* in the *species* 'work in movement') there exist works which, though organically completed, are 'open' to a continuous generation of internal relations which the addressee must uncover and select in his act of perceiving the totality of incoming stimuli. (iii) *Every* work of art, even though it is produced by following an explicit or implicit poetics of necessity, is effectively open to a virtually unlimited range of possible readings, each of which causes the work to acquire new vitality in terms of one particular taste, or perspective, or personal *performance.*

Contemporary aesthetics has frequently pointed out this last characteristic of *every* work of art. According to Luigi Pareyson:

> The work of art . . . is a form, namely of movement, that has been concluded; or we can see it as an infinite contained within finiteness.
> . . . The work therefore has infinite aspects, which are not just 'parts' or fragments of it, because each of them contains the totality of the work, and reveals it according to a given perspective. So the variety of performances is founded both in the complex factor of the performer's in-

dividuality and in that of the work to be performed. . . . The infinite points of view of the performers and the infinite aspects of the work interact with each other, come into juxtaposition and clarify each other by a reciprocal process, in such a way that a given point of view is capable of revealing the whole work only if it grasps it in the relevant, highly personalized aspect. Analogously, a single aspect of the work can only reveal the totality of the work in a new light if it is prepared to wait for the right point of view capable of grasping and proposing the work in all its vitality.

The foregoing allows Pareyson to move on to the assertion that

. . . all performances are definitive in the sense that each one is for the performer, tantamount to the work itself; equally all performances are bound to be provisional in the sense that each performer knows that he must always try to deepen his own interpretation of the work. Insofar as they are definitive, these interpretations are parallel, and each of them is such as to exclude the others without in any way negating them. . . .[15]

This doctrine can be applied to all artistic phenomena and to art works throughout the ages. But it is useful to have underlined that now is the period when aesthetics has paid especial attention to the whole notion of 'openness' and sought to expand it. In a sense these requirements, which aesthetics have referred widely to every type of artistic production, are the same as those posed by the poetics of the 'open work' in a more decisive and explicit fashion. Yet this does not mean that the existence of 'open' works and of *works in movement* adds absolutely nothing to our experience because everything in the world is already implied and subsumed by everything else, from the beginning of time, in the same way that it now appears that every discovery has already been made by the Chinese. Here we have to distinguish between the theoretical level of aesthetics as a philosophical discipline which attempts to formulate definitions and the practical level of poetics as programmatic projects for creation. While aesthetics brings to light one of the fundamental demands of contemporary culture, it also reveals the latent possibilities of a certain type of experience in every artistic product, independently of the operative criteria which presided over its moment of inception.

The poetic theory or practice of the *work in movement* senses this possibility as a specific vocation. It allies itself openly and self-consciously to current trends in scientific method and puts into action and tangible form the very trend which aesthetics has already acknowledged as the general background to performance. These poetic systems recognize 'openness' as *the* fundamental possibility of the contemporary artist or consumer. The aesthetic theoretician, in his turn, will see a confirmation of his own intuitions in these practical manifestations: they constitute the ultimate realization of a receptive mode which can function at many different levels of intensity.

Certainly this new receptive mode vis-à-vis the work of art opens up a much vaster phase in culture and in this sense is not intellectually confined to the problems of aesthetics. The poetics of the *work in movement* (and partly that of the 'open' work) sets in motion a new cycle of relations between the artist and his audience, a new mechanics of aesthetic perception, a different status for the artistic product in contemporary society. It opens a new page in sociology and in pedagogy, as well as a new chapter in the history of art. It poses new practical problems by organizing new communicative situations. In short, it installs a new relationship between the *contemplation* and the *utilization* of a work of art.

Seen in these terms and against the background of historical influences and cultural interplay which links it by analogy to widely diversified aspects of the contemporary world view, the situation of art has now become a situation in the process of development. Far from being fully accounted for and catalogued, it deploys and poses problems in several dimensions. In short, it is an 'open' situation, *in movement*. A work in progress.

NOTES

1. Here we must eliminate a possible misunderstanding straightaway: the practical intervention of a 'performer' (the instrumentalist who plays a piece of music or the actor who recites a passage) is different from that of an interpreter in the sense of consumer (somebody who looks at a picture, silently reads a poem, or listens to a musical composition performed by somebody else). For the purposes of aesthetic analysis, however, both cases can be seen as different manifestations of the same interpretative attitude. Every 'reading', 'contemplation', or 'enjoyment' of a work of art represents a tacit or private form of 'performance'.

2. "La nuova sensibilità musicale," *Incontri Musicali,* no. 2 (May 1958): 25.

3. For the evolution of pre-Romantic and Romantic poets in this sense, see L. Anceschi, *Autonomia ed eteronomia dell'arte,* 2d ed. (Florence: Vallecchi, 1959).

4. See W. Y. Tindall, *The Literary Symbol* (New York: Columbia University Press, 1955). For an analysis of the aesthetic importance of the notion of ambiguity, see the useful observations and bibliographical references in Gillo Dorfles, *Il divenire delle arti* (Turin: Einaudi, 1959), pp. 51ff.

5. Edmund Wilson, *Axel's Castle* (London: Collins, Fontana Library, 1961), p. 178.

6. Pousseur, p. 25.

7. J. Schérer, Le 'Livre' de Mallarmé (Premières recherches sur des documents inédits) (Paris: Gallimard, 1957); see in particular the third chapter, "Physique du livre."

8. Werner Heisenberg, Physics and Philosophy (London: Allen and Unwin, 1959), chapter 3.

9. Niels Bohr, in his epistemological debate with Einstein (see P. A. Schlipp, ed., Albert Einstein: Philosopher-Scientist [Evanston, Ill.: Library of Living Philosophers, 1949]). Epistemological thinkers connected with quantum methodology have rightly warned against an ingenuous transposition of physical categories into the fields of ethics and psychology (for example, the identification of indeterminacy with moral freedom; see P. Frank, Present Role of Science, Opening Address to the Seventh International Congress of Philosophy, Venice, September 1958). Hence it would not be justified to understand my formulation as analogy between the structures of the work of art and the supposed structures of the world. Indeterminacy, complementarity, non-causality are not modes of being in the physical world, but systems for describing it in a convenient way. The relationship which concerns my exposition is not the supposed nexus between an 'ontological' situation and a morphological feature in the work of art, but the relation between an operative procedure for explaining physical processes and an operative procedure for explaining the processes of artistic production and reception. In other words, the relationship between a scientific methodology and a poetics.

10. Edmund Husserl, Médiations cartésiennes, Med. 2, par. 19 (Paris: Vrin, 1953), p. 39; the translation of this passage is by Anne Fabre-Luce.

11. J. P. Sartre, L'être et le néant (Paris: Gallimard, 1943), chapter 1.

12. M. Merleau-Ponty, Phénoménologie de la perception (Paris: Gallimard, 1945), pp. 381–83.

13. Ibid., p. 384.

14. On this 'éclatement multidirectionnel des structures', see A. Boucourechliev, "Problèmes de la musique moderne," Nouvelle Revue Française (December-January, 1960–1).

15. Luigi Pareyson, Estetica—Teoria della formatività, 2d ed. (Bologna: Zanichelli, 1960), pp. 194ff, and in general the whole of chapter 8, "Lettura, interpretazione e critica."

CHAPTER TWO

The Semantics of Metaphor

2.1. Foreword

If a code allowed us only to generate semiotic judgments, all linguistic systems would serve to enunciate exclusively that which has already been determined by the system's conventions: each and every utterance (*énoncé*) would be—even though through a series of mediations—tautological. On the contrary, however, codes allow us to enunciate events that the code did not anticipate as well as *metasemiotic* judgments that call into question the legitimacy of the code itself.

If all codes were as simple and univocal as Morse code, there would be no problem. It is true that a great deal which the code cannot anticipate can be said with Morse code; it is equally true that one can transmit in Morse code instructions capable of modifying the code itself. This can occur because Morse code's signifiers take, as the signified, alphabetical signifiers which in turn refer us to that complex system of systems known as language—by language meaning, in this case, the total competence of a speaking subject and thus the system of semantic systems as well, that is, the total form of the content. Yet it is precisely this sort of competence, not entirely analyzable, which we have decided to call 'code' as well, not for the sake of simple analogy but in order to broaden the scope of the term.[1]

How can it be, then, that this code, which in principle ought to have structured the speaking subject's entire cultural system, is able to generate both factual messages which refer to original experiences and, above all, messages which place in doubt the very structure of the code itself?

The fact that the code, in referring to predictable cultural entities, nonetheless allows us to assign new semiotic marks to them, is singular

"Semantica della metafora," in *Le forme del contenuto* (Milan: Bompiani, 1971). This chapter is a revised version of the Italian original. Translated by John Snyder.

[67]

to that feature of the code called 'rule-governed creativity'. That the code allows for factual judgments poses no difficulties either; the very nature of the code, which is arbitrary, explains how it can, by manipulating signifiers, refer to new signifieds produced in response to new experiences. It also explains why, once issued, factual judgments can be integrated into the code in such a way as to create new possibilities for semiotic judgment. How, though, does this 'rule-changing creativity' work?

Even prior to the specifically aesthetic usage of language, the first example of such creativity is provided in common speech by the use of different types of metaphors and thus of rhetorical figures. A series of problems that touch on rhetorical devices will allow us to respond to these questions. In the case under consideration we will at present deal with the problem of interaction between metaphoric mechanisms and metonymic mechanisms; to these one can probably ascribe the entire range of tropes, figures of speech, and figures of thought.[2]

The goal of this discussion is to show that each metaphor can be traced back to a subjacent chain of metonymic connections which constitute the framework of the code and upon which is based the constitution of any semantic field, whether partial or (in theory) global. This investigation takes as its point of origin a specific metaphoric substitution located in *Finnegans Wake* and explainable only through the exposure of a metonymic chain beneath the metaphoric level. A second check on a typical Joycean *mot-valise* (which, for the variety and polyvalence of its connotations, assumes a metaphoric value) will uncover, here too, a much more vast and articulate network of metonymies that have been wrapped in silence or revealed in another part of the work.

Finnegans Wake, at this point, presents itself as an excellent model of a Global Semantic System (since it posits itself, quite explicitly, as the Ersatz of the historical universe of language) and confronts us with a methodological exigency of the sort found in a study of general semantics proposing to illuminate the ways in which language can generate metaphors. The conclusion is that the mechanism of metaphor, reduced to that of metonymy, relies on the existence (or on the hypothesis of existence) of partial semantic fields that permit two types of metonymic relation: (i) the *codified* metonymic relation, inferable from the very structure of the semantic field; (ii) the *codifying* metonymic relation, born when the structure of a semantic field is culturally experienced as deficient and reorganizes itself in order to produce another structure. Relations of type (i) imply *semiotic judgments,* whereas relations of type (ii) imply *factual judgments.*[3]

The usefulness of such an analysis, which traces each metaphoric substitution back to a metonymic chain founded on codified semantic fields, is as follows: any explanation which restores language to metaphor or which shows that, in the domain of language, it is possible to invent metaphors returns to an analogical (and hence metaphorical) explanation of language and presumes an idealist doctrine of linguistic creativity. If, on the other hand, the explanation of the creativity of language (presupposed by the existence of metaphors) is based on metonymic chains based in turn on identifiable semantic structures, it is then possible to bring the problem of creativity back to a description of language which depends upon a model susceptible to translation in binary terms. In other words, it is possible (even though for experimental purposes and only for limited parts of the Global Semantic System) to construct an automaton capable of generating and understanding metaphors.

A last important qualification: this study is concerned not only with poetic metaphor but with metaphor in general. The majority of our messages, in everyday life or in academic philosophy, are lined with metaphors. The problem of the creativity of language emerges, not only in the privileged domain of poetic discourse, but each time that language—in order to designate something that culture has not yet assimilated (and this 'something' may be external or internal to the circle of semiosis)— must *invent* combinatory possibilities or semantic couplings not anticipated by the code.

Metaphor, in this sense, appears as a new semantic coupling not preceded by any stipulation of the code (but which generates a new stipulation of the code). In this sense, as we shall see, it assumes a value in regard to communication and, indirectly, to knowledge.

What remains to be defined is the particular status of its cognitive function.

This study is centered, therefore, on the semantic aspect of metaphor. The semantic aspect does not explain how metaphor can also have an aesthetic function. The aesthetic nature of a given metaphor is also produced by contextual elements or by the articulation of supersegmental features. This means, then, that, if on the one hand our study considers metaphor capable of segmenting in different ways the substance of content to the point of transforming it into a new form of content, on the other hand it does not explain by what segmentations of the substance of expression a given metaphor can obtain aesthetic effect. In other words, one's interest lies in knowing in what sense the fact of saying that the eyes of Leopardi's Silvia are /*fuggitivi*/ (fugitive) increases (in legitimizing the operation) the adjectival possibilities of the Italian language. It is not my purpose in this text to establish how and why the position of /*fuggitivi*/ (fugitive) after /*ridenti*/ (laughing) or the use of /*fuggitivi*/ instead of /*fuggenti*/ (fleeing) or /*fuggiaschi*/ (runaway) imparts to Leopardi's metaphor the aesthetic impact with which it is generally credited.

Not by chance have I chosen *Finnegans Wake* (hereafter *FW*) as our field of inquiry: as a literary work it produces sufficiently violent metaphors without interruption or reservation; at the same time, in proposing itself as a model of language in general, it focuses our attention specifically on semantic values. In other words, since *FW* is itself a metaphor for the process of unlimited semiosis, I have chosen it for metaphoric reasons as a field of inquiry in order to cover certain itineraries of knowledge more quickly. After this test we will be able to pass on to a more technical discourse that touches on the real linguistic mechanisms outside of the pilot text.

2.2.   Mandrake makes a gesture

In part 3, chapter 3 of *FW,* Shaun, in the form of Yawn, undergoes a trial in the course of which the Four Old Men bombard him with questions. The Old Men say to Shaun: "Now, fix on the little fellow on my eye, Minucius Mandrake, and follow my little psychosinology, poor armer in slingslang."[4] James Atherton, who has identified an enormous number of bibliographical references hidden in *FW,* recognizes in this passage a clear reference to a father of the church, Minucius Felix, an author whom Joyce perhaps knew.[5] But as for the meaning of /Mandrake/, he simply gives up: "I do not understand the allusion." The English meaning of /mandrake/ is a clue that only leads us to a dead end.

Probably Atherton had not thought of the world of comic strips (a world which Joyce—as Richard Ellman informs us—knew very well through the daily comics in the newspapers of the time); otherwise, he would have realized that Mandrake could be Mandrake the Magician, the famous character of Lee Falk and Phil Davis. Joyce, who in *FW* resorted to cartoon characters such as Mutt and Jeff, for instance, could not have been ignorant of this character. Let us hypothesize that the Mandrake of the text is the Mandrake of the comic strips and see what comes of it.

Mandrake is a master of prestidigitation, a hypnotist, an illusionist. With a simple gesture (the recurrent phrase is "Mandrake makes a gesture"), his eyes glued to those of his adversary, Mandrake forces him to see nonexistent situations, to mistake the pistol in his hand for a banana, to hear objects talking. Mandrake the Magician is a master of persuasion, a master of diabolic tricks (even if he uses his 'white' magic for good); in short, he is a 'devil's advocate'. In this regard it is interesting to note that Minucius Felix, too, was an advocate, professionally speaking (*Octavius* is a harangue in favor of Christianity), and an apologist father, whose historic function was to convince the Gentiles of the truth of the Christian faith.

From this point on, the relation between the two characters, in the interior of the Joycean context, becomes crystal clear.

At issue in the passage under consideration is the struggle between the ancient Irish church and the Catholic church, and the Four Old Men specifically ask Shaun whether or not he is a Roman Catholic. However, in a typical Joycean pun, they ask him if he is "roman cawthrick." Now, /to caw/ is the crow's cry and, even if we put to one side the fact that Joyce, in Trieste, perhaps learned the anticlerical sense of the word /cornacchia/, 'crow' (used in Italy to designate priests), there is still the problem of this /thrick/ which deforms (in order to echo one of the phonemes of 'catholic') the verb /to trick/. That Minucius Mandrake (alias Shaun) is a *trickster* is repeated several times in the context; for example, we find /Mr. Trickpat/.

Here let us put aside the other fascinating clue, one that could lead us to the character of the 'practical joker' in many primitive sagas, the *Schelm* or Trickster God (and we don't know if Joyce knew about him) that could trace Shaun back to archetypes of the gnome-like joker, such as Till Eulenspiegel. Let us only consider for the moment, without dealing with other problems, that Shaun has been accused of being a *trickster*. When he is called /Minucius Mandrake/ (afterwards we will see why), he—Catholic priest, expert in tricks and other persuasions more or less occult, crafty rhetorician, master of chicanery—must submit to a typical Dantean *contrappasso*. As an advocate he must undergo a trial; as a hypnotist he is asked to fix his eyes on the eyes of his interrogator. In this manner his art is neutralized and turned back against itself. The magical gesticulation (the gesture which presumably accompanies the words "Look at me with your eyes!"), too, is turned against itself, and the following gesticulation is ascribed to him: "Again I am deliciated by the picaresqueness of your irmages"—where the root /arm/ (the arm that makes the gesture) is inserted in the key word /image/, which is found at the base of all illusion.[6]

It is therefore reasonable to consider him, whether Minucius or Mandrake, as a metaphoric substitution in the place of something else, that is, the series of attributes and faults proper to Shaun.

But at this stage it is necessary to verify the credibility of this interpretation and the mechanism of this substitution.

2.3. Felix the Cat

The first version of the passage under consideration dates from 1924. In this version the name Mandrake does not appear.[7] The reason seems (to me) simple enough: the comic strip character appeared for the first time in 1934. And, in fact, the aforementioned passage was revised and expanded between 1936 and 1939. Thus the origin of the metaphoric 'vehicle' is plausible. But why couple Mandrake with Minucius? In other words, from the moment in which they first appear together in the text, they seem to us eminently well matched. But how did the idea of matching them come about? Once matched they seem to cause a short circuit of associations, but we know that for the most part the short circuit arises *a posteriori* and does not motivate the act of association. Minucius is like Mandrake: the coupling institutes between the two an elisional similitude which generates a metaphor (in which vehicle and tenor are exceptionally co-present and interchangeable).

But why specifically Minucius and Mandrake? The comic strip itself supplies the key which allows us to give a new answer (which in turn reinforces our original hypothesis). Minucius is also called Felix. And Felix is another typical comic strip character, Pat Sullivan's cat, appearing in the daily comics from 1923 and thus probably known to Joyce.

Here, then, is the mechanism subjacent to the metaphoric substitution: Minucius refers by contiguity to Felix, Felix refers by contiguity (belonging to the same universe of comic strips) to Mandrake. Once the middle term has fallen, there remains a coupling that does not seem justified by any contiguity and thus appears to be metaphoric. The always possible substitution between Minucius and Mandrake is attributable no longer to the possibility of passing from one to the other through a series of successive choices but to the fact that they seem to possess characteristics which are 'similar' (advocates, rhetoricians, and so on) and thus 'analogous'.

This example explains to us how the metaphor came about, but not why it functions. In point of fact, the reader grasps the analogies between Minucius and Mandrake and does not depend upon the existence of a third term. However, it could be said that he depends upon an extremely long series of third terms that exist in the general context of the book, some of which we have already examined: *trickster, arm, image,* and so on. We should therefore be able to show that each metaphor produced in *FW* is, in the last analysis, comprehensible because the entire book, read in different directions, actually furnishes the metonymic chains that justify it. We can test this hypothesis on the atomic element of *FW, the pun,* which constitutes a particular form of metaphor founded on subjacent chains of metonymies.

2.4. Morphology of the meandertale

The pun constitutes a forced contiguity between two or more words: *sang* plus *sans* plus *glorians* plus *riant* makes 'Sanglorians'.

It is a contiguity made of reciprocal elisions, whose result is an ambiguous deformation; but, even in the form of fragments, there are words that nonetheless are related to one another. This *forced contiguity* frees a series of possible readings—hence interpretations—which lead to an acceptance of the term as a metaphoric *vehicle* of different *tenors*. At this point the lexemes (or the lexematic fragments) thrust into forced contiguity acquire a kind of natural kinship and often become mutually substitutable. However, in the pun the metaphoric substitution assumes a particular type of status: vehicles coexist with tenors—for example, 'Jungfraud messonge': 'Jung' plus 'Freud' plus 'young' plus 'fraud' plus 'Jungfrau'; message plus *songe* plus *mensonge*.

All the terms present stand in a relationship of *mutual substitution*. This is the case with 'Minucius Mandrake' and also with a pun such as the one mentioned above: the reading 'young message' replaces 'virginal fraud', and vice versa. Each term is at the same time vehicle and tenor, while the entire pun is a multiple metaphor. At other times the forced coexistence does not imply possible substitution; think, for instance, of 'cawthrick'. A shadow of predicability remains, however, since one term appears to qualify the other (the crow is a trickster himself), and thus it can be said that the pun nevertheless decides the fate of future reciprocal substitution affecting the two terms in a position of forced contiguity.

One can object to our discourse that, if Jung and Freud or the crow and the trickster are placed in a position of contiguity, it is because they already stood in a prior analogical (and thus metaphoric) relation to each other.

Just as in the quarrel between analogic and digital, the quarrel between metaphor and metonym can generate a flight to infinity, in which one moment establishes the other, and vice versa.[8]

We can in theory distinguish between two types of puns, in accordance with the reasons that established the contiguity of the terms:

> *contiguity by resemblance of signifiers:* for example, 'nightiness' contains 'mightiness' by phonetic analogy ('m/n'); 'slipping' contains, for the same reasons, 'sleep' and 'slip';
> *contiguity by resemblance of signifieds:* 'scherzarade', for the playful analogies between *'scherzo'* and 'charade' (sememes in which 'game' would be the archisememe); but it is also true that the origin could lie in the simple phonetic similarity between /cha/ and /za/. One could then ask if the allusion to 'Scheerazade' is born first from the phonetic similarity or from the semantic similarity (the tale of Scheherazade as game and enigma, and so on).

As one can see, the two types refer to each other, even as contiguity seems to refer to the instituting resemblance, and vice versa.

In truth, though, the force of the pun (and of every successful and inventive metaphor) consists in the fact that prior to it no one had grasped the resemblance. Prior to 'Jungfraud' there was no reason to suspect a relationship between Freud, psychoanalysis, fraud, lie, and lapsus (*linguae* or *calami*). The resemblance becomes necessary only after the contiguity is realized. Actually (*FW* itself is the proof), it is enough to find the means of rendering two terms phonetically contiguous for the resemblance to impose itself; at best, the similitude of signifiers (at least in the place of encounter) is that which precedes, and the similitude of signifieds is a consequence of it.

The exploration of the field of *FW* as a contracted model of the global semantic field is at once useful and derisive. It is useful because nothing can show us better than a reading of *FW* that, even when semantic kinship seems to precede the coercion to coexist in the pun, in point of fact a network of subjacent contiguities makes necessary the resemblance which was presumed to be spontaneous. It is derisive because, everything being given in the text already, it is difficult to discover the 'before' and the 'after'. But, before arriving at any theoretical conclusions, let us make an incursion into the text, with all the risks that that involves.

Let us take the lexeme /Neanderthal/ (not found as such in the text) and see what mechanisms led the author to modify it into /meandertale/. Naturally, we could also follow the inverse process: we could take the pun found in the text and trace it back to its original components. But the very fact that we can conceive of two possible courses indicates that, in this case (as opposed to /Minucius Mandrake/), the two moments coincide: it was possible to invent the pun because it is possible to read it; language, as a cultural base, should be able to allow both operations. It should be noted also that, for reasons of a simple operative convention, we will start from one of the component words of the pun in order to deduce the other; probably another one would serve our purposes equally well. But this is the very characteristic of a language considered as the place of unlimited semiosis (as for Peirce), where each term is explained by other terms and where each one is, through an infinite chain of interpretants, potentially explainable by all the others.[9]

Our experiment thus has two senses: first, to see if, from a point outside Joyce's linguistic universe, we can enter into the universe; then, departing from a point internal to that universe, to see whether or not we can connect, through multiple and continuous pathways, as in a garden where the paths fork, all the other points. It will then come down to defining whether or not this entrance and this traversability are based on simple relationships of contiguity. For the moment, however, we will attempt to reason in terms—however imperfectly defined—of 'association' (phonetic and semantic).

Let us take the word /Neanderthal/. In the following schema we will notice how the lexeme generates, through a phonetic association, three other lexemes: /meander/, /tal/ (in German, 'valley'), and /tale/, which combine to form the pun /meandertale/. In the associative course, how-

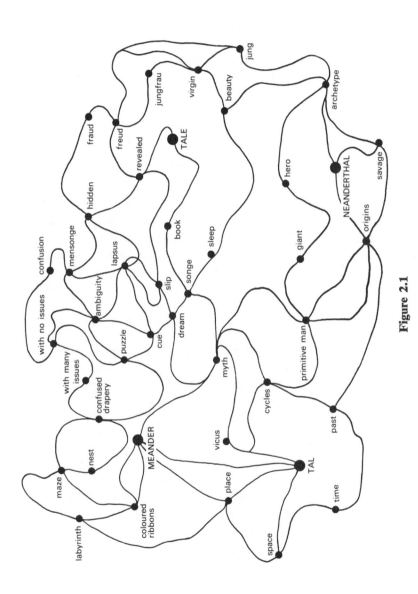

Figure 2.1

ever, intermediate modes create themselves from terms that are all present in the text of *FW*. Here the associations can be of either a phonetic or a semantic type.

It should be noted that all the lexemes mentioned here are only those which are to be found in the text of *FW*. The same psycholinguistic test might have generated, in another subject, other equally plausible responses. Here we have limited ourselves to this type of response, not only because it is the Joycean one (in which case the experiment would only seek to understand how the pun is born, not how it is read), but also for reasons of economy and, in addition, because the reader of *FW*, controlled by the text, is in fact led into a game of associations that were previously suggested to him by the co-text (which means that every text, however 'open' it is, is constituted, not as the place of all possibilities, but rather as the field of oriented possibilities).

The interconnections show, moreover, the way in which every lexeme can in this turn become the archetype of an associative series which would lead to the recuperation, sooner or later, of the associative terminals of another lexeme. The whole diagram (Figure 2.1) has a purely orientative value, in the sense that it impoverishes the associations in terms of both number and dimension: a bidimensional graph cannot reproduce the game of interconnections produced when lexemes are brought into contact with their respective sememes. We should consider as multidimensional, not only the game of interconnections produced in the global semantic system of real language, but also the game of that Ersatz field —the literary work, the text (in our case *FW*, more open to interconnections than are many other texts and thus more fit for experimentation).

If we pass from the diagram to Joyce's text, we can see how all the associations have been developed. They actually produce the puns which define the book. The book is a /slipping beauty/ (and thus a beautiful sleeper who, in sleeping, generates lapsus by semantic slippages, in remembering a flaw, and so on), a /jungfraud's messongebook/ (where, to the previously cited associations, is added that of a 'message'), a labyrinth in which is found /a word as cunningly hidden in its maze of confused drapery as a fieldmouse in a nest of coloured ribbons/, and thus at last a /Meandertale/.

The pun-lexeme /meanderthaltale/ becomes, in the end, the metaphoric substitution for everything that can be said about the book and that is said by the associative chains indicated in the diagram.

2.5. The games of the Swedish stall-bars

Once again we can foresee the objection that can be made to the diagram under consideration. The associative sequences, except for the first quadripartition, have a semantic character. The sememes associate among themselves through semic identity. Through a componential investigation it can be proved that all the associated sememes have in common a series of *semes*.[10] To explain the association by a partial identity of meaning means once again to explain it by similitude or by analogy. Thus the diagram would confirm the fact that, at the roots of the pun's forced contiguity, previous resemblances are found.

However, in its historic development, semantic theory has provided a series of explanations capable of capsizing our problem once again. If we reread the associative sequences, we see that each one of them could be constructed in retracing itself to a 'field of notions' accepted in a given culture or to one of the typical linguistic crossroads theorized by Trier, Matoré, and others.

Let us look, for example, at the sequence generated by /*Tal*/: 'space' and 'place' are the archisememes codified by the dictionary itself; the relationship between space and time is a typical antonymic relation by complementarity, which one imagines to be already acquired by a culture in the form of a semantic axis (the antonymic relationship is the structural precondition for comprehension of the signified of one of the two lexemes: the opposition /*space* vs. *time*/ precedes the semantic constitution of the two sememes; the antonym should be considered as one of the possible immediate connotations of the lexeme and thus as one of its most curious semantic marks; not by chance do more sophisticated dictionaries define a lexeme by its opposite as well as by its synonym). The time-past relationship is also acquired in the interior of a very obvious field of notions, registrable in advance. Vico's past-cycles relationship is born out of a type of classbook-like contiguity, somewhat like one's visual memory of a page out of Monarch Notes. Thus all associations, before being grasped as identity or similarity of meaning, are grasped as contiguity internal to semantic fields and axes or to a componential spectrum of the lexeme that considers even the most peripheral connotations.

This means that all connections were already codified before the artist could recognize them by pretending to institute or discover them. This allows us to affirm that it is in theory possible to construct an automaton whose memory would conserve all the semantic fields and axes which we have just mentioned; it is thus within its capacity to establish the connections which we have indicated (or, as it were, to attempt to make others; this could mean writing a new *FW* or reading *FW* in a way different from our own).

What makes the pun creative is not the series of connections (which precedes it as already codified); it is the decision of the short circuit, the so-called metaphoric one. Because, in fact, between /*mensonge*/ and

/*songe*/, except for the phonetic similarity, there is no contiguity; in order to unite them, a leap was first necessary from one to another of the diagram's discontinuous points. But, if the points are discontinuous, it is because the diagram is incomplete. A review of the fields of notions acquired by a given culture would have rapidly led us from /Freud/ to /*songe*/, or from /fraud/ to /Freud/ (independently of the phonetic similarity), or from /Freud/ to /Jung/. This means that, under the apparent metaphoric short circuit (for here the similarity between two senses seems to click for the first time), there is an uninterrupted web of culturalized contiguity that our hypothetical automaton might be able to traverse through a sequence of binary choices.

A metaphor can be invented because language, in its process of unlimited semiosis, constitutes a multidimensional network of metonymies, each of which is explained by a cultural convention rather than by an original resemblance. The imagination would be incapable of inventing (or recognizing) a metaphor if culture, under the form of a possible structure of the Global Semantic System, did not provide it with the subjacent network of arbitrarily stipulated contiguities. The imagination is nothing other than a ratiocination that traverses the paths of the semantic labyrinth in a hurry and, in its haste, loses the sense of their rigid structure. The 'creative' imagination can perform such dangerous exercises only because there exist 'Swedish stall-bars' which support it and which suggest movements to it, thanks to their grill of parallel and perpendicular bars.[11] The Swedish stall-bars are Language [*langue*]. On them plays Speech [*parole*], performing the competence.

2.6.   Rhetoric of the Swedish stall-bars

A semiotic explanation of different rhetorical figures can be attempted through the development of the theory of interpretants as represented in the Model Q.[12]

Suppose a code is formed that posits a system of paradigmatic relations of the following sort:

$$\begin{array}{cccccc}
A & vs. & B & vs. & C & vs. & D \\
\downarrow & & \downarrow & & \downarrow & & \downarrow \\
k & & y & & z & & k
\end{array}$$

where the horizontal line constitutes a paradigm of different sememes and the vertical correlation constitutes relations from sememe to seme or semantic mark (k is a semantic mark of A; obviously, according to the Model Q, k can become in its turn a sememe k to be analyzed through other semantic marks, among which even a could be considered).

To name A by k is a case of synecdoche (the veil for the ship, *pars pro toto*). Since k could even be the seme «crown» characterizing the sememe «king», to name A by k can also be a case of metonymy (in traditional terms; in the terms of our present approach, such a difference tends to disappear). But k happens to be also a seme of another sememe, namely, D. Therefore, by an amalgamation through k, one can substitute A with /D/. This is a case of metaphor. A long white neck being a property both of a beautiful woman and of a swan, the woman can be metaphorically substituted for by the swan. Apparently, one entity is in the place of the other by virtue of a mutual resemblance. But the resemblance is due to the fact that in the code there exist already fixed relations of substitution which, in some way or other, link the substitute entities to those substituted for.

Now suppose that there exists a practice of language in which A is *habitually* substituted for k. In this case k becomes, by convention, one of the possible connotations of A. The metaphor, once it has become usual, enters as part of the code and in the long run can fix itself in a *catachresis* ('the neck of the bottle', 'the leg of the table'). The fact remains, however, that the substitution took place because of the existence, in the code, of connections and therefore contiguities. This would lead us to state that the metaphor rests on a metonymy. If Model Q is based upon unlimited semiosis, every sign, sooner or later, must depend upon a connection anticipated by the code. Obviously there can be produced connections of which no one had ever thought. We then have an ambiguous message. The aesthetic function of language seeks to create connections which as of yet do not exist; thus it also seeks to enrich the code's possibilities. Even in this case metaphoric substitution can rely upon metonymic practice.

2.7. The crown and the white collar

At this point we need to elucidate the terms 'metaphor' and 'metonymy', since it seems that up to now the latter term has been used in a metaphoric sense.

Every theory of metaphor defines this figure as the substitution of one element of language for another (the operation is completely internal to the semiotic circle), but *by virtue of a resemblance between their referents*. It is this necessary recourse to referents (and to their presumed relations of analogy or resemblance) that has prodded us to criticize the notion of metaphor as something that cannot be founded on autonomously semiotic terms. The risk is now that (reconducting every metaphor to a chain of metonymies) even these will demand to be founded on a recourse to referents. In reality, rhetoric—in having recourse to referents—explains metonymy to us. We name the king by the crown only because there is a *factual* contiguity between king and crown (the fact that the king wears a crown is a fact, not a linguistic phenomenon). But then, again, if the fact of naming the crown refers us by force of analogy to the king, it also retransforms the metonymic explanation into an explanation founded on similarity. There is a natural resemblance, due to the habit of contiguity, that pushes for recognition of the king in the crown.

Notice, however, that if by some chance an employee of the property-tax office whom I know wears spectacles, I cannot name, in a figurative discourse, the employees of the property-tax office by spectacles. This contiguity would not be recognizable and, in any case, even if recognized, it would not be sufficient to found the metonymic substitution. It must be that (by recognized and *codified* habit) all (or a large number of) employees of the property-tax office wear spectacles for it to be possible to operate the substitution by contiguity. Now, there was a time when all (or most) of the employees wore white collars on their shirts. This contiguity was codified, and only at that moment was it possible to designate the employees as 'white-collar workers'; even if today there are no employees wearing white collars, one can recognize that this contiguity is capable of founding a metonymic substitution. This is a sign that the contiguity is no longer factual, but semiotic. What matters is, not that in reality someone wears white collars, but that in a semantic representation of the lexeme /employee/ there exists the connotation «wears white collars».

The contiguity on which the metonymic transposition is founded is thus transformed from factual (empirical) contiguity to *contiguity of code*. The referent no longer carries any weight, and neither does the possibility of recognizing the metonymized term by a natural kinship with the metonymizing term. The kinship is not natural; it is *cultural*. The two terms refer to each other because they are conventionally situated each in the place of the other. The metonymizing term is already part of the semantic representation of the metonymized term, as one of its *interpretants*. The rhetorical rule presupposes, then, that one can name a lexeme by one of the semantic components of the corresponding sememe. A study of efficient and comprehensible metonymies would lead to the discovery that they employ, as metonymizing, a semantic component that belongs exclusively to one particular lexeme and not another. The mark «male» is also a semantic component of the lexeme /king/, but no one would use /male/ as a metonymy of /king/. /Crown/ is used because *only the king* wears a crown. We can thus imagine a robot constructed in order to recognize metonymies, provided that it has been programmed for the following: "replace the metonymizing term with that sememe, unique among the others (or the only one allowed by the context), which possesses it as a semantic component." The correction between parentheses should serve in such cases as 'i veloci legni' (the swift woods); without a doubt, 'di legno' (of wood) enters into the semantic spectrum of many lexemes, but, in a naval context, it is obvious that the lexeme in question is /nave/ (ship).

The extreme traversability of the chains we have called 'metonymic' (and it would be better to say 'of contiguity in the code')—chains that allow metaphoric substitutions with leaps which are apparent ones, but which in fact are short circuits of a preestablished path—results from the fact that these chains are already entirely constituted *inside the code* and do not refer to connections attained in the referents. We can then establish that every metonymic connection refers to one of these three types of contiguity:

> *contiguity in the code:* the most common type, it corresponds to some of the examples given in the preceding pages, such as /crown/, /white-collar/, and so on;
> *contiguity in the co-text:* an example could be as follows: "out of the getaway car came some pistol shots; that car had to be silenced" (where the car is substituted for the pistol, and vice versa);
> *contiguity in the referent:* according to what has already been said, this genre of contiguity should be practically nonexistent. However, since there are some special cases, let us see if it is a question of *contiguity through the referent* or *contiguity through the signified* (and thus it can revert back to the two preceding cases of contiguity in the code or contiguity in the co-text).

Let us examine the case of a particular type of lapsus, also studied by psychoanalysis, which is born not out of the comparison of two words but, rather, out of the comparison of two given facts of experience. That is to say, in a situation of lapsus, I can say 'ho colto il morto' (I have picked up the dead body) in the place of 'ho colto il mirto' (I have picked up the myrtle), because I know that a corpse is buried under the myrtle bush (or because I remember a corpse buried under another bush). In this case the contiguity, which would appear to be linguistic, cannot be explained without recourse to the referent. In the same way, one cannot explain the fact that in seeing a dagger an individual has erotic fantasies, unless one knows for certain that he saw his own mother kill her lover with a dagger during intercourse.

This type of contiguity—imposed by some sort of violence done to the code—remains so inexplicable that the need emerges for an 'interpretation' of dreams, until, once the dream is explained, the contiguity is institutionalized and becomes *part of the culture*. In this sense the hermeneutic work of the psychoanalyst, when applied to the contiguity of the referent, is a case of code making and not of code observing.[13]

2.8. Language makes a gesture

Since we suppose that, in the making and unmaking of particular semantic fields, the entire Global Semantic System is never completely structurable (and even if it were, it would not be structured; and even if it were structured, we could not describe it in its globality), we should assume that *only in theory* does each semantic unit refer to all others. In practice there are millions of empty valences and millions of units that *cannot* be connected to the others. To do so would mean to emit factual judgments (of the type 'A is the same as D') that the Global Semantic System can accept only at the cost of exploding.

Let us imagine that the scheme envisaged in section 2.6 does not anticipate only four terms (A, B, C, D) and two levels of correlated entities but, rather, an infinite number of terms and levels. And let us also imagine that D is not segregated from A by only four passages (A→k→ k→D), but rather by millions of passages. If culture has never made these passages, A and D have never been connected. We can connect them without any good reason (the bad reason being immediately evident) or for reasons as yet difficult to realize, and we can do this either by disturbing or not disturbing the semantic system we rely upon. Let us try to throw a first and tentative light upon this web of intertwined semiotic problems—our attempt aiming only at being a first approach to a much more complex question.

First, what is a 'good' reason to establish a metaphorical connection? Let us distinguish two kinds of successful metaphor, the merely 'acceptable' and the 'rewarding'. A metaphor is (at least) acceptable when its metonymic foundation is immediately (or only after more mediation) evident. The substitution of /sleep/ for «death» constitutes an acceptable metaphor (many semes or marks in common). No one would say that it is 'beautiful'; it is missing the tension, the ambiguity, and the difficulty which are characteristic of the aesthetic message.

Let us suppose, on the other hand, that there is issued a metaphor whose metonymic foundation is not evident—for example, the 'selva oscura' (dark wood) of Dante. In this case the semantic necessity that connects the vehicle (as the signified), which is of a physico-geographical sort, to the moral entity that constitutes the tenor is quite occult—at least to the extent that it allows a series of hermeneutic games aimed at discovering an interpretation, a reliable reading. What is instead immediately apparent? The rhythmico-phonetic necessity in the order of signifiers— in other words, the necessity caused by meter and rhyme, which makes 'reasonable', for reasons of a 'musical' sort, the occurrence of the signifier /*selva oscura*/ in relation to the signifiers /*dura*/ (hard) and /*paura*/ (fear). Faced with one possible, although still unthinkable, relation on the level of the form of content, a clear relation stands out on the level of the form of expression, so that we are led to believe that a relation *should* exist also on the level of the form of content. This metaphor is 'rewarding' because it prefigures a semantic necessity before that necessity has ever been defined and located.

When, though, does it happen that a metaphor is 'deceiving' or 'defaulting'? Whenever a weak necessity on the level of the form of expression corresponds to the incommensurable distance between vehicle and tenor on the level of content, and despite this distance the amount of new knowledge provided is disappointing. Many Baroque metaphors are of this type.

In Artale's sonnet about Mary Magdalen, the fact that her hair is named /*fiumi*/(rivers) without a doubt presents a necessity in terms of the form of expression—the rhyme necessarily links /*fiumi*/ (rivers) to /*lumi*/ (lights) and /*allumi*/ (he lights):

> L'occhio e la chioma in amorosa arsura
> Se' l bagna e 'l terge, avvien ch'amante allumi
> Stupefatto il fattor di sua fattura;
> Ché il crin s' è un Tago e son due Soli i lumi,
> Prodigio tal non rimirò natura:
> Bagnar coi Soli e rasciugar coi fiumi.

But this necessity serves only to induce a search for the metonymic connection between rivers and hair. When it is discovered (thanks in part to a preceding revelatory verse, which prepared the metaphor with a similitude), we see that the seme «fluency», which could unify the two sememes, is rather peripheral to those semes characterizing the two sememes in a mutually exclusive sense, since hair in effect is dry and solid and rivers are wet and liquid. It is nonetheless true that—still in the order of content—the semantic necessity of /*fiumi*/ (rivers) could be reinforced by its opposition to /*soli*/ (suns), which has replaced /*occhi*/ (eyes). But, here too, since eyes seem as 'necessarily' connected to /*soli*/ (suns) as hair is to rivers, two wrongs clearly do not make a right, and two weak and isolated necessities in the form of metaphors do not reinforce the joint necessity of their chiasmatic and oppositional occurrence. This means that, while we ask the form of expression to guarantee the supposed or proposed semantic necessity, we ask the form of content to insure that the necessity, once discovered, will enrich in some manner the knowledge of either the signifieds of the message or the operational possibilities of the code.

As for Mary Magdalen, the facts that her eyes are suns and that her hair is a river do not help us at all to a better understanding of this woman's personality; thus the expressive artifice that led us to discover metaphoric relations at the semantic level seems wasted to us, or deceptive. From this moment on our possibility of using the code no longer seems enriched, because we will rarely find ourselves in a situation that will allow us to reuse a metaphor of this genre. The poetic effect is recognized as null, since in this case poetry seems 'to serve no purpose'. Dante's 'selva oscura', on the other hand, refers us to an open chain of semantic associations whose roots run deep in a symbolic and theologic tradition and which allows us to speak of life, sin, and man's situation on earth. Here is what some have intuitively called 'the universality of poetry': its capacity to provoke, in the order of content, alterations that become operative even beyond the concrete occasion which generated the seman-example of 'defaulting' metaphor (from the point of view of content) tic substitution.

Achillini, another eighteenth-century author, provides a different example of 'defaulting' metaphor (from the point of view of content) which, this time, finds no support on the level of expression. But Achillini does not fail because of a too 'distant' connection; on the contrary, he is matching something that our common knowledge has long since matched, and without exciting results. 'Sudate, o fochi, a preparar metalli' (sweat, O fires, to prepare metals), imposes no expressive necessity that justifies the use of the verb 'sudare' (to sweat). One might very well have said, without detracting from the rhyme or the meter, 'bruciate o fochi' (burn, O fires). The whole discourse then displaces itself to the level of content. And here again, even if the subjacent metonymic chain exists and is visible (fire-heat-sweat, the fire which receives as its own seme the effect that it has on whoever is subjected to its action, and so on), it appears as rather contorted, demanding a pathway, a tiresome short circuit that *does not pay* sufficiently well, so much exertion in order to learn what was already known—that fire causes sweat. The reader refuses the invitation to an adventure without worthwhile results, to a linguistic operation that, with the pretense of making language function in a creative direction, actually creates nothing and succeeds only in the realization of a wearisome tautology.

A different series of judgments might be of the sort, 'The chemical composition of hair is similar to that of water; fire secretes, through glands similar to the sweat glands of humans, a sort of liquid with homeostatic functions . . .'. Here we confront a series of *factual* judgments. As has already been said, it is not up to semiotics to establish whether they are true or false, but it is up to semiotics to establish whether or not they are socially acceptable. Many factual judgments seem unacceptable, not because they are false, but rather because to accept them would mean to impose a restructuration of the Global Semantic System or large parts of it. This explains why, under particular historical conditions, physical proof of the truth of certain judgments could not stand up before the social necessity of rejecting these same judgments. Galileo was condemned not for logical reasons (in terms of True or False) but for semiotic reasons—inasmuch as the falsity of his factual judgments is proved by recourse to contrary semiotic judgments of the type 'this does not correspond to what is said in the Bible'.

Nevertheless, it can be the case that unacceptable factual judgments are enunciated in metaphoric form before being enunciated in referential form. For example, whoever before Copernicus used the metaphor 'the peripheral sphere' in order to describe the Earth would have forced the receiver of the message to face the necessity of inferring substitutibility between two sememes which, on the contrary, presented completely opposite semes: the Earth has a seme of centrality and no semes of periphericity (in regard to the solar system). In this case we would find ourselves before a metaphor which, in a confused way, anticipated a restructuration of the future code and which allowed the inference of the possibility of factual judgments that, however, could not yet be enunciated. In this case the creativity of language would have encouraged a new structuration of semantic fields and axes, without being able to guarantee the necessity of the formulation. Language is full of such metaphoric anticipations, whose hermeneutic value—the capacity to uncover new metonymic chains—is revealed afterwards and whose fortune is determined by historic circumstances not grasped by semiotics.

Another case is that of a metaphoric anticipation which installs a short circuit between two semantic units hitherto foreign to each other and which, however, sustains it by a sort of necessity at the level of the form of expression. Some years before the development of nuclear fission, when /atom/ was still burdened with a seme of «indivisibility» (at least at the level of common knowledge), Joyce spoke in *FW* of the "abnihilation of the ethym." Here we find a substitution between 'atom' and /etymon/ (*etym-* = the root of a word) that depends upon something we have called *contiguity by resemblance of signifiers*. Once the substitution is made, we can begin to verify, at the semantic level, a series of inspections into the possible realization of a destructive atomic process which, in regard to the "etyma" (roots), seems to have been completely developed in the text in front of us (and thus a *contiguity in the co-text* develops as a reinforcement); semes that are common to the two sememes (their elementary radicality and their originality that make the atom an 'etymon' of physical events and the 'etyma' a verbal atom; the very structure of the code makes all these associations reasonable ones) begin to lend credibility to a possible factual judgment that would overturn the entire semantic field. The poet anticipates a future scientific and conceptual discovery because—even if through expressive artifices, or conceptual chains set in motion to put cultural units into play and to disconnect them—he uproots them from their habitual semiotic situation.

Here is how and why, to return to our explanatory schema, A and D can be connected *with some reason*. This means that, sooner or later, someone understands in some way the reason for the connection and the necessity for a factual judgment that does not yet exist. Then, and only then, is it shown that the course of successive contiguities, however tiresome, was traversable or that it was possible to institute certain traversals. Here is how the factual judgment, anticipated in the form of an unusual metaphor, overturns and restructures the semantic system in introducing circuits not previously in existence. And thus here is why it is possible to anticipate the creative functions of language which, rather than depend upon the existence of already culturalized courses, take advantage of some of these courses in order to institute new ones. All of this clarifies at last what really separates the inventive metaphor from the true factual judgment, even if both seem to have the same function of establishing new connections in the semantic system.

The factual judgment draws, perceptively or intellectually, the disturbing data *from the exterior of language*. The metaphor, on the other hand, draws the idea of a possible connection *from the interior* of the circle of unlimited semiosis, even if the new connection restructures the circle itself in its structuring connections.

The factual judgment is born from a physical mutation of the world and only afterwards is transformed into semiotic knowledge. The metaphor is born from an internal disturbance of semiosis. If it succeeds in its game, it produces knowledge because it produces new semiotic judgments and, in the final outcome, obtains results which do not differ from factual judgments. What is different is the amount of time spent in order to produce knowledge. Factual judgments as such die as soon as they are transformed into semiotic judgments. Once accepted as true, the factual judgment ('the earth is not the center of the solar system') dies as such in order to generate a stipulation of code (*'earth entails periphery'*).

Successful factual judgments are remembered as such only when they become famous ('the famous discovery of Copernicus'; but it is clear that this famous discovery is henceforth part of the codes of a first-grader). On the other hand, metaphors (which, after all, are *metasemiotic judgments*) tend to resist acquisition. If they are inventive (and thus original), they cannot be easily accepted; the system tends not to absorb them. Thus they produce, prior to knowledge, something which, psychologically speaking, we could call 'excitation' and which, from a semiotic point of view, is none other than 'information' in the most proper sense of the term: an excess of disorder in respect to existing codes. When faced with metaphor, we sense that it is turning into a vehicle of knowledge, and intuitively (in surveying the subjacent metonymic chains) we grasp its legitimacy; but until analysis has brought these subjacent metonymic chains to light, we must recognize that metaphors imply additional knowledge without knowing how to demonstrate the legitimacy of the argument.

The coupling between the new vehicle and the new (or old, or unsuspected) tenor is still not a part of our culture. The sense of this still unrecognized codification, nevertheless felt in a confused way to be necessary, confers to metaphor its memorability and exemplariness. When united to other contextual or supersegmental artifices involving operations on the substance of expression and thus aesthetic metaphors, this confused sense becomes exactly that which naive aestheticians choose to call 'poetry', 'lyricism', or 'the miracle of art'. It is the sense of availability, of a valence not yet saturated by culture. It is the moment that new codes *could* (*should*) be born and that the old codes cannot resist the impact. When, finally, metaphors are transformed into knowledge, they will at least have completed their cycle: they become catachreses. The field has been restructured, semiosis rearranged, and metaphor (from the invention which it was) turned into culture.

In any case, in order to arrive at these results, metaphor has had to rely upon possible contradictions of the code. It has obtained subversive value, thanks to the existence of two conditions in the code, one linked to the level of expression and the other to the level of content:

(i) It was necessary for the code's fundamental arbitrariness that there be correspondences between signifying systems and signified systems (not strictly univocal correspondences, not in a single sense, not predetermined once and for all; but, on the contrary, open to slippages of different sorts), by virtue of which we could conceive of the possibility of using a signifier to indicate a signified which, in the current game of couplings, is not its own.

(ii) In the second place, it was necessary—in passing from one semantic field to another and in putting them in relationship to each other —to discover in the interior of the Global Semantic System that it is possible to attribute contradictory semes to a single sememe.

Given once again the schema

$$A \quad vs. \quad B \quad vs. \quad C \quad vs. \quad D$$
$$\downarrow \qquad \downarrow \qquad \downarrow \qquad \downarrow$$
$$k \qquad y \qquad z \qquad k$$

there should be a possibility (and, in fact, it exists) that, once we begin to substitute D for A by metonymic connections, we discover that D has some semes in contradiction with those of A and that, nevertheless, it is possible, once the substitution of D for A is done, to formulate the meta-semiotic judgment A = non-D.

In order for the Global Semantic System to be able to produce creative utterances, *it is necessary* that it be self-contradictory and that no *Form* of content exist, only *forms* of content.

NOTES

1. See U. Eco, "The Code: Metaphor or Interdisciplinary Category?" *Yale Italian Studies* 1, no. 1 (1977).

2. See H. Lausberg, *Handbuch der literarischen Rhetorik* (Munich: Huerber, 1960) and Pierre Fontanier, *Les Figures du discours* (Paris: Flammarion, 1968).

3. See Umberto Eco, *A Theory of Semiotics* (Bloomington: Indiana University Press, 1976), section 3.2.

4. P. 486 (London: Faber and Faber, 1957).

5. See James Atherton, *The Books the Wake* (New York: Viking, 1960). A further note of interest: Minucius Felix's *Octavius* in the same way as *Ulysses*. A group of young intellectuals talk of Christ while walking by the edge of the sea, whose incessant movement they describe. Meanwhile, in the distance, some children are at play. The analogy is perhaps a causal one, but it would not be wrong to suspect one further pastiche-reminiscence on the part of Joyce, that insatiable reader.

6. P. 486 (London: Faber and Faber, 1957). Another clue: The reference to the picaresque might just be a reference to the Trickster as a leprechaun-like jester.

7. See D. Hayman, *A First Draft Version of F. W.* (London: Faber and Faber, 1963).

8. See Umberto Eco, *Le poetiche di Joyce,* 2d ed. (Milan: Bompiani, 1965), where the same mechanism seems to rule the phenomenon of *epiphany.* In effect, this is no different from what happens with the epiphanic relation.

9. See Chapter 7 of this book.

10. See Eco, *A Theory . . . ,* sections 2.5–2.11.

11. See Ross M. Quillian, "Semantic Memory," in *Semantic Information Processing,* ed. Marvin Minsky (Cambridge: M.I.T. Press, 1968) and *Theory,* section 2.12.

12. The Quillian model (Model Q) is based on a mass of nodes interconnected by different types of associative links. For the meaning of every lexeme, memory should contain a node which has as its 'patriarch' the term to be defined here called *type.* The definition of a type A foresees the use of a series

of other signifiers (as its own interpretants) which are included as *tokens* (and which, in the model, constitute other lexemes).

The configuration of the meaning of the lexeme is given by the multiplicity of its links with several 'tokens', each of which becomes, in its turn, a type B. Type B is the patriarch of a new configuration which includes many other lexemes as tokens; some of these lexemes were also tokens of type A. Thus type B can actually take type A as one among its own tokens.

"The over-all structure of the complete memory forms an enormous aggregation of planes, each consisting entirely of token nodes except for its 'head' node" (Quillian, p. 327).

This model therefore anticipates the definition of every sign, thanks to its interconnection with the universe of all other signs that function as interpretants, each of which is ready to become the sign interpreted by all the others: the model, in its complexity, is based upon a process of *unlimited semiosis*. Starting with a sign that is considered as a 'type', one can retraverse, from the center to the extreme periphery, the entire universe of cultural units. Each of these can in turn become the center and generate infinite peripheries.

13. See Eco, *A Theory* . . . , section 3.1.2.

CHAPTER THREE

On the Possibility of Generating Aesthetic Messages in an Edenic Language

According to Jakobson the aesthetic use of language is marked by the *ambiguity* and the *self-focusing character* of the messages articulated by it. By ambiguity the message is rendered creative in relation to the acknowledged possibilities of the code. The same is true of the metaphorical —not necessarily the same thing as aesthetic—applications of language. For an aesthetic message to come into being, it is not enough to establish ambiguity at the level of the *content-form;* here, inside the formal symmetry of metonymic relationships, metaphorical replacements are operated, enforcing a fresh conception of the semantic system and the universe of meanings coordinated by it. But, to create an aesthetic message, there must also be alterations in the form in which it is expressed, and these alterations must be significant enough to require the addressee of the message, though aware of a change in the *content-form,* to refer back to the message itself as a physical entity. This will allow him to detect alterations in the form of expression, for there is a kind of solidarity binding together the alteration in content with any change in its mode of expression. This is the sense in which an aesthetic message becomes self-focusing; it also conveys information about its own physical make-up, and this justifies the proposition that in all art there is inseparability of form and content. However, this principle does not necessarily mean that one cannot distinguish between the two levels and pick out the specific opera-

"Sulla possibilità di generare messaggi estetici in una lingusa edenica," *Strumenti Critici* 5, no. 11 (1971). Bruce Merry, trans., "On the Possibility of Generating Esthetic Messages in an Edenic Language," *Twentieth Century Studies* 6, no. 7 (1972). This chapter is a revised version of the translation.

[90]

tions which are being carried on at each; it simply establishes that any changes occurring at the two levels are functionally related to each other.

In aesthetic debate there is always a temptation to support the above propositions at an abstract level. When the analyst moves on to practical demonstration, he tends to work with aesthetic messages which have already been elaborated and which therefore present special complexities; in this case, distinctions between different levels, changes in code and system, innovatory devices—all become very difficult to examine accurately. So it is a useful exercise to set up a small-scale working model of aesthetic language; this would involve an extremely simple language/ code and demonstrate the rules by which aesthetic messages can be generated. These rules will have to arise from inside the code itself, but then be capable of generating an alteration of the code, both in its form of expression and in its form of content. The working model must therefore be equipped to demonstrate a language's own capacity for generating self-contradiction. It must also show how the aesthetic use of the given language is one of the most appropriate devices for generating these contradictions. Finally, the model must prove that any contradictions generated by the aesthetic use of language at the level of its form of expression equally involve contradictions in the form of its content; ultimately, they entail a complete reorganizing of our conceptual vision of the universe.

To set this experiment in motion, we shall imagine a primordial predicament: life in the Garden of Eden, where the inhabitants speak in Edenic language.

My model for this language is borrowed from G. Miller's Grammarama project (*Psychology and Communication,* New York, 1967), except that Miller did not plan his model specifically as an Edenic language. He was merely concerned to study an individual speaker who is producing casual sequences by means of two base symbols (D and R) and receiving control responses designed to clarify which of his sequences are grammatically well formed; then Miller checked the speaker's capacity for piecing together the generative rule of the correct sequences. His model in fact constituted a language-learning test, whereas my experiment presents us with Adam and Eve, who already know which are the correct sequences and who employ them in conversation, even though they entertain unclear notions about the underlying generative rules.

3.1.   Semantic units and significant sequences in the Garden of Eden

Although they are surrounded by a luxuriant environment, Adam and Eve have managed to devise a restricted series of semantic units which give preferential status to their emotional responses to flora and fauna, rather than a naming and exact classification of each of them. These semantic units can be organized under six main headings:

Yes vs. No

Edible vs. Inedible   (Where Edible stands for «to be eaten», «comestible», «I want to eat», and so on.)

Good vs. Bad   (This antithesis covers both moral and physical experiences.)

Beautiful vs. Ugly   (This antithesis covers every degree of pleasure, amusement, desirability.)

Red vs. Blue   (This antithesis covers the whole gamut of chromatic experience: the ground is perceived as red and the sky as blue, meat is red and stones are blue, and so on.)

Serpent vs. Apple   (This is the only antithesis which denotes objects rather than qualities of objects or responses to them. We must take note that, while all other objects are ready to hand, these latter two emerge exceptionally on account of their alien character; indeed, we can acknowledge that these two cultural units are incorporated in the code only after a factual judgment issued by God about the nontouchable status of the apple. So when the serpent appears round the tree on which the apple is hanging, the animal is somehow registered as complementary to the fruit and becomes a specific cultural unit, whereas all other animals are perceived as 'edible' or 'bad' or 'blue' or even 'red', without the intervention of further specifications from the global continuum of perception.)

Obviously, one cultural unit inevitably leads to another, and this sets up a series of connotative chains:

(1) Red   = Edible   = Good   = Beautiful
     Blue   = Inedible   = Bad   = Ugly

Nevertheless, Adam and Eve are unable to designate, hence conceive of, these units unless they route them by way of significant forms. This is why they are provided with (or perhaps acquire by slow stages) an extremely elementary language which is adequate to express these concepts.

The repertoire of this language is built up out of two sounds, A and B, which can be arranged in a variety of sequences following the combinatory rule X, nY, X. This means that every sequence must start with one of the two elements and carry on with n repetitions of the other, ending up with one further occurrence of the first element. This kind of rule allows the production of an infinite series of syntactically correct sequences. But Adam and Eve have a strictly finite repertoire which exactly fits the cultural units mentioned above. So their code works out as follows:

(2) ABA   Edible
     BAB   Inedible
     ABBA   Good
     BAAB   Bad
     ABBBA   Serpent
     BAAAB   Apple
     ABBBBA   Beautiful
     BAAAAB   Ugly
     ABBBBBA   Red
     BAAAAAB   Blue

Furthermore, this code incorporates two all-purpose operators:

$$AA = Yes$$
$$BB = No$$

which can stand for Permission/Interdiction or, alternatively, Existence/Nonexistence, and even denote such oppositions as Approval/Disapproval, and so forth.

There are no further syntactical rules, apart from the fact that, if two sequences are joined to each other, their cultural units are thus brought into reciprocal predication: BAAAB, ABBBBBA, for example, means 'the apple is red', but also 'red apple'.

Adam and Eve are fully competent at handling their Edenic language, yet there is one thing they find hard to form a clear idea of: the generative rule behind the sequences. They can grasp this intuitively, but with the consequence that the AA and BB sequences become anomalous. What is more, they fail to realize that other correct sequences could be granted. This is partly because they feel no particular need for them, since there is nothing else they want to put a name to. The world they find themselves living in is full, harmonious, and satisfying, so that they register no sense of crisis or of necessity.

Therefore the connotative chains referred to in (1) assume the following structures:

(3) ABA = ABBA = ABBBBA = ABBBBBA = BAAAB = AA
     Eat   Good   Beautiful   Red   Apple   Yes

BAB	=	BAAB	=	BAAAAB	=	BAAAAAB	=	ABBBA	=	BB
No Eat		Bad		Ugly		Blue		Serpent		No

Words thus equal things (or rather the sensations which Adam and Eve are aware of) and things equal words. This makes it natural for them to envisage a number of connotative associations such as

(4) ABA = Red

Evidently this presents us already with a rudimentary use of metaphor, based on the possibility of extrapolating from metonymic chains of the type (3), and constitutes an embryonic inventive use of language. The inventiveness shown in this operation is still minimal because all the chains involve known elements, which have been fully explored, this semiotic universe being so diminutive both in the form of its content and in its expressive possibilities.

Any judgment which Adam and Eve pass on the universe is automatically bound to be a semiotic judgment, which is equivalent to calling it a judgment inside the normative cycle set up by the semiosis. It is true that they also pronounce factual judgments of the kind /. . . red/ when, for example, they find themselves confronted by a cherry. But this kind of factual information is exhausted instantly, since there is no linguistic mechanism for uttering /. . . /, and therefore this sensation is not susceptible of formal insertion into their referential system. Ultimately, judgments of this sort can only generate tautology, because the cherry, once it is perceived and denoted as /red/, prepares the ground for evaluative statements such as /red is red/ or, alternatively, /red is good/, which had already been rendered homologous by the system, as we saw above in (3). We are entitled to assume that they can point at things with their fingers, that is, use physical gestures to designate an object to the other person, which is the equivalent of /this/. In much the same way, the shifter /I/ or /you/ or /he/ is added to any statement by means of pointed fingers designed to function as pronouns. Hence the statement /ABBBBBA. ABA/ means, if accompanied by two stabbing gestures with the finger, 'I eat this red'. But no doubt Adam and Eve perceive those indexical devices as nonlinguistic ones: they consider them as *existential qualifiers* or *circumstantial arrows* used for referring a message (meaningful in itself) to an actual object or situation.

3.2. Formulation of the first factual judgment with semiotic consequences

Adam and Eve have only just settled down in the Garden of Eden. They have learned to find their way around with the help of language—when out comes God, who pronounces the first factual judgment. The general sense of what God is trying to tell them is as follows: "You two probably imagine that the apple belongs to the class of good, edible things, because it happens to be red. Well, I've got news for you. The apple is not to be considered edible because it is bad." Obviously, God is above providing an explanation of why the apple is evil; he is himself the yardstick of all values and knows it. For Adam and Eve the whole thing is rather more tricky: they have grown into the habit of associating the Good with the Edible and the Red. Yet they cannot possibly ignore a commandment coming from God. His status in their eyes is that of an AA: he constitutes 'yes', an incarnation of the Positive. In fact, whereas the sequence AA is used with all other occurrences only for the purpose of connoting pairings of different sequences, in the case of God ('I am that I am'), AA is more than a mere formula of predication: it is his name. If they were a little more versed in theology, Adam and Eve would come to the conclusion that the serpent should be referred to as BB, but they are blissfully ignorant of such subtleties. Anyway, the serpent is blue and inedible, and only after God's commandment does it become a pertinent detail among all the items of Eden's resources.

God spoke and his words were /BAAAB. BAB—BAAAB. BAAB/ (apple inedible, apple bad).

This constitutes a factual judgment, as it affords a notion which is as yet unfamiliar to those God has addressed; for God is both referent and source of the referent—his pronouncements are a court of reference. Yet God's judgment is in part semiotic, for it posits a new type of connotative pairing between semantic units which had previously been coupled together differently.

Nevertheless, we shall see shortly how God committed a grave error by providing those very elements which could throw the whole code out of joint. In an effort to elaborate a prohibition which would put his creatures to the test, God provides the fundamental example of a subversion in the presumed natural order of things. Why should an apple which is red be inedible as if it were blue?

Alas, God wanted to bring into existence the cultural tradition, and culture is born, apparently, to the sound of an institutional taboo. It would be possible to argue that culture was implicitly present, granted the existence of language and that all God's creative activity was already a norm, a source of authority, a law. But who will ever be able to trace the precise order of events at that turning point in history? What if language was formed at a stage later than the issue of the prohibition? My present task is, not to solve the problem of the origins of language, but to manipulate a hypothetical speech model. All the same, we are entitled to insist that God acted rashly; it is too soon to establish where he went wrong. First, we must return to the evolving crisis in the Garden.

Now that Adam and Eve have been served with the apple interdict, they find themselves obliged to adjust the connotative chains established in (3) and set up new chains as follows:

(5) Red = Edible = Good = Beautiful = Yes
    Blue = Inedible = Bad = Ugly = No = Serpent and Apple

from which it is only a short step to

Serpent = Apple

This shows that the semantic universe rapidly becomes unbalanced by comparison with the pristine situation. Nonetheless, it would seem that modern man's semantic universe bears more resemblance to (5) than to (3). This imbalance within their system insinuates the first contradictions into Adam and Eve's wonderland.

3.3. In which the contradiction takes shape inside the semantic universe of Eden

It is perfectly true that certain habits of perception entitle us to go on referring to the apple as a /red/, even when we are quite conscious that it has been connotatively assimilated to that which is bad and inedible and, therefore, to Blue. The sentence,

(6) BAAAB. ABBBBBA (the apple is red),

is directly contradicted by the other sentence,

(7) BAAAB. BAAAAAB (the apple is blue).

Adam and Eve suddenly realize they have hit on an anomaly, by which a denoting term establishes a straight contrast with those connotations which it inevitably produces; this contradiction cannot possibly be expressed in their standard denotative vocabulary. They are unable to point out the apple by saying /this is red/. They are naturally quite reluctant to formulate the contradictory proposition «the apple is red, it is blue», so they are confined to pointing out the peculiar phenomenon of the apple by a crude metaphor such as /the thing which is red and blue/ or, preferably, /the thing which is named red-blue/. Instead of the cacophonous proposition /BAAAB. ABBBBBA. BAAAAAB/ (the apple is red, it is blue), they prefer to devise a metaphor, a compound substitutional name. This releases them from the logical contradiction and also opens up the possibility of an intuitive and ambiguous grasp of the concept (by way of a fairly ambiguous use of the code). Hence they refer to the apple by

(8) ABBBBBABAAAAAB (the redblue).

This new term expresses a contradictory fact without obliging the speaker to formulate it in accordance with the habitual logical rules, which would in fact exclude it. But it stimulates an unprecedented sensation in Adam and Eve. They find such an unusual sound fascinating, as well as the unprecedented form they have devised for the sequence. The message in (8) is obviously ambiguous from the viewpoint of the form of content, but the form of its expression is also ambiguous. It thus becomes embryonically self-focusing. Adam says /redblue/, and then, instead of looking at the apple, he repeats to himself in a slightly dazed and childish way that lump of curious sounds. For the first time perhaps he is observing words rather than the things they stand for.

3.4.   The generation of aesthetic messages

When he takes another look at (8), Adam makes a startling discovery: ABBBB*BAB*AAAAAB contains at its very center the sequence BAB (which means 'inedible'). How odd: the apple, *qua redblue,* structurally incorporates a formal indication of the inedibility which previously seemed to be simply one of its connotations at the level of the form of content. Now, on the contrary, the apple turns out to be 'inedible' even at the level of expression. Adam and Eve have at last discovered the aesthetic use of language. But they are not completely absorbed in it. Desire for the apple has yet to grow stronger; the apple experience still has to acquire a growing fascination if it is to produce an aesthetic impulse. The Romantics were well aware of this: art is created only by the upsurge of grand passions (even if the object of this passion is merely the language). Adam has now acquired the language passion. The whole business is most enticing. But the apple also triggers off another passion in Adam: the apple is Forbidden Fruit, and, being the only such article in the Garden of Eden, it holds a special appeal for him, an apple appeal, so to speak. It certainly makes one want to ask "Why?" Yet it is the forbidden fruit which has caused the birth of a previously unprecedented word—a forbidden word? There is now a close correlation between passionate desire for the apple and passion for language; we have a situation permeated with a physical and mental excitation which seems to mirror the whole process we moderns call the creative urge.

   The following stage in Adam's experiment confers special status on the *substance of expression.* He finds a chunk of rock and scribbles on it

(9) ABBBBBA, which means 'red'. But he writes this with the juice of blue berries.

Next he writes

(10) BAAAAAB, which means 'blue'. This time he writes it in red juice.

Now he steps back and admires his work with a certain satisfaction. Surely the expressions in (9) and (10) are both metaphors for the apple. However, their metaphoric status is heightened by the presence of a physical element, namely, the particular emphasis inherent in the matter of expression itself. Still, this operation has transformed the substance of expression (the particular way of handling it) from a purely optional variant into a pertinent feature: it is now *form of expression,* though Adam is dealing with form of expression in a language of colors, as opposed to words. Also, something rather curious has happened: up to this point red objects were imprecise referents which the sign-vehicle ABBBBBA ('red') could be applied to. But now a red something, the red of the berry's juice, has itself become the sign-vehicle of an element which has as one of its meanings the very same word ABBBBBA which previously stood for it. In fact, the limitless possibilities of semiosis allow any meaning to become the sign-vehicle of another meaning, even of its own erstwhile sign-vehicle. There can even come about a situation where an object (that is, referent) becomes itself a sign. In any case, that redness means, not only «red», nor even merely «ABBBBBA», but also «edible» and «beautiful», and so on. Meanwhile the verbal equivalent of what is actually scribbled on the rock is «blue» and, consequently, «bad», «inedible». What a marvelous discovery! It certainly renders the whole force of ambiguity in the concept of apple. For hours on end Adam and Eve sit back and contemplate those signs written out on the rock; they are in an ecstasy of admiration. "How very baroque," Eve would like to comment, but she cannot. She has no critical metalanguage at her disposal. But Adam is bursting to have another go. He writes up

(11) ABBBBB*B*A.

Here are six B's. This sequence does not exist in the terms of his vocabulary, yet it is closest of all to the sequence ABBBBBA (red). Adam has written up the word /red/, but with added graphic emphasis. Perhaps this emphasis of the form of expression has a parallel at the level of the form of content? Surely it is a heavily emphasized red? A red which is redder than other reds? Blood, for example? It is odd that this very moment, when Adam is casting around for a function for his new word, is the first occasion when he has had to take note of the various shades of red in the world that surrounds him. The innovation which he has established at the level of form of expression actually induces him to isolate specific detail in the form of content. If he has come this far, then we may say that the extra B is, not a variant in the form of expression, but rather a fresh feature to add to it. Adam puts the problem to one side for the time being. His immediate interest is to continue the language experiment dealing with the apple, and this recent discovery has sidetracked him. He now wants to try writing (or saying) something more complex. He wants to say «inedible is bad, which is apple ugly and blue», and here is how he sets about writing it:

(12)   BAB
         BAAB
         BAAAB
         BAAAAB
         BAAAAAB

The text is now in a vertical column. And two curious formal characteristics of the message force themselves onto Adam's attention: there is a progressive increase in the length of words (this represents the establishment of a rhythm), and, second, each of the five sequences ends with the same letter (this represents a primitive model of rhyme). All of a sudden Adam is swept away by the incantatory power (the *epode*) of language. So God's commandment was justified, he thinks to himself: the sinfulness of the apple is underlined and emphasized by a kind of formal necessity which *requires* that the apple be ugly and blue. Adam is so persuaded by this apparent indivisibility of form and content that he begins to believe that *nomina sint numina*. He decides to go even further than this: he decides to reinforce both the rhythm and the rhyme by inserting elements of calculated redundancy in his already unquestionably poetic statement:

(13)   BAB   BAB
         BAAAB   BAB
         BAAB   BAB
         BAB   BAAAAAB

By now his 'poetic' ambitions are clearly aroused! The idea that *nomina sint numina* has fired his imagination. With an almost Heideggerian sense of false etymology, he starts by noticing that the word for «apple» (BAAAB) ends with the letter B, just like all those words which refer specifically to BB things, bad things, like badness, ugliness, and blue. The first impression made on Adam by the poetic use of language is a growing conviction that language is part of the natural order of things, easily conceived by analogy with the world it depicts and held in gestation by obscure onomatopoeic impulses of the soul; language is the authorized voice of God. We can see that Adam tends to use poetic experience to put the clock back, in a rather reactionary key: through language the gods speak themselves! Furthermore, the whole process is flattering to his ego: ever since he started to manipulate language, he has been inclined to see himself as being on the side of God. It is beginning to occur to him that he may be one up on dear Eve. He begins to think that the poetic power is *la différence*.

However, Eve is by no means indifferent to her partner's passion for language. She just dabbles in it for different motives. Her meeting with the Serpent has already taken place, and the little which he can have told her (in the impoverished idiom of the Garden) has probably been charged with a mutual liking we investigators are in no position to speculate about, since semiotics has "to pass over in silence what it cannot speak about."

At any rate, Eve joins in the game. And she explains to Adam that if words are Gods, then it's odd how the Serpent (ABBBA) has the same ending as the words which stand for beautiful, good, and red. Eve goes on to explain that poetry allows all sorts of language games:

(14) ABBA
      ABBBBA
      ABBBBBA
      ABBBA

«Good, beautiful and red—is the Serpent» goes Eve's poem, and it entails just the same formal identity between expression and content as the one produced by Adam (12). Eve's sensitiveness has allowed her to go even further and to display the anaphorical smoothness of the beginning as a counterpoint to the rhymed gentleness of the end. Eve's approach reopens the whole problem of self-contradiction, which Adam's poem seems to have papered over. Just how can the Serpent be the formal equivalent of things which the language system excludes as his predicates?

Eve's success goes to her head. She vaguely imagines a new device for creating hidden homologies between form and content and for using these to produce new contradictions. She could, for example, try out a sequence where every letter, if analyzed against a microscopic grid, proved to be composed by one semantically opposed to it. But to carry off this type of 'concrete poetry' successfully would require a level of graphic sophistication which is quite beyond Eve's power. Adam therefore takes things into his own hands and conceives a still more ambiguous sequence:

(15) BAA—B.

Now what does the blank space stand for? If it really is a blank, then Adam has uttered the concept «bad» with a slight hesitation; but if the blank is really a proper space (which has been muffled by some chance noise), then it could only contain an extra A, which means he has uttered «apple». At this stage Eve devises her own *recitar cantando,* an Edenic Sprachgesang: in other words, a kind of musical theater:

(16) ABB*B*A.

Here the sing-song voice hovers at a heightened tone on the last B, with the result that we cannot tell whether she has sung out ABBBA (Serpent), or simply doubled the final B of «beautiful». This considerably upsets Adam, because it suggests a real possibility that language is responsible for ambiguities and deceptions. So he transfers his anxiety away from the pitfalls of language onto the meanings which the commandment issued by God had put into question: 'to be or not to be' can only result in 'edible/inedible', in Adam's situation, but, when he sings out his dilemma, he is fascinated by its rhythm, for language is beginning to crumble to pieces in his mouth; he has found the way to give it a totally free rein:

```
(17) ABA    BAB
     ABA    BAB
     ABA    BAB   BAB   BB   B   A
     BBBBBBAAAAAABBBBBB
     BAAAA
     AA
```

The poem sets free an explosion of words, the Futurist *parole in libertà.*

But, at the very moment he recognizes that he has invented incorrect words, Adam begins to see more clearly why the others were correct. At last he can visualize the generative rule which stood at the center of his language system (X, nY, X). It is only when he violates the system that Adam comes to understand its structure. At this precise moment, while he is wondering if the last line is the acme of grammatical disorderliness, he is bound to realize that the sequence AA does in fact exist, so he will ask himself how and why the language system can allow it. He therefore thinks back to (15) and the problem which occurred to him in that case, concerning the blank space. It comes clear to him that even a blank constitutes a full space in the system, and that the sequences AA or BB, which both struck him originally as anomalous, are actually correct, because the rule (X, nY, X) certainly does not prevent the value of n from being *Zero.*

Adam has arrived at a comprehension of the system at the very moment in which he is calling the system into question and therefore destroying it. Just as he comes to understand the rigid generative law of the code which had governed him, so he realizes that here is technically nothing to stop him from proposing a new code (for example, nX, nY, nX): such a code would legitimize sequences of the type BBBBBBAAAAAABBBBBB, as in the fourth line of (17). While bent on destroying the system, he comprehends its full range of possibilities and discovers that he is master of it. Only a short while ago, he fondly imagined that poetry was a medium through which spoke Gods. Now he is becoming aware of the *arbitrariness of signs*.

At first he loses control of his own exuberance. He continually takes to pieces and puts together again this crazy gadget that he has found in his control; he composes totally implausible gibberish and then hums it admiringly to himself for hours on end; he invents the colors of the vowels, flatters himself that he has created a poetic language accessible, some days, to all senses; he writes of silences and of nights; he defines vertigos. He says, An apple! and, out of the forgetfulness where his voice banishes any contour, inasmuch as it is something other than known calyxes, musically arises, an idea itself and fragrant, the one absent from all baskets. *Le suggérer, voilà le rêve!* He wants to make himself a *seer,* by a long, prodigious and rational disordering of all the senses. But then, step by step, he escapes from emotion, expressing it through its objective correlative and, as does the God of the Creation, remains within or behind or above his handiwork, invisible, refined out of existence, indifferent, paring his fingernails.

3.5. The reformulation of content

Eventually, Adam calms down. At least one thing has become clear during his manic explorations: the order of language is not absolute. This gives rise to the legitimate doubt that the pairing off of denoting sequences against the cultural universe of meanings, which was provided as the system in (2), may not be an unquestionable absolute after all. Finally, he feels inclined to question the very totality of the cultural units which the System had neatly paired off against the series of sequences which he has so recently destroyed.

Now Adam passes on to an investigation of the form of content. Whoever actually said that Blue was Inedible? From conventionalized meanings Adam takes a short step back to the world of experience and stages another encounter with its physical referents. He picks a blue berry for himself and eats it; the berry tastes good. So far he has been in the habit of drawing all the liquid he needed from (red) fruit, but now he discovers that (blue) water is eminently drinkable and develops a pronounced taste for it. Again, he is influenced by the curiosity which he first felt after the experiment in (11): probably there are different gradations of red, blood red, the sun's red, the red of apples or of certain plants and bushes. Again, Adam resegments the content and discovers fresh cultural categories (this means new perceptive realities), which oblige him to provide new names for them, although these are quite easy to invent. He composes complex sequences to denote these new categories and devises new verbal formulae in order to express this experience in factual judgments. The experience is subsequently assigned to the expanding language system by way of semiotic judgments. His language is beginning to swell in his hands, and his whole world is growing fuller. Clearly, neither language nor the world is so harmonious or single-voiced as both were during the period of situation (1), but at least he is no longer afraid of the contradictions concealed inside their language system; this is because from one side the contradictions force him to reenvisage the form which he assigns to the world, while from the other they induce him to exploit them for their potential poetic effects.

As a result of all this, Adam discovers that Order, as such, is non-existent; it is just one of the infinite possible states of repose which disorder occasionally arrives at.

It would be superfluous to add that Eve goes on to encourage him to eat the apple. Once Adam has eaten it, he is in a position to issue a judgment of the kind «the apple is good», which reestablishes, at least for one item, the equilibrium which the language system enjoyed before the Prohibition. But this detail is irrelevant at the stage we have now reached. Adam was obliged to exit from the Garden of Eden after his first nervous manipulation of language. This was the mistake God made by disturbing the univocal harmony of the primitive language system by an ambiguously phrased prohibition; but, like all prohibitions, it was supposed to forbid something desirable. From that moment onward (not from the time when Adam really ate the apple), world history commenced.

Unless God was fully aware of this and issued his prohibition precisely to stimulate the birth of history. Or again, perhaps God did not exist, and the prohibition was simply invented by Adam and Eve for the specific purpose of introducing a contradiction into the language system and producing inventive modes of discussion. Perhaps the language system incorporated this contradiction from its very beginnings and the prohibition myth was invented by our forefathers simply to explain such a scandalous state of affairs.

Evidently these observations have taken us outside the strict terms of our inquiry, which is concerned with language creativity, its poetic applications, and the interaction between the world's form and language's form.

At any rate, it goes without saying that, once Adam had redeemed language's pledge to Order and Singleness of Voice, it was handed down to his descendants in a considerably richer form.

Hence Cain and Abel, having discovered the existence of other orders precisely by means of language, pass on logically to the murder of Adam. This latter detail draws us even further away from our habitual exegetical tradition and plumps us in a midway position between the myth of Saturn and the myth of Sigmund. But there is a method to all this madness, for Adam taught mankind that, in order to restructure codes, one needs to rewrite messages.

Part Two   Closed

CHAPTER FOUR

The Myth of Superman

The hero equipped with powers superior to those of the common man has been a constant of the popular imagination—from Hercules to Siegfried, from Roland to Pantagruel, all the way to Peter Pan. Often the hero's virtue is humanized, and his powers, rather than being supernatural, are the extreme realization of natural endowments such as astuteness, swiftness, fighting ability, or even the logical faculties and the pure spirit of observation found in Sherlock Holmes. In an industrial society, however, where man becomes a number in the realm of the organization which has usurped his decision-making role, he has no means of production and is thus deprived of his power to decide. Individual strength, if not exerted in sports activities, is left abased when confronted with the strength of machines which determine man's very movements. In such a society the positive hero must embody to an unthinkable degree the power demands that the average citizen nurtures but cannot satisfy.

Superman is not from Earth; he arrived here as a youth from the planet Krypton. Growing up on Earth, Superman finds he is gifted with superhuman powers. His strength is practically unlimited. He can fly through space at the speed of light, and, when he surpasses that speed, he breaks through the time barrier and can transfer himself to other epochs. With no more than the pressure of his hands, he can subject coal to the temperature required to change it into diamond; in a matter of seconds, at supersonic speed, he can fell an entire forest, make lumber from trees, and construct a ship or a town; he can bore through mountains, lift

"Il mito di Superman e la dissoluzione del tempo," in *Demitizzazione e immagine,* ed. E. Castelli (Padua: Cedam, 1962). Natalie Chilton, trans., "The Myth of Superman," *Diacritics* (spring 1972). This chapter, with minor alterations, reproduces the translation.

ocean liners, destroy or construct dams; his X-ray vision allows him to see through any object to almost unlimited distances and to melt metal objects at a glance; his superhearing puts him in extremely advantageous situations permitting him to tune in on conversations however far away. He is kind, handsome, modest, and helpful; his life is dedicated to the battle against the forces of evil; and the police find him an untiring collaborator.

Nevertheless, the image of Superman is not entirely beyond the reach of the reader's self-identification. In fact, Superman lives among men disguised as the journalist Clark Kent; as such, he appears fearful, timid, not overintelligent, awkward, nearsighted, and submissive to his matriarchal colleague, Lois Lane, who, in turn, despises him, since she is madly in love with Superman. In terms of narrative, Superman's double identity has a function, since it permits the suspense characteristic of a detective story and great variation in the mode of narrating our hero's adventures, his ambiguities, his histrionics. But, from a mythopoeic point of view, the device is even subtle: in fact, Clark Kent personifies fairly typically the average reader who is harassed by complexes and despised by his fellow men; though an obvious process of self-identification, any accountant in any American city secretly feeds the hope that one day, from the slough of his actual personality, there can spring forth a superman who is capable of redeeming years of mediocre existence.

4.1. The structure of myth and the 'civilization' of the novel

With the undeniable mythological connotation of our hero established, it is necessary to specify the narrative structure through which the myth is offered daily or weekly to the public. There is, in fact, a fundamental difference between the figure of Superman and the traditional heroic figures of classical and nordic mythology or the figures of Messianic religions.

The traditional figure of religion was a character of human or divine origin, whose image had immutable characteristics and an irreversible destiny. It was possible that a story, as well as a number of traits, backed up the character; but the story followed a line of development already established, and it filled in the character's features in a gradual, but definitive, manner.

In other words, a Greek statue could represent Hercules or a scene of Hercules' labors; in both cases, but more so in the latter, Hercules would be seen as someone who has a story, and this story would characterize his divine features. The story has taken place and can no longer be denied. Hercules has been made real through a development of temporal events. But once the development ended his image symbolized, along with the character, the story of his development, and it became the substance of the definitive record and judgments about him. Even the account greatly favored by antiquity was almost always the story of something which had already happened and of which the public was aware.

One could recount for the nth time the story of Roland the Paladin, but the public already knew what happened to the hero. New additions and romantic embellishments were not lacking, but neither would they have impaired the substance of the myth being narrated. A similar situation existed in the plastic arts and the paintings of Gothic cathedrals or of Counter-Reformation and Renaissance churches. What had already happened was often narrated in moving and dramatic ways.

The 'civilization' of the modern novel offers a story in which the reader's main interest is transferred to the unpredictable nature of *what will happen* and, therefore, to the plot invention which now holds our attention. The event has not happened *before* the story; it happens *while* it is being told, and usually even the author does not know what will take place.

At the time of its origin, the *coup de théâtre* where Oedipus finds himself guilty as a result of Tiresias' revelation 'worked' for the public, not because it caught them unaware of the myth, but because the mechanism of the 'plot', in accordance with Aristotelian rules, succeeded in making them once more co-participants through pity and terror. The reader is brought to identify both with the situation and with the character. In contrast, there is Julien Sorel shooting Madame de Rênal, or Poe's detective discovering the party guilty of the double crime in Rue de la Morgue, or Javert paying his debt of gratitude to Jean Valjean, where we are spectators to a *coup de théâtre* whose unpredictable nature is part of the invention and, as such, takes on aesthetic value. This phenomenon becomes important in direct proportion to the popularity of the novel, and the *feuilleton,* for the masses—the adventures of Rocambole and of Arsène Lupin—have, as craft, no other value than the ingenious invention of unexpected events.

This new dimension of the story sacrifices for the most part the mythic potential of the character. The mythic character embodies a law, or a universal demand, and therefore must be in part *predictable* and cannot hold surprises for us; the character of a novel wants, rather, to be a man like anyone else, and what could befall him is as unforeseeable as what may happen to us. Such a character will take on what we will call an 'aesthetic universality', a capacity to serve as a reference point for behavior and feelings which belong to us all. He does not contain the universality of myth, nor does he become an archetype, the emblem of a supernatural reality. He is the result of a universal rendering of a particular and eternal event. The character of a novel is a 'historic type'. Therefore, to accommodate this character, the aesthetics of the novel must revive an old category particularly necessary when art abandons the territory of myth; this we may term the 'typical'.

The mythological character of comic strips finds himself in this singular situation: he must be an archetype, the totality of certain collective aspirations, and therefore he must necessarily become immobilized in an emblematic and fixed nature which renders him easily recognizable (this is what happens to Superman); but, since he is marketed in the sphere of a 'romantic' production for a public that consumes 'romances', he must be subjected to a development which is typical, as we have seen, of novelistic characters.

4.2. The plot and the 'consumption' of the character

A tragic plot, according to Aristotle, involves the character in a series of events, reversals, recognitions, pitiful and terrifying cases that culminate in a catastrophe; a novelistic plot, let us add, develops these dramatic units in a continuous and narrated series which, in the popular novel, becomes an end in itself. They must proliferate as much as possible *ad infinitum. The Three Musketeers,* whose adventures continue in *Twenty Years Later* and conclude finally in *The Vicomte de Bragelonne* (but here intervene parasitic narrators who continue to tell us about the adventures of the Musketeers' sons, or the clash between d'Artagnan and Cyrano de Bergerac, and so on), is an example of narrative plot which multiplies like a tapeworm; the greater its capacity to sustain itself through an indefinite series of contrasts, oppositions, crises, and solutions, the more vital it seems.

Superman, by definition the character whom nothing can impede, finds himself in the worrisome narrative situation of being a hero without an adversary and therefore without the possibility of any development. A further difficulty arises because his public, for precise psychological reasons, cannot keep together the various moments of a narrative process over the space of several days. Each story concludes within the limits of a few pages; or, rather, every weekly edition is composed of two or three complete stories in which a particular narrative episode is presented, developed, and resolved. Aesthetically and commercially deprived of the possibility of narrative development, Superman gives serious problems to his script writers. Little by little, varying formulae are offered to provoke and justify a contrast; Superman, for example, does have a weakness. He is rendered almost helpless by the radiation of Kryptonite, a metal of meteoric origin, which his adversaries naturally procure at any cost in order to neutralize their avenger. But a creature gifted with superhuman intellectual and physical powers easily finds a means to get out of such scrapes, and that is what Superman does. Furthermore, one must consider that as a narrative theme the attempt to weaken him through the employment of kryptonite does not offer a broad range of solutions, and it must be used sparingly.

There is nothing left to do except to put Superman to the test of several obstacles which are intriguing because they are unforeseen but which are, however, surmountable by the hero. In that case two effects are obtained. First, the reader is struck by the strangeness of the obstacles—diabolically conceived inventions, curiously equipped apparitions from outer space, machines that can transmit one through time, teratological results of new experiments, the cunning of evil scientists to overwhelm Superman with kryptonite, the hero's struggles with creatures endowed with powers equal to his, such as Mxyzptlk, the gnome, who comes from the fifth dimension and who can be countered only if Superman manages to make him pronounce his own name backwards (Kltpzyxm), and so on. Second, thanks to the hero's unquestionable superiority, the crisis is rapidly resolved and the account is maintained within the bounds of the short story.

But this resolves nothing. In fact, the obstacle once conquered (and within the space allotted by commercial requirements), Superman has still *accomplished something*. Consequently, the character has made a gesture which is inscribed in his past and which weighs on his future. He has taken a step toward death, he has gotten older, if only by an hour; his storehouse of personal experiences has irreversibly enlarged. *To act,* then, for Superman, as for any other character (or for each of us), means to 'consume' himself.

Now, Superman cannot 'consume' himself, since a myth is 'inconsumable'. The hero of the classical myth became 'inconsumable' precisely because he was already 'consumed' in some exemplary action. Or else he had the possibility of a continuing rebirth or of symbolizing some vegetative cycle—or at least a certain circularity of events or even of life itself. But Superman is myth on condition of being a creature immersed in everyday life, in the present, apparently tied to our own conditions of life and death, even if endowed with superior faculties. An immortal Superman would no longer be a man, but a god, and the public's identification with his double identity would fall by the wayside.

Superman, then, must remain 'inconsumable' and at the same time be 'consumed' according to the ways of everyday life. He possesses the characteristics of timeless myth, but is accepted only because his activities take place in our human and everyday world of time. The narrative paradox that Superman's scriptwriters must resolve somehow, even without being aware of it, demands a paradoxical solution with regard to time.

4.3. Temporality and 'consumption'

The Aristotelian definition of time is "the amount of movement from before to after," and since antiquity time has implied the idea of *succession;* the Kantian analysis has established unequivocally that this idea must be associated with an idea of *causality:* "It is a necessary law of our sensibility and therefore a condition of all perception that preceding Time necessarily determines what follows."[1] This idea has been maintained even by relativistic physics, not in the study of the transcendental conditions of the perceptions, but in the definition of the nature of time in terms of cosmological objectivity, in such a way that time would appear as the *order of causal chains*. Reverting to these Einsteinian concepts, Reichenbach recently redefined the order of time as the order of causes, the order of open causal chains which we see verified in our universe, and the *direction* of time in terms of *growing entropy* (taking up in terms even of information theory the thermodynamic concept which had recurrently interested philosophers and which they adopted as their own in speaking of the irreversibility of time.[2]

Before causally determines *after,* and the series of these determinations cannot be traced back, at least in our universe (according to the epistemological model that explains the world in which we live), but is irreversible. That other cosmological models can foresee other solutions to this problem is well known; but, in the sphere of our daily understanding of events (and, consequently, in the structural sphere of a narrative character), this concept of time is what permits us to move around and to recognize events and their directions.

Expressing themselves in other words, but always on the basis of the order of *before* and *after* and of the causality of the before on the after (emphasizing variously the determination of the before on the after), existentialism and phenomenology have shifted the problem of time into the sphere of the structures of subjectivity, and discussions about action, possibility, plan, and liberty have been based on time. Time as a *structure of possibility* is, in fact, the problem of our moving toward a future, having behind us a past, whether this past is seen as a block with respect to our freedom to plan (planning which forces us to choose necessarily what we have already been) or is understood as a basis of future possibilities and therefore possibilities of conserving or changing what has been, within certain limits of freedom, yet always within the terms of positive processes.

Sartre says that "the past is the ever-growing totality of the in-itself which we are." When I want to tend toward a possible future, I must be and cannot not be this past. My possibilities of choosing or not choosing a future depend upon acts already accomplished, and they constitute the point of departure for my possible decisions. And as soon as I make another decision, it, in turn, belongs to the past and modifies what I am and offers another platform for successive projects. If it is meaningful to put the problem of freedom and of the responsibility of our decisions in philosophical terms, the basis of the discussion and the point of departure for a phenomenology of these acts is always the structure of temporality.[3]

For Husserl, the 'I' is free inasmuch as it is in the past. In effect, the past determines me and therefore also determines my future, but the future, in turn, 'frees' the past. My temporality is my freedom, and on my freedom depends my 'Being-having-been' which determines me. But, in its continuous synthesis with the future, the content of my 'Being-having-been' depends on the future. Now, if the 'I' is free because it is already determined together with the 'I-that-should-be', there exists within this freedom (so encumbered by conditions, so burdened with what was and is hence irreversible) a 'sorrowfulness' (*Schmerzhaftigkeit*) which is none other than 'facticity'. (Compare with Sartre: "I am my future in the continuous prospective of the possibility of not being it. In this is the suffering which we described before and which gives sense to my present; I am a being whose sense is always problematic.")[4] Each time I plan I notice the tragic nature of the condition in which I find myself, without being able to avoid it. Nevertheless, I plan to oppose the tragic elements with the possibility of something positive, which is a change from that which is and which I put into effect as I direct myself toward the future. Plan, freedom, and condition are articulated while I observe this connection of structures in my actions, according to a dimension of *responsibility*. This is what Husserl observes when he says that, in this 'directed' being of the 'I' toward possible scopes, an ideal 'teleology' is established and that the future as possible 'having' with respect to the original futurity in which I already always *am* is the universal prefiguration of the aim of life.

In other words, the subject situated in a temporal dimension is aware of the gravity and difficulty of his decisions, but at the same time he is aware that he must decide, that it is he who must decide, and that this process is linked to an indefinite series of necessary decision making that involves all other men.

4.4. A plot which does not 'consume' itself

If contemporary discussions which involve man in meditation upon his destiny and his condition are based on this concept of time, the narrative structure of Superman certainly evades it in order to save the situation which we have already discussed. In Superman it is the concept of time that breaks down. The very structure of time falls apart, not in the time *about which,* but, rather, in the time *in which the story is told.*

In Superman stories the time that breaks down is the *time of the story,* that is, the notion of time which ties one episode to another. In the sphere of a story, Superman accomplishes a given job (he routs a band of gangsters); at this point the story ends. In the same comic book, or in the edition of the following week, a new story begins. If it took Superman up again at the point where he left off, he would have taken a step toward death. On the other hand, to begin a story without showing that another had preceded it would manage, momentarily, to remove Superman from the law that leads from life to death through time. In the end (Superman has been around since 1938), the public would realize the comicality of the situation—as happened in the case of Little Orphan Annie, who prolonged her disaster-ridden childhood for decades.

Superman's scriptwriters have devised a solution which is much shrewder and undoubtedly more original. The stories develop in a kind of oneiric climate—of which the reader is not aware at all—where what has happened before and what has happened after appear extremely hazy. The narrator picks up the strand of the event again and again, as if he had forgotten to say something and wanted to add details to what had already been said.

It occurs, then, that along with Superman stories, Superboy stories are told, that is, stories of Superman when he was a boy, or a tiny child under the name of Superbaby. At a certain point, Supergirl appears on the scene. She is Superman's cousin, and she, too, escaped from the destruction of Krypton. All of the events concerning Superman are retold in one way or another in order to account for the presence of this new character (who has hitherto not been mentioned, because, it is explained, she has lived in disguise in a girls' school, awaiting puberty, at which time she could come out into the world; the narrator goes back in time to tell in how many and in which cases she, of whom nothing was said, participated during those many adventures where we saw Superman alone involved). One imagines, using the solution of travel through time, that Supergirl, Superman's contemporary, can encounter Superboy in the past and be his playmate; and even Superboy, having broken the time barrier by sheer accident, can encounter Superman, his own self of many years later.

But, since such a fact could comprise the character in a series of developments capable of influencing his future actions, the story ends here and insinuates that Superboy has dreamed, and one's approval of what has been said is deferred. Along these lines the most original solution is undoubtedly that of the *Imaginary Tales.* It happens, in fact, that the public will often request delightful new developments of the scriptwriters; for example, why doesn't Superman marry Lois Lane, the journalist, who has loved him for so long? If Superman married Lois Lane, it would of course be another step toward his death, as it would lay down another irreversible premise; nevertheless, it is necessary to find continually new narrative stimuli and to satisfy the 'romantic' demands of the public. And so it is told "what would have happened *if* Superman had married Lois." The premise is developed in all of its dramatic implications, and at the end is the warning: Remember, this is an 'imaginary' story which in truth has not taken place. (In this respect, note Roberto Giammanco's remarks about the consistently homosexual nature of characters like Superman or Batman—another variation of the theme of 'superpowers'. This aspect undoubtedly exists, particularly in Batman, and Giammanco offers reasons for it which we refer to later; but, in the specific case of Superman, it seems that we must speak not so much of homosexuality as of 'parsifalism'. In Superman the element of masculine societies is nearly absent, though it is quite evident in characters like Batman and Robin, Green Arrow and his partner, and so on. Even if he often collaborates with the Legion of Super Heroes of the Future—youngsters gifted with extraordinary powers, usually ephebic but of both sexes—Superman does not neglect working with his cousin, Supergirl, as well, nor can one say that Lois Lane's advances, or those of Lana Lang, an old schoolmate and rival of Lois, are received by Superman with the disgust of a misogynist. He shows, instead, the bashful embarrassment of an average young man in a matriarchal society. On the other hand, the most perceptive philologists have not overlooked his unhappy love for Lois Lemaris, who, being a mermaid, could offer him only an underwater *ménage* corresponding to a paradisiacal exile which Superman must refuse because of his sense of duty and the indispensable nature of his mission. What characterizes Superman is, instead, the platonic dimension of his affections, the implicit vow of chastity which depends less on his will than on the state of things, and the singularity of his situation. If we have to look for a structural reason for this narrative fact, we cannot but go back to our preceding observations: the 'parsifalism' of Superman is one of the conditions that prevents his slowly 'consuming' himself, and it protects him from the events, and therefore from the passing of time, connected with erotic ventures.)

The *Imaginary Tales* are numerous, and so are the *Untold Tales* or those stories that concern events already told but in which 'something was left out', so they are told again from another point of view, and in the process lateral aspects come to the fore. In this massive bombardment of events which are no longer tied together by any strand of logic, whose interaction is ruled no longer by any necessity, the reader, without realizing it, of course, loses the notion of temporal progression. Superman happens to live in an imaginary universe in which, as opposed to ours, causal chains are not open (A provokes B, B provokes C, C provokes D, and so on, *ad infinitum*), but closed (A provokes B, B provokes C, C provokes D, and D provokes A), and it no longer makes sense to talk about temporal progression on the basis of which we usually describe the happenings of the macrocosm.[5]

One could observe that, apart from the mythopoeic and commercial necessities which together force such a situation, a similar structural assessment of Superman stories reflects, even though at a low level, a series of diffuse persuasions in our culture about the problem of concepts of causality, temporality, and the irreversibility of events; and, in fact, a great deal of contemporary art, from Joyce to Robbe-Grillet, or a film such as *Last Year at Marienbad,* reflects paradoxical temporal situations, whose models, nevertheless, exist in the epistemological discussions of our times. But it is a fact that, in works such as *Finnegans Wake* or Robbe-Grillet's *In the Labyrinth,* the breakdown of familiar temporal relations happens in a conscious manner, on the part both of the writer and of the one who derives aesthetic satisfaction from the operation. The disintegration of temporality has the function both of quest and of denunciation and tends to furnish the reader with imaginative models capable of making him accept situations of the new science and of reconciling the activity of an imagination accustomed to old schemes with the activity of an intelligence which ventures to hypothesize or to describe universes that are not reducible to an image or a scheme. In consequence, these works (but here another problem opens up) carry out a mythopoeic function, offering the inhabitant of the contemporary world a kind of symbolic suggestion or allegorical diagram of that absolute which science has resolved, not so much in a metaphysical modality of the world, but in a possible way of establishing our relation with the world and, therefore, in a possible way of describing the world.[6]

The adventures of Superman, however, do not have this critical intention, and the temporal paradox on which they are sustained should not be obvious to the reader (just as the authors themselves are probably unaware of it), since a confused notion of time is the only condition which makes the story credible. Superman comes off as a myth only if the reader loses control of the temporal relationships and renounces the need to reason on their basis, thereby giving himself up to the uncontrollable flux of the stories which are accessible to him and, at the same time, holding on to the illusion of a continuous present. Since the myth is not isolated exemplarily in a dimension of eternity, but, in order to be assimilated, must enter into the flux of the story in question, this same story is refuted as flux and seen instead as an immobile present.

In growing accustomed to the idea of events happening in an ever-continuing present, the reader loses track of the fact that they should develop according to the dictates of time. Losing consciousness of it, he forgets the problems which are at its base, that is, the existence of freedom, the possibility of planning, the necessity of carrying plans out, the sorrow that such planning entails, the responsibility that it implies, and, finally, the existence of an entire human community whose progressiveness is based on making plans.

4.5. Superman as a model of 'heterodirection'

The proposed analysis would be greatly abstracted and could appear apocalyptic if the man who reads Superman, and for whom Superman is produced, were not that selfsame man with whom several sociological reports have dealt and who has been defined as 'other directed man'.

In advertising, as in propaganda, and in the area of human relations, the absence of the dimension of 'planning' is essential to establishing a paternalistic pedagogy, which requires the hidden persuasion that the subject is not responsible for his past, nor master of his future, nor even subject to the laws of planning according to the three 'ecstasies' of temporality (Heidegger). All of this would imply pain and labor, while society is capable of offering to the heterodirected man the results of projects already accomplished. Such are they as to respond to man's desires, which themselves have been introduced in man in order to make him recognize that what he is offered is precisely what he would have planned.

The analysis of temporal structures in Superman has offered us the image of a *way of telling stories* which would seem to be fundamentally tied to pedagogic principles that govern that type of society. Is it possible to establish connections between the two phenomena affirming that Superman is no other than one of the pedagogic instruments of this society and that the destruction of time that it pursues is part of a plan to make obsolete the idea of planning and of personal responsibility?

4.6. Defense of the iterative scheme

A series of events repeated according to a set scheme (iteratively, in such a way that each event takes up again from a sort of virtual beginning, ignoring where the preceding event left off) is nothing new in popular narrative. In fact, this scheme constitutes one of its more characteristic forms.

The device of iteration is one on which certain escape mechanisms are founded, particularly the types realized in television commercials: one distractedly watches the playing out of a sketch, then focuses one's attention on the punch line that reappears at the end of the episode. It is precisely on this foreseen and awaited reappearance that our modest but irrefutable pleasure is based.

This attitude does not belong only to the television spectator. The reader of detective stories can easily make an honest self-analysis to establish the modalities that explain his 'consuming' them. First, from the beginning the reading of a traditional detective story presumes the enjoyment of following a scheme: from the crime to the discovery and the resolution through a chain of deductions. The scheme is so important that the most famous authors have founded their fortune on its very immutability. Nor are we dealing only with a schematism in the order of a 'plot', but with a fixed schematism involving the same sentiments and the same psychological attitudes: in Simenon's Maigret or in Agatha Christie's Poirot, there is a recurrent movement of compassion to which the detective is led by his discovery of the facts and which merges into an empathy with the motives of the guilty party, an act of *caritas* which is combined with, if not opposed to, the act of justice that unveils and condemns.

Furthermore, the writer of stories then introduces a continuous series of connotations (for example, the characteristics of the policeman and of his immediate 'entourage') to such an extent that their reappearance in each story is an essential condition of its reading pleasure. And so we have the by now historical 'tics' of Sherlock Holmes, the punctilious vanity of Hercule Poirot, the pipe and the familiar fixes of Maigret, on up to the daily idiosyncrasies of the most unabashed heroes of postwar detective stories, such as the cologne water and Player's #6 of Peter Cheyney's Slim Callaghan or the cognac with a glass of cold water of Brett Halliday's Michael Shayne. Vices, gestures, nervous tics permit us to find an old friend in the character portrayed, and they are the principal conditions which allow us to 'enter into' the event. Proof of this is when our favorite author writes a story in which the usual character does not appear and we are not even aware that the fundamental scheme of the book is still like the others: we read the book with a certain detachment and are immediately prone to judge it a 'minor' work, a momentary phenomenon, or an interlocutory remark.

All this becomes very clear if we take a famous character such as Nero Wolfe, immortalized by Rex Stout. For sheer preterition and by way of caution, in the likelihood of one of our readers' being so 'highbrow' as to have never encountered our character, let us briefly recall the elements which combine to form Nero Wolfe's "type" and his environment. Nero Wolfe, from Montenegro, a naturalized American from time immemorial, is outlandishly fat, so much so that his leather easy chair must be expressly designed for him. He is fearfully lazy. In fact, he never leaves the house and depends, for his investigations, on the open-minded Archie Goodwin, with whom he indulges in a continuous relationship of a sharp and tensely polemic nature, tempered somewhat by their mutual sense of humor. Nero Wolfe is an absolute glutton, and his cook, Fritz, is the vestal virgin in the pantry, devoted to the unending care of this highly cultivated palate and equally greedy stomach; but along with the pleasures of the table, Wolfe cultivates an all-absorbing and exclusive passion for orchids; he has a priceless collection of them in the greenhouse on the top floor of the villa where he lives. Quite possessed by gluttony and flowers, assailed by a series of accessory tics (love of scholarly literature, systematic misogyny, insatiable thirst for money), Nero Wolfe conducts his investigations, masterpieces of psychological penetration, sitting in his office, carefully weighing the information with which the enterprising Archie furnishes him, studying the protagonists of each event who are obliged to visit him in his office, arguing with Inspector Cramer (attention: he always holds a methodically extinguished cigar in his mouth), quarreling with the odious Sergeant Purley Stebbins; and, finally, in a fixed setting from which he never veers, he summons the protagonists of the case to a meeting in his studio, usually in the evening. There, with skillful dialectical subterfuges, almost always before he himself knows the truth, he drives the guilty one into a public demonstration of hysteria and thus into giving himself away.

Those who know Rex Stout's stories know that these details hardly scratch the surface of the repertoire of *topoi,* of recurrent stock situations which animate these stories. The gamut is much more ample: Archie's almost canonic arrest under suspicion of reticence and false testimony; the legal diatribes about the conditions on which Wolfe will take on a client; the hiring of part-time agents like Saul Panzer or Orrie Carther; the painting in the studio behind which Wolfe or Archie can watch, through a peephole, the behavior and reactions of a subject put to the test in the office itself; the scenes with Wolfe and an insincere client—one could go on forever; we realize, at the end, that the list of these *topoi* is such that it could exhaust almost every possibility of the events permitted within the number of pages allowed to each story. Nevertheless, there are infinite variations of the theme; each crime has new psychological and economic motivations, each time the author devises what appears as a new situation. We say 'appear'; the fact is that the reader is never brought to verify the extent to which something new is told. The noteworthy moments are those when Wolfe repeats his usual gestures, when he goes up for the nth time to take care of his orchids while the case itself is reaching its dramatic climax, when Inspector Cramer threateningly enters with one foot between the door and the wall, pushing aside Goodwin and warning Wolfe with a shake of his finger that this time things will not go so smoothly. The attraction of the book, the sense of repose, of psychological extension which it is capable of conferring, lies in the fact that, plopped in an easy chair or in the seat of a train compartment, the reader continuously recovers, point by point, what he already knows, what he wants to know again: that is why he has purchased the book. He derives pleasure from the nonstory (if indeed a story is a development of events which should bring us from the point of departure to a point of arrival where we would never have dreamed of arriving); the distraction consists in the refutation of a development of events, in a withdrawal from the tension of past-present-future to the focus on an *instant,* which is loved because it is recurrent.

4.7.   The iterative scheme as a redundant message

It is certain that mechanisms of this kind proliferate more widely in the popular narrative of today than in the eighteenth-century romantic *feuilleton,* where, as we have seen, the event was founded upon a *development* and where the character was required to 'consume' himself through to death. Perhaps one of the first inexhaustible characters during the decline of the *feuilleton* and bridging the two centuries at the close of *la belle époque* is Fantomas. (Each episode of Fantomas closes with a kind of 'unsuccessful catharsis'; Juve and Fandor finally come to get their hands on the elusive one when he, with an unforeseeable move, foils the arrest. Another singular fact: Fantomas—responsible for blackmail and sensational kidnappings—at the beginning of each episode finds himself inexplicably poor and in need of money and, therefore, also of new 'action'. In this way the cycle can keep going.) With him the epoch ends. It remains to be asked if modern iterative mechanisms do not answer some profound need in contemporary man and, therefore, do not seem more justifiable and better motivated than we are inclined to admit at first glance.

If we examine the iterative scheme from a structural point of view, we realize that we are in the presence of a typical *high-redundance message.* A novel by Souvestre and Allain or by Rex Stout is a message which informs us very little and which, on the contrary, thanks to the use of redundant elements, keeps hammering away at the same meaning which we have peacefully acquired upon reading the first work of the series (in the case in point, the meaning is a certain mechanism of the action, due to the intervention of 'topical' characters). The taste for the iterative scheme is presented then as a taste for redundance. The hunger for entertaining narrative based on these mechanisms is a *hunger for redundance.* From this viewpoint, the greater part of popular narrative is a narrative of redundance.

Paradoxically, the same detective story that one is tempted to ascribe to the products that satisfy the taste for the unforeseen or the sensational is, in fact, read for exactly the opposite reason, as an invitation to that which is taken for granted, familiar, expected. Not knowing who the guilty party is becomes an accessory element, almost a pretext; certainly, it is true that in the action detective story (where the iteration of the scheme triumphs as much as in the investigation detective story), the suspense surrounding the guilty one often does not even exist; it is not a matter of discovering who committed the crime, but, rather, of following certain 'topical' gestures of 'topical' characters whose stock behavior we already love. To explain this 'hunger for redundance', extremely subtle hypotheses are not needed. The *feuilleton*, founded on the triumph of information, represented the preferred fare of a society that lived in the midst of messages loaded with redundance; the sense of tradition, the norms of associative living, moral principles, the valid rules of proper comportment in the environment of eighteenth-century bourgeois society, of the typical public which represented the consumers of the *feuilleton*— all this constituted a system of foreseeable communication that the social system provided for its members and which allowed life to flow smoothly without unexpected jolts and without upsets in its value system. In this sphere the 'informative' shock of a short story by Poe or the *coup de théâtre* of Ponson du Terrail acquired a precise meaning. In a contemporary industrial society, instead, the alternation of standards, the dissolution of tradition, social mobility, the fact that models and principles are 'consumable'—everything can be summed up under the sign of a continuous load of information which proceeds by way of massive jolts, implying a continual reassessment of sensibilities, adaptation of psychological assumptions, and requalification of intelligence. Narrative of a redundant nature would appear in this panorama as an indulgent invitation to repose, the only occasion of true relaxation offered to the consumer. Conversely, 'superior' art only proposes schemes in evolution, grammars which mutually eliminate each other, and codes of continuous alternations.

Is it not also natural that the cultured person who in moments of intellectual tension seeks a stimulus in an action painting or in a piece of serial music should in moments of relaxation and escape (healthy and indispensable) tend toward triumphant infantile laziness and turn to the consumer product for pacification in an orgy of redundance?

As soon as we consider the problem from this angle, we are tempted to show more indulgence toward escape entertainments (among which is included our myth of Superman), reproving ourselves for having exercised an acid moralism on what is innocuous and perhaps even beneficial.

The problem changes according to the degree to which pleasure in redundance breaks the convulsed rhythm of an intellectual existence based upon the reception of information and becomes the *norm* of every imaginative activity.

The problem is not to ask ourselves if different ideological contents conveyed by the same narrative scheme can elicit different effects. Rather, an iterative scheme becomes and remains that *only* to the extent that the scheme sustains and expresses a world; we realize this even more, once we understand how the world has the same configuration as the structure which expressed it. The case of Superman reconfirms this hypothesis. If we examine the ideological contents of Superman stories, we realize that, on the one hand, that content sustains itself and functions communicatively thanks to the narrative structure; on the other hand, the stories help define their expressive structure as the circular, static conveyance of a pedagogic message which is substantially immobilistic.

4.8.   Civic consciousness and political consciousness

Superman stories have a characteristic in common with a series of other adventures that hinge on heroes gifted with *superpowers*. In Superman the real elements blend into a more homogeneous totality, which justifies the fact that we have devoted special attention to him; and it is no accident that Superman is the most popular of the heroes we talk about: he not only represents the forerunner of the group (in 1938), but of all the characters he is still the one who is most carefully sketched, endowed with a recognizable personality, dug out of longstanding anecdote, and so he can be seen as the representative of all his similars. (In any case, the observation that follows can be applied to a whole series of superheroes, from Batman and Robin to Green Arrow, Flash, the Manhunter from Mars, Green Lantern, and Aquaman up to the more recent Fantastic Four, Devil, and Spider Man, where the literary 'genre', however, has acquired a more sophisticated form of self-irony.)

Each of these heroes is gifted with such powers that he could actually take over the government, defeat the army, or alter the equilibrium of planetary politics. On the other hand, it is clear that each of these characters is profoundly kind, moral, faithful to human and natural laws, and therefore it is right (and it is nice) that he use his powers only to the end of good. In this sense the pedagogic message of these stories would be, at least on the plane of children's literature, highly acceptable, and the same episodes of violence with which the various stories are interspersed would appear directed toward this final indictment of evil and the triumph of honest people.

The ambiguity of the teaching appears when we ask ourselves, *What is Good?* It is enough to reexamine in depth the situation of Superman, who encompasses the others, at least in their fundamental structure.

Superman is practically omnipotent, as we have said, in his physical, mental, and technological capacities. His operative capacity extends to a cosmic scale. A being gifted with such capacities offered to the good of humanity (let us pose the problem with a maximum of candor and of responsibility, taking everything as probable) would have an enormous field of action in front of him. From a man who could produce work and wealth in astronomic dimensions in a few seconds, one could expect the most bewildering political, economic, and technological upheavals in the world. From the solution of hunger problems to the tilling of uninhabitable regions, from the destruction of inhuman systems (if we read Superman into the 'spirit of Dallas', why does he not go to liberate six hundred million Chinese from the yoke of Mao?), Superman could exercise good on a cosmic level, or on a galactic level, and furnish us in the meantime with a definition that through fantastic amplification could clarify precise ethical lines everywhere.

Instead, Superman carries on his activity on the level of the small community where he lives (Smallville as a youth, Metropolis as an adult), and—as in the case of the medieval countryman who could have happened to visit the Sacred Land, but not the closed and separate community which flourished fifty kilometers from the center of his life—if he takes trips to other galaxies with ease, he practically ignores, not exactly the dimension of the 'world', but that of the "United States" (only once, but in one of the *Imaginary Tales,* he becomes president of the United States).

In the sphere of his own little town, evil, the only evil to combat, is incarnate in a species which adheres to the underworld, that of organized crime. He is busy by preference, not against blackmarket drugs, nor, obviously, against corrupt administrators or politicians, but against bank and mail-truck robbers. In other words, *the only visible form that evil assumes is an attempt on private property.* Outerspace evil is added spice; it is casual, and it always assumes unforeseeable and transitory forms; the underworld is an endemic evil, like some kind of impure stream that pervades the course of human history, clearly divided into zones of Manichaean incontrovertibility—where each authority is fundamentally pure and good and where each wicked man is rotten to the core without hope of redemption.

As others have said, in Superman we have a perfect example of civic consciousness, completely split from political consciousness. Superman's civic attitude is perfect, but it is exercised and structured in the sphere of a small, closed community (a 'brother' of Superman—as a model of absolute fidelity to establish values—might appear in someone such as the movie and television hero Dr. Kildare).

It is strange that Superman, devoting himself to good deeds, spends enormous amounts of energy organizing benefit performances in order to collect money for orphans and indigents. The paradoxical waste of means (the same energy could be employed to produce directly riches or to modify radically larger situations) never ceases to astound the reader who sees Superman forever employed in parochial performances. As evil assumes only the form of an offense to private property, *good is repre-sented only as charity.* This simple equivalent is sufficient to characterize Superman's moral world. In fact, we realize that Superman is obliged to continue his activities in the sphere of small and infinitesimal modifica-tions of the immediately visible for the same motives noted in regard to the static nature of his plots: each general modification would draw the world, and Superman with it, toward final consumption.

On the other hand, it would be inexact to say that Superman's judicious and measured virtue depends only on the structure of the plot, that is, on the need to forbid the release of excessive and irretrievable develop-ments. The contrary is also true: the immobilizing metaphysics underlying this kind of conceptual plot is the direct, though not the desired, conse-quence of a total structural mechanism which seems to be the only one suited to communicate, through the themes discussed, a particular kind of teaching. The plot must be static and must evade any development, because Superman *must* make virtue consist of many little activities on a small scale, never achieving a total awareness. Conversely, virtue must be characterized in the accomplishment of only partial acts, so that the plot can remain static. Again, the discussion does not take on the features of the authors' preferences as much as their adaptation to a concept of 'order' which pervades the cultural model in which the authors live and where they construct on a small scale "analogous" models which mirror the larger one.

NOTES

1. *Critique of Pure Reason,* "Analytic of Principles," chapter 2, section 3.
2. See in particular Hans Reichenbach, *The Direction of Time* (Berkeley and Los Angeles: University of California Press, 1956).
3. For the Sartrian discussion, see *Being and Nothingness,* chapter 2.
4. Ibid.
5. Reichenbach, pp. 36–40.
6. See Chapter 1 of this book.

CHAPTER FIVE

Rhetoric and Ideology in Sue's
Les Mystères de Paris

Terms such as 'the sociological study of literature' or 'the sociology of literature' often serve, and have served in the past, to indicate sometimes quite opposite lines of research. One can take a literary work simply as documentary evidence of a historical period; one can consider the social element as the explanatory cause of the aesthetic solution adopted for a literary work; finally, one can invent a dialectic between two points of view (the work as an aesthetic phenomenon and society as its explanatory context) in which, on the one hand, the social element explains each aesthetic choice that has been made and, on the other, a study of the work and of its structural features leads to a clearer understanding of the state of a society.[1]

Of what use, in this third method we envisage, is the kind of semiotic research which examines narrative structures? If the description of the work as a system of signs helped us to shed an absolutely 'neutral' and 'objective' light on its structures (leaving aside the complex of meanings that history continually attributes to the work as message), then even the social context would be excluded—if only temporarily—from this semiological study. And with it would go that ideological nucleus which the whole work implies. But this singleness of approach to the research only appears feasible. In point of fact, we cannot select and isolate (or, in other words, emphasize or make prominent) any formal element without attributing to it—at least implicitly—further significance. Insofar as the

"Eugène Sue, il socialismo e la consolazione," introduction to E. Sue, *I misteri di Parigi* (Milan: Sugar, 1965). English translation as "Rhetoric and Ideology in Sue's *Les Mystères de Paris*," *International Social Sciences Journal* 14, no. 4 (1967). This chapter is a revised version of the translation.

description claims to be objective (by revealing structures that exist within the work), the structures which are brought to light are those that seem relevant only if we consider the work from a certain point of view *ideologically overcoded*. In this way any examination of the semiotic structures of the work becomes *ipso facto* the corroboration of both historical and sociological hypotheses—and this happens even when the critic neither knows it is happening nor wants it to. It is better, then, to be aware of it, in order to correct as far as possible the distortion produced by the angle of perspective and to take the greatest possible advantage of such distortion as cannot be corrected.

So the structural analysis of the work describes a circular motion apparently typical of all research into acts of communication.[2] The method is scientific insofar as it admits this conditioning of the research, instead of ignoring it, and insofar as it gives it a critical basis and uses it as an opportunity for a better understanding of the work.

Once these basic principles of the method to be employed have been admitted, the description of the structures of the work shows itself to be one of the most rewarding ways in which to bring out the connections between a work and its sociohistorical context. In other words, it appears highly desirable that any sociological study of literature worthy of the name should resort to semiotics for its corroboration. The circular character of our method consists in moving then from the external social context to the internal structural context of the work under analysis, in building up the description of both contexts (or of other facts which play a part in the interpretation) by using uniform instruments of definition in each case and in revealing, next, structural correspondences between the co-text of the work, its sociohistorical context, and any other contexts which may come under examination. Thus one perceives that the way in which the work 'reflects' the social context, if we may be allowed once again to use the ambiguous category of 'reflection', may be characterized in structural terms, by building up complementary systems (or series) which, since it was possible to describe them by homogeneous means, appear structurally homologous.

The investigation will be to reveal correspondences and not causal relations. This does not mean that causal relations should not be introduced in a historical examination of wider scope; but, at this stage of the research, it would be inappropriate and rash to demonstrate them. Our examination is only to bring out parallelisms between the ideological and the rhetorical aspects of a given literary work.[3]

The above details of a method of analysis may be illustrated by the results of a study of the narrative structures of *Les Mystères de Paris* by Eugène Sue. In the pages that follow, we shall isolate three "series," or "systems," which play a part in the work: (i) the author's ideology;

(ii) the market conditions which determined or favored the conception, the writing, and the circulation of the book; and (iii) the narrative devices.

5.1. Eugène Sue: An ideological standpoint

In order to understand Sue's ideological attitude at the time he wrote *Les Mystères de Paris* (hereafter *Les Mystères*), it is necessary to make a brief resumé of his intellectual evolution—a subject which has already been treated fully and very ably elsewhere.[4] Sue himself gives a short summary of this evolution in a work composed toward the end of his life.

> I began to write sea stories because I had seen the sea; these early novels have a political and philosophical side to them (*La Salamandre, Atar-Gull, La Vigie de Koat-Ven* and others) which is radically opposed to the convictions I held from 1844 onwards (*Les Mystères de Paris*); it would perhaps be interesting to trace by what successive transformations in my intellect, studies, ideas, tastes and the liaisons I formed—after having believed firmly in the religious and absolutist doctrine embodied in the works of Bonald, de Maistre and Lamennais (*De l'indifference en matière de religion*), my masters at the time—I came, guided only by justice, truth and virtue, to a direct recognition of the supremacy of democratic and social republicanism.[5]

By way of political legitimism, and of dandyism both in public and in private life, Sue arrived at a profession of faith in socialism. Of what kind was his socialism? A brief glimpse at his biography tells us that at first he was moved by occasional fits of enthusiasm, the result of meeting a cultured and politically mature member of the working class, whose class consciousness, rectitude, simple behavior, and revolutionary ardor drove Sue to a confession of faith that was purely emotional. There is reason to believe that at first socialism represented for Sue merely a new and exciting way of displaying his eccentric dandyism. At the beginning of *Les Mystères,* a taste for the diabolical, for morbid situations, for the horrific and the grotesque is predominant in his narrative. He describes the sordid *tapis-francs* of the Ile de la Cité and reproduces the thieves' slang used in the Paris underworld, yet continually begs his readers' forgiveness for the horrors and miseries of which he speaks—an indication that he still imagines himself addressing an aristocratic and bourgeois public, eager for emotions but having nothing to do with the protagonists of his novel. But, as the novel advances, and as one instalment follows another in the *Journal des Débats,* Sue gradually succumbs to public approbation. The classes *of whom* he writes become the classes *for whom* he writes; *the* author is suddenly promoted to the rank of poet of the proletariat, the same proletariat he describes in his book. As public approval mounts ever higher, Sue is gradually won over by the very sentiments he has himself invoked. As Bory has remarked, "The popular novel (popular in its aim) as it becomes popular (in terms of its success) soon becomes popular in its ideas and its form."⁶

In the third part of the work, Sue is already proposing models of social reform (the farm at Bouquenval); in the fifth, the action slows down and gives place to long, moralizing lectures and 'revolutionary' propositions (though, as will be seen, these are really only reformist); as the work draws to a close, the tirades become more and more frequent, almost intolerably so. As the action and the essayistic perorations develop, Sue's new ideological position becomes clear: *Les Mystères* reveals to the reader the iniquitous social conditions which out of poverty produce crime—a mystery with the veil torn away. If this misery can be alleviated —if the prisoner can be reeducated, the virtuous girl rescued from the wealthy seducer, the honest workman released from the debtors' prison, and all given a chance of redemption and helped in a spirit of Christian brotherhood towards reform—then the world will become a better place. Evil is only a social ill. The book, which might at first have been entitled The Gangsters' Epic, ends up as the Epic of the Unfortunate Workman and A Manual of Redemption. It is clear that this outlook does not appear 'revolutionary' in the sense in which we understand that word since the advent of Marxism; but even so these views aroused scandalized reactions in the conservative press in Paris, though other, more malicious critics perceived the bourgeois limits of Sue's supposed socialism.

In one of his *Marginalia,* written after *Les Mystères* had been translated into English, Edgar Allan Poe notes that the philosophical motives ascribed to Sue are in the highest degree absurd. Sue's first, and really his only, care was to write an exciting and therefore saleable story. His tirades (implicit and explicit) to improve society, and so on, are a mere stratagem, very common in authors who hope to impart a note of dignity or utilitarianism to their pages by gilding their licentiousness. Poe's criticism cannot be called 'leftist'; the American poet confines himself to pointing out a falseness in the tone of the book and to attributing to its author intentions which remain unconfessed.

A far more penetrating, and ideologically more apposite, criticism was made of Sue in the same year by Belinskij. After a rapid survey of lower-class conditions in Western industrial civilization, Belinskij opens fire: Eugène Sue was a man of fortune whose first and foremost intention was the very lucrative one of speculating, quite literally, at the expense of the people. A respectable bourgeois in the full sense of the term and a petit-bourgeois constitutional philistine—if he could have become a deputy, he would have been one such as we find everywhere today. When in his novel he describes the French people, Sue considers them as a real bourgeois does, oversimplifying everything: in his eyes they are the starving masses, doomed to crime through ignorance and poverty. He ignores the true virtues and vices of the people; nor does he suspect that the people may have a future which the party at present triumphantly in power will never see, because the people have faith, enthusiasm, and moral strength. Eugène Sue has compassion for the sufferings of the people; why refuse him the novel faculty of compassion—particularly when it brings in such sure profits? But what sort of compassion is it? That is another question entirely. Sue hopes that the people will one day be freed from poverty and that they will cease to be starving masses driven to crime against their will, becoming instead a fully satisfied community that is presentable and behaves as it should, while the bourgeoisie and the present lawgivers remain the masters of France, a race of highly cultivated speculators. Sue demonstrates in his novel how French laws offer an involuntary protection to crime and debauchery, and it must be said his argument is exact and plausible. But what he does not realize is that the evil is inherent, not only in certain laws, but in the entire system of French legislation, in the organization of society as a whole.[7]

The charge made against him is clear: Sue's attitude is typical of the reformer who aims at changing something in order that in the end everything will stay the same. In political terms he is a social democrat; from a literary point of view, he is a sensation monger who speculates on human misery.

If at this point we turn back and reread the pages of Marx and Engels' *Die Heilige Familie,* we shall find the same polemical elements.[8] The work aims at the systematic satirization of the young Hegelians of the *Allgemeine Literaturzeitung* and, in particular, of Szeliga, who presented *Les Mystères* as the epic of the straits which divide the ephemeral from the immortal and which are continually being narrowed. It is Szeliga, not Sue, who is the central target. But in order to succeed and to be convincing, Marx and Engels' analysis must discredit Sue's work by showing it as a kind of ideological hoax that could look like a message of salvation only to Bruno Bauer and his associates. The reformist and petit-bourgeois character of the work is vividly illustrated in the words spoken by the unfortunate Morel at the height of his financial misfortunes: "Oh, if only the rich knew of it!" The moral of the book is that the rich can know of it and can intervene to heal by their munificence the wounds of society.

Marx and Engels go further: not content with stressing Sue's reformist roots (they are not satisfied, for example, with judging the value of the idea of a paupers' bank, as suggested by Prince Rodolphe, on purely economic grounds), they point out that Rodolphe's executioner's revenge is an act of hypocrisy; hypocritical, too, is the description of the social regeneration of the Ripper; Sue's new penal theory is entirely vitiated by religious hypocrisy, as the punishment of the Schoolmaster shows; finally, the redemption of Fleur-de-Marie is not only hypocritical, but a typical example of religious alienation in Feuerbach's sense of the term. Thus Sue is branded, not as a naive social democrat, but as a reactionary, a legitimist, and a follower of de Maistre, at least in youth, when he wrote in praise of slave-trading colonialism.

If we wanted to trace the personality of Sue along the curve formed by his life, we should have to modify the negative judgment passed on him by Marx and Engels. Already in 1845, when *Le Juif Errant* was published, the languid, easygoing humanitarianism of the former dandy had given place to a clearer, sterner vision of the struggle between the working-class world and officialdom. And if in *Le Juif Errant* this dissension still wears the imaginative disguise of a symbolic struggle between the characters of the novel (the wicked, intriguing Jesuit and the virtuous, heroic priest), if it is expressed in terms of a Fourierist Utopia, in his next long, unshapely but revealing work, *Les Mystères du Peuple,* Sue shows that he has seen to the bottom of the class conflict. The period of composition of this book extends from the time when he first threw himself body and soul into the political struggle, as a candidate for the socialist republican party, when he opposed Louis Napoleon's *coup d'état,* until he went to spend the last years of his life in exile at Annecy, by then the universally recognized laureate of the proletarian revolution.

Marx and Engels' verdict is limited to *Les Mystères de Paris,* however. Our study of the text should likewise leave aside other, earlier and later writings and concentrate on expounding the plot structures and stylistic devices which correspond to given ideological attitudes.

5.2.   The 'consolatory' structure

The author of a popular novel never expresses his own problems of composition to himself in purely structural terms (How to write a narrative work?), but in terms of social psychology (What sort of problems must I solve in order to write a narrative which I intend will appeal to a large public and arouse both the concern of the masses and the curiosity of the well-to-do?).

I suggest a possible solution: let us suppose an existing everyday situation in which are to be found elements of unresolved tension (Paris and its poverty); then let us suppose a factor capable of resolving this tension, a factor contrasting with the initial reality and opposing it by offering an immediate and consolatory solution to the initial contradictions. If the initial reality is authentic and if the conditions necessary for the resolution of its contradictions do not already exist within it, then the resolutive factor must be fictitious. Insofar as it is fictitious, it can be readily presented from the beginning as already in being: so it can go into action straightway, without having to pass through the restrictive intermediary of concrete events. Such an element is Rodolphe of Gerolstein, who is endowed with all the traits required by fable: he is a prince (and a sovereign one, even if Marx and Engels ridicule this little German Serene Highness, treated as a king by Sue; but it is well known that no one is a prophet in his own country); he rules according to the dictates of prudence and virtue;[9] he is very rich. He is stricken with incurable remorse and a fatal nostalgia (his unhappy love for the adventuress Sarah Mac-Gregor; the supposed death of the daughter born of this union; the fact that he raised his arm against his father). Though good-natured, this character has connotations of the romantic hero popularized by Sue himself in earlier books: an adept of vengeance, he does not shrink from violent solutions; he delights, if only in the cause of justice, in the most horrible cruelty (he puts out the Schoolmaster's eyes and causes Jacques Ferrand to die of unassuaged lust). Being put forward as the immediate solution to the evils of society, he cannot simply obey its laws, which in any case are defective enough; so he invents his own. Rodolphe, judge and executioner, benefactor and reformer without the law, is a superman. A direct descendant of the satanic hero of the romantic period, he is perhaps the first superman in the history of the serial story, the prototype for Monte Cristo, a contemporary of Vautrin (who though created earlier came to full development only at that time).

Antonio Gramsci had already noted with insight and irony that the superman, having been molded from the clay of the serial novel, proceeded thence to philosophy.[10] Some other prototypes also can be discerned in the composition of this particular superman, as Bory observes: Rodolphe is a kind of God the Father (those who benefit from his goodness never tire of repeating this) who takes human form and enters the world disguised as a workman. God becomes the Worker. Marx and Engels had not considered quite thoroughly enough the problem of a superman in action, and thus they complain that Rodolphe, whom they take to be a model of humanity, is guided, not at all by disinterested and charitable motives, but by a predilection for vengeance and prevarication. This is true: Rodolphe is a cruel and vindictive God, a Christ with the spirit of Jehovah.

In order to solve by imaginative means the real dramas of the poverty-stricken Parisian underworld, Rodolphe had to (i) convert the Ripper, (ii) punish the Owl and the Schoolmaster, (iii) redeem Fleur-de-Marie, (iv) console Madame d'Harville by giving her life a new purpose, (v) save the Morels from despair, (vi) overthrow the sinister power of

Jacques Ferrand and restore what he had taken from the weak and helpless, (vii) find his lost daughter, who had fled from the wiles of Sarah
MacGregor. Then come various tasks of less moment, though connected
with the main ones, such as punishing evil-doers of secondary importance
such as Polidori, the Martials, and the young Saint-Rémy; redeeming
those who, like La Louve and the good Martial, have started on the
downward path; and rescuing a few good people such as the young
Germain, the young Fermont, and so on.

The element of reality (Paris and its poor) and the element of fantasy
(Rodolphe's solutions) must strike the reader at each step, gripping his
attention and torturing his sensibilities. The plot must be so arranged,
therefore, so as to present climaxes of disclosure, that is, surprises. Since
the reader may identify himself either with the characters and situations
of the initial circumstances, that is, before the denouement, or with those
present at the end of the book, after the denouement, the features which
characterize them must be reiterated so as to make this identification possible. Long stretches of redundant material must therefore be inserted
into the plot; in other words, the author must dwell at length on the unexpected in order to render it familiar.

The author must of necessity rely on *coups de théâtre* to further his task
of disclosing information, and the need for repetition leads perforce to
the reiteration of these *coups de théâtre* at regular intervals. It is in this
way that *Les Mystères* is related, not to those narrative works which we
may define as showing a constant curve (where the various elements of
the plot are woven more and more closely together until a climax of tension is reached—at which point the denouement intervenes to break and
resolve this tension), but to those we may describe as of *sinusoidal structure:* tension, resolution, renewed tension, further resolution, and so on.

In point of fact, *Les Mystères* abounds in minor dramas, set in motion,
partially resolved, and then abandoned so that we may return to the wind-
ings of the main narrative. It is as though the story were a large tree whose
trunk is Rodolphe's search for his lost daughter, and whose different
branches are the story of the Ripper, the story of Saint-Rémy, the relationship of Clémence d'Harville to her husband, and her old father, and
to her stepmother, the episode of Germain and Rigolette, and the vicissi-
tudes of the Morels.

It is now time to ask whether this sinusoidal structure corresponds to
an explicit narrative program or depends on external circumstances. If we
read what was said by the young Sue on the subject of composition, it
would appear that the structure is intentional. Early on, when writing of
his sea adventure stories (from *Kernok* to *Atar-Gull* and *La Salamandre*),
he propounds a theory of the episodic novel: "Instead of keeping strictly
to a unity of interest shared out among a chosen number of characters

who, starting out at the beginning of the book, must all willy-nilly reach the end to contribute their mite to the dénouement . . ." it would be better not to fix the characters too firmly in the story, since, "as they are not an essential accompaniment of the abstract moral idea upon which the work turns, they may be abandoned half-way, as the opportunity offers itself or the logical sequence of events demands."[11] Hence the author is free to switch the reader's attention and to transfer the main thread of the story from one character to another. Bory calls this type of novel (which shows a multiplicity, rather than a unity, of time, place, and action) *centrifugal* and sees it as a typical example of the serial novel, which by reason of its piecemeal publication, is forced to keep the reader's interest alive from week to week or from day to day. But it is not only a question of a natural adaptation of the novel structure to the conditions peculiar to a particular genre (within which differentiations might also be made according to the particular type of serial publication adopted). The determining influence of the market goes deeper than this. As Bory also observed, "success prolongs the novels." New episodes are invented one after another, because the public claims that it cannot bear to say good-bye to its characters. A dialectic is established between market demands, and the plot's structure is so important that at a certain point even fundamental laws of plot construction, which might have been thought inviolate for any commercial novel, are transgressed.

Whether the plot describes a constant curve or shows a sinusoidal structure, the essential features of a story as enumerated by Aristotle in the *Poetics* remain unchanged: beginning, tension, climax, denouement, catharsis. The most one can say of the sinusoidal structure is that it is the product of an amalgamation of several plots, a problem which had already been discussed by the theorists of the twelfth and thirteenth centuries, the first masters of French structural criticism.[12] So strong is the psychological need felt by the reader for this tension-resolution dialectic that the worst kind of serial story ends by producing false tensions and false denouements. In *Le Forgeron de la Cour-Dieu* by Ponson du Terrail, for instance, there are about ten cases of fictitious recognitions, in the sense that the reader's expectations are built up only to be revealed to him facts he already knew but which were unknown to one particular character. By contrast, in *Les Mystères* something else happens—something quite staggering: Rodolphe, lamenting his lost daughter, meets the prostitute Fleur-de-Marie; is she Rodolphe's daughter?—an excellent theme on which to ring the changes for page after page and a subject which Sue himself must have considered the mainspring of his whole book. But abruptly, in part 2, chapter 15, scarcely a fifth of the way through the whole book, Sue, seeing that the reader will have guessed that Fleur-de-Marie is Rodolphe's daughter, comes to a decision and announces: now let us leave this theme aside, to be resumed later. It is so clear that a good story has been thrown away and that a kind of totally inexplicable narrative suicide has been committed that the present-day reader is left utterly bewildered. Things must have been different, however, when the book was being published in instalments. Sue must have been suddenly obliged to prolong his narrative; the machine had been geared for a much shorter journey and the tension could not have been maintained to the end; the public was clamoring to be told. So he threw them this revelation as a sop and went on to explore other paths. The public is satisfied, but the plot as an organism has broken down. The kind of commercial distribution which can in some cases provide the serial story with good rules will at other times prevaricate, and the author in his capacity as an artist must submit to this. *Les Mystères* is no longer a novel but a series of montages designed for the continual and renewable gratification of its readers. From here on Sue is no longer concerned with obeying the laws of good narration and as the story advances introduces into it certain convenient artifices, of which the great nineteenth-century narrative was mercifully ignorant. They are to be found curiously enough in certain comic strip publications such as the stories of Superman.[13]

For example, Sue starts explaining in footnotes what he can no longer express by means of the plot alone. In part 9, chapter 9, the note tells us that Madame d'Harville asks a particular question because, having only arrived the night before, she could not know that Rodolphe had recognized Fleur-de-Marie, who is here called Amélie, because her father had changed her name a few days earlier. In part 9, chapter 2, the note points out that "the reader will not have forgotten that the instant before he struck Sarah, the Owl believed and had told her that. . . ." In part 2, chapter 17, a note reminds us that the youthful passion of Rodolphe and Sarah is unknown in Paris. And so on. The author records what has already been said, for fear his audience may have forgotten it by then, and establishes late in the day facts he has not been able to tell us because it is impossible to say everything; his book is a macrocosm in which there are too many characters, and Sue can no longer manage to keep track of them all. It may be observed that all these notes occur after the revelation of the identity of Fleur-de-Marie; it is here that the plot breaks down.

Thus it happens that Sue behaves sometimes like a mere observer who has no power over a world that escapes him, whereas at other times he lays claims to the divine right of the novelist to be omniscient and to make luscious advance disclosures to the reader. Poe had already noted that Sue did not know the *ars celandi artem* and that he never missed an opportunity of saying to the reader: "Now, in a moment you will see what you will see. I am going to give you a most extraordinary surprise. Prepare yourselves, for it will work strongly on your imagination and excite your pity." A criticism that is unkind, but pertinent. Sue behaves like this because one of the principal aims of the 'novel of reassurance' is to produce a dramatic effect. This effect can be obtained in two ways, and one—the easier of the two—is "Look out for what is going to happen next." The other involves recourse to Kitsch.[14]

Les Mystères is clearly dripping with Kitsch. The author asks himself, What will be certain of producing an effect because it has already been tested? The answer is, The literary styleme which has already proved itself in another context. A styleme duly 'quoted' is not only successful, but confers dignity on its context. It habituates the aesthetic thrill, made inseparable from it now by repetition. For the use of this device, too, there are two possible solutions. First, one can directly evoke a sensation that others have tried and described. In part 7, chapter 14, we read as follows: "To complete the effect of this picture, the reader should recall the mysterious, almost fantastic appearance of a room where the flame in the grate strives to conquer the great black shadows that flicker on ceiling and walls. . . ." The writer dispenses with direct evocation by dint of simple representation and enlists the reader's help by referring him to the *déjà vu*. Second, one can introduce already acknowledged common-places. The whole character of Cécily, the beauty and the perfidy of the mulatto girl, is part of an exotic-erotic paraphernalia of romantic origin. Briefly, her portrait is a typological oleograph: "Everyone has heard of those coloured girls, fatal to Europeans, of those enchanting vampires, who by their fearful powers of seduction intoxicate their victim and drain his gold or his blood to the last drop, leaving him, as that telling native phrase has it, nought but his tears to drink or his heart to fret away." Here it is perhaps worse, for it is not a literary locution that is taken at second-hand but quite simply a popular commonplace; and in this Sue shows great ingenuity, inventing, so to speak, a Kitsch for the poor. In other words, he does not make his oleograph by setting on the canvas the constituent elements of Art, but merely by making a mosaic of previous oleographs—what in fact would today be called a work of 'pop' art and would then be intentionally ironic.

Even a feature which some critics, Bory among them, consider as the basic and powerful interplay of archetypes is reduced to this kind of stylistic pastiche: the wicked characters are related back to animal proto-types after the manner of Lavater and often even bear their names (the Owl; the cross between Harpagon and Tartuffe to be seen in Jacques Ferrand; the couple formed by the Schoolmaster once he is blinded; the abominable monster Tortillard, a vile reversal of the Oedipus-Antigone motif; and, finally, Fleur-de-Marie, the *vierge souillée,* a genuine 'type' of romantic derivation). Sue certainly makes use of archetypes and in so doing reveals his culture and inventive genius. But he does not thereby make of his novel a journey through myth towards knowledge, as we might say Mann did; it is really in order to have 'models' which he knows will produce a desired effect. Kitsch is thus an imaginative device which provides solutions to a real situation according to a predetermined plan.

A last device that allows the reiteration of an effect, and guarantees its effectiveness, is the undue drawing out of certain scenes. The death of Jacques Ferrand, victim of satyriasis, is described with the precision of a clinical manual and the exactitude of a tape recording. Instead of giving an imaginative synthesis of the event, he records it 'live': he makes it last as long as it would in reality; he has his character saying lines over and over again as often as a dying man would repeat them in real life. But this repetition does not resolve itself into any pattern. Sue quite simply records everything and does not stop until every reader, even the dullest, is up to his neck in the drama and feels suffocated along with the fictional character.

Within narrative structures of this type, the ideological choices which, as we have already shown, Sue makes in *Les Mystères* can but make themselves felt. If the method of solving the problem of narration by frequent disclosures is suddenly to be lost in a morass of moving and conciliatory redundancy, solutions must likewise be found for the description of events which, without divorcing them from their origins, will channel them in obedience to the reader's wishes. We do not, however, need to ask ourselves whether in the work of Sue the ideological argument preceded the invention of the story or whether the kind of story he invented as he yielded to public demand imposed on him a certain ideological attitude. In reality the different factors in question are often interactive, and the only *raison d'être* of an investigation is given us by the book itself as it is. It would similarly be quite incorrect to say that the choice of the *roman-feuilleton* as one's medium necessarily entails the adoption of a conservative and blandly reformist ideology or that a conservative and reformist ideology must of necessity produce a *roman-feuilleton*. All that we can say is that the various ingredients of the mixture are blended in such and such a way.

If we consider the education of Fleur-de-Marie, we find ourselves face to face with a problem that presents itself in the same way on the ideological as on the narrative level: (i) we have a prostitute (a 'type' that bourgeois society has firmly established according to certain canonical rules); (ii) this prostitute has been reduced to this level by the force of circumstances (she is innocent), but she has nevertheless prostituted herself (and bears the mark of this); (iii) Rodolphe convinces her that she can rise above her condition, and the prostitute is redeemed; (iv) Rodolphe discovers that she is his daughter, a princess of the blood.

The reader is stunned by a series of *coups de théâtre* which correspond to so many moments of disclosure. As narrative this is successful, but, from the viewpoint of the public's moral code, it oversteps the limits. One could not stand another such shock. It would be too much that Fleur-de-Marie should also reign happy and contented. Every possible identification with the novel situation as a whole would break down. So Fleur-de-Marie dies, worn out by remorse. It is what every respectable reader should expect in accordance with divine justice and his own sense of what is right. What new ideas we have acquired fade away as a few choice principles of ethic and polite behavior are quietly reiterated and wisely corroborated. After surprising the reader by telling him what he did not yet know, the author reassures him by repeating what he knows already. The machinery of the novel demands that Fleur-de-Marie should end as she in fact does. It is Sue's own ideological training, then, which, in order to articulate these episodes, causes him to resort to a religious solution.

Here Marx and Engels' analysis appears to us in all its perfection. Fleur-de-Marie has discovered that regeneration is possible and, thanks to the resources of youth, begins to enjoy real, human happiness. When Rodolphe tells her that she is going to live on the farm at Bouquenval, she goes almost mad with joy. But gradually, under the influence of the pious insinuations of Madame Georges and the curate, the girl's 'natural' happiness is turned into a 'supernatural' anxiety: the idea that her sin cannot be wiped out, that God's mercy must be extended to her 'despite' the enormity, the heinousness, of her crime, and the certainty that full remission will be denied her on this earth draw the unhappy 'Goualeuse' slowly down into the depths of despair. "From this moment Marie is enslaved by the consciousness of her sin. And whereas in a far less happy situation she knew how to make herself lovable and human, and though outwardly disgraced was conscious of her real human self, now the stain of modern society, which has touched her outwardly, attaches to her intimate self, and she torments herself unceasingly with this stain, imagining an illness that is not hers, the stain becomes a burden to be borne, a life-mission allotted her by God Himself."[15]

The conversion of the Ripper follows the same pattern. He has killed and, though fundamentally honest, is an outcast from society. Rodolphe saves him by telling him he still has courage and honor. He shakes hands with him. *Coup de théâtre*. Now the discrepancy must be attenuated and the tale be brought down to earth again. We can ignore Marx and Engels' first remark that Rodolphe turns the Ripper into an *agent-provocateur* and uses him to entrap the Schoolmaster; we have already accepted the conduct of the superman as legitimate at the outset. The fact remains that he makes of him a 'dog', a slave who is from then on incapable of living except under the protection of his new master and idol, for whom he dies. The Ripper is redeemed by his acceptance of Rodolphe's fatherly beneficence, not by acquiring a new, independent conscience that can plan life for itself.

Madame d'Harville's education required a subtler solution: Rodolphe urges her on to social activity, but this choice must appear credible in the eyes of the general public. So Clémence is made to give herself to the poor because charity constitutes for her a pleasure, a noble and subtle kind of joy. It can be enjoyable to do good.[16] The poor are to become the rich man's diversion.

Ferrand's punishment, too, turns out to be just what is expected. After licentious living it is of lust unappeased that he dies. He stole money from widows and orphans, only to see this money restored to them by the will Rodolphe forces him to make, bequeathing his goods for the founding of a paupers' bank.

Here we see the main features of Sue's, alias Rodolphe's, social doctrine. Its chief manifestation is the model farm at Bouquenval, the perfect example of successful paternalism. The reader has only to look again at part 3, chapter 6. The farm is an ideal phalanstery that nevertheless functions according to the decrees of a master who comes to the aid of all who find themselves without work. The paupers' bank, with related theories on the reform of pawnbrokers, is similarly inspired: seeing that poverty exists and that the workman can find himself out of work, we must set up systems of providential help to supply him with money in times of unemployment. When he gets work he will pay this back. "During the times he has work," as Marx and Engels put it in their commentary, "he gives back to me what he had from me during his unemployment." Sue's plans for the prevention of crime, and for the reduction of legal costs for the indigent, proceed along the same lines. So, too, does his project for an honest citizens' police force, which, just as the law keeps the wicked under observation, arrests them and brings them to judgment, would keep a close watch on the good, 'denounce' them to the community for their virtuous actions, and summon them to the public courts, where their good deeds would receive due recognition and reward. The basis of Sue's ideology is this: to try to discover what we can do for the humble (by means of brotherly collaboration between classes) while leaving the present structure of society unchanged.

That this ideology has a right to be considered for its political merits quite outside the sphere of the serial novel is both obvious and well known. Whether it has anything to do with the pleasure the novel affords us is a question that should be looked into more closely, and we have already supplied the means of doing so. Once again it is a question of reassuring the reader by showing him that the dramatic situation is both posed and capable of solution, yet in such a way that he does not cease to identify himself with the situation described in the novel as a whole.

The society operated on by Rodolphe in the guise of a miraculous healer remains the same society as at the beginning of the book. If it were otherwise the reader would lose his bearings, and the purely fictitious solution would lack verisimilitude. Or at any rate, the reader would feel he could not participate in it.[17] In all events, none of these reforms provides for a new autonomy to be placed in the hands of the 'people', whether considered as 'laboring classes' or as 'dangerous classes'. Faced with the honesty of Morel, Sue exclaims: "Is it not uplifting and consoling to think that it is not force or terrorization, but sound moral sense which alone restrains this formidable human ocean, whose overflow might drown the whole of society, making light of its laws and its power, as the sea in its rage scorns dikes and ramparts!" Thus reform is to be used to strengthen and encourage the common sense and foresight of the working masses. This is to be achieved by an act of enlightened intelligence on the part of the rich, who recognize their role as depositaries of wealth to be used for the common good, "by the salutary example of capital associated with hard work . . . an honest, intelligent and just pooling of resources which would ensure the well-being of the artisan without danger to the fortune of the rich man . . . and which, by creating bonds of affection between these two classes, would permanently safeguard the peace of the State."

Peace, in the commercial novel, takes the form of reassurance by reiteration of what the reader expects, and, when expressed in ideological terms, it assumes the aspect of a reform which changes something so that everything will remain the same, that is, the system of order that grows out of the constant repetition of the same things and out of the stability of acknowledged values. Ideology and rhetoric here fuse perfectly.

This is borne out by a particular technical feature of Sue's novel, a narrative device that is obvious to the reader and that we cannot do better than describe as the mechanism "Oh Lord, how thirsty I am!" The reference is to an old joke about a man in a railway carriage who was irritating his traveling companions by incessantly repeating "Oh Lord, how thirsty I am!" Driven crazy by this refrain, at the first stop the other travelers rushed to the windows to get the poor creature drinks of all kinds. When the train set off again, there was a moment's silence and then the wretched man began again, repeating endlessly "Lord, how thirsty I was!" A typical scene in Sue's novel occurs when unfortunate characters (the Morels, La Louve in prison, or Fleur-de-Marie on at least two or three occasions) weep and wail for pages and pages describing the most painful and distressing situations. When the reader's tension has reached its limit, Rodolphe arrives, or someone in his place, and sets things right for everyone. Immediately the doleful story starts up again, while for page after page the same actors, retelling their woes to each other or to new arrivals, describe how badly off they were the moment before and how Rodolphe saved them from the blackest despair.

Now, it is true that Sue's public loved to have events repeated and confirmed over and over again and that every reader who wept over a character's misfortunes would in similar circumstances have behaved in the same way. But the reason for the 'Lord, how thirsty I was!' trick is apparently something else: this device allows the author to put the clock back so that the situation returns exactly to the status quo just before the change occurred. The transformation unties a knot, but removes nothing essential (the rope is not changed so to speak). Balance and order are disturbed by the informative violence of the *coup de théâtre,* but are reestablished on the same emotional bases as before. Above all, the characters do not 'evolve'. No one 'evolves' in *Les Mystères.* The character who undergoes conversion was basically good to begin with; the villain dies impenitent. Nothing happens that could possibly cause anyone any anxiety. The reader is comforted either because hundreds of marvelous things happen or because these events do not alter the up-and-down course of things. The sea continues to ebb and flow, except that for an instant there has been weeping, joy, suffering, or pleasure. The narrative sets in motion a series of devices for gratifying the reader, the most completely satisfactory and reassuring of which is that all remains in order, even those changes that take place in the realm of the imagination: Marie ascends the throne, Cinderella leaves her hearth. Nevertheless, she dies, from excess of scruple.

Within this mechanism one is free to dream; Rudolph is at the corner of the street for every reader—it is enough to stand and wait. It has already been noted that the year of Sue's death was the same that saw the publication of *Madame Bovary.* And *Madame Bovary* is the critical account of the life of a woman who read 'consolatory novels' in the style of Sue, from which she learned to wait for something that would never happen. It would be unfair to regard Sue the man and Sue the writer only in the symbolic light of this merciless dialectic. But it is useful to see the problem of the commercial novel, from Sue's day to our own, threatened by the obscurantist shadow of 'consolation'.

5.3. Conclusion

The whole of the foregoing examination represents a method of study employed by one particular reader relying on the 'cultivated' codes that were supposedly shared by the author and his contemporary critics. We know perfectly well that other readers in Sue's day did not use this key to decipher the book. They did not grasp its reformist implications, and from the total message only certain more obvious meanings filtered through to them (the dramatic situation of the working classes, the depravity of some of those in power, the necessity for change of no matter what kind, and so on). Hence the influence, which seems proved, of *Les Mystères* on the popular uprising of 1848. As Bory remarks: "It cannot be denied that Sue is certainly in part responsible for the revolution of February 1848. February 1848 was like an irresistible saturnalia celebrated by Sue's heroes, the labouring classes and the dangerous classes in the Paris of *Les Mystères*."[18] For this reason we must keep in mind a principle, characteristic of any examination of mass communication media (of which the popular novel is one of the most spectacular examples): the message which has been evolved by an educated elite (in a cultural group or a kind of communications headquarters, which takes its lead from the political or economic group in power) is expressed at the outset in terms of a fixed code, but it is caught by divers groups of receivers and deciphered on the basis of other codes. The sense of the message often undergoes a kind of filtration or distortion in the process, which completely alters its 'pragmatic' function. This means that every semiotic study of such a work should be complemented by a field research. The semiotic analysis reveals the implications of the message at the moment of emission; the check on the spot should establish what new meanings have been attributed to the message at the moment of reception.

NOTES

1. See Lucien Goldmann, *Pour une sociologie du roman* (Paris: Gallimard, 1964).

2. See two critical theories which stress the circular movement of this method: Leo Spitzer, *Essays in Stylistics* (Princeton: Princeton University Press, 1948), pp. 1–39; and Erwin Panofsky, "The History of Art as a Humanistic Discipline," in *Meaning in the Visual Arts* (New York: Doubleday, 1955).

3. I have in mind the meaning that Roland Barthes attributes to these two terms in "Rhetorique de l'image," *Communications* 4 (1964): 40–51.

4. For these and other biographical data, the reader is referred to Jean-Louis Bory's excellent work, *Eugène Sue—Le roi du roman populaire* (Paris: Hachette, 1962). See also Bory's "Presentation" in Eugène Sue, *Les Mystères de Paris* (Paris: Pauvert, 1963), and "Introduction," chronology, and notes to the anthology, *Les plus belles pages—Eugène Sue* (Paris: Mercure de France, 1963).

5. Quoted in S. Parmenie and C. Bonnier de la Chapelle, *Histoire d'un Editeur et de ses Auteurs: P. J. Hetzel* (Paris: Albin Michel, 1963). See also Bory, *Eugène Sue...*, pp. 370ff.

6. See Bory, ibid., p. 248.

7. V. V. Belinskij, *Textes Philosophique Choisis* (Moscow, 1951), pp. 394ff.

8. K. Marx and F. Engels, *Die Heilige Familie oder Kritik der Kritischen Kritik: Gegen Bruno Bauer und Consorten* (Frankfurt, 1945).

9. "These good people enjoyed such profound happiness and were so entirely satisfied with their log, that the Grand Duke, in his enlightened solicitude, had no trouble preserving them from the craze for constitutional innovations" (part 2, chapter 12).

10. "In any case, it seems possible to assert that the prototype and pattern for many Nietzschean 'supermen' is not Zarathustra, but the Count of Monte Cristo, by Alexandre Dumas," notes Gramsci. He does not take into account here that Rodolphe as a prototype precedes Monte Cristo (as in the *Three Musketeers,* in which the second superman in Gramsci's theory, Athos, appears, whereas the third, Giuseppe Balsamo, dates from 1849), though he is certainly thinking of Sue's work and makes several analyses of it: "Perhaps the popular superman of the Dumas type is properly to be understood as a democratic reaction to the concept of racialism, which is of feudal origin, and to be linked with the glorification of 'Gallicism' to be found in the novels of Eugène Sue (while in Nietzsche one should also see those influences which later culminate in Gobineau and the Pangermanism of Treitschke)"; see *Letteratura e Vita Nazionale. III: Letteratura popolare* (Turin: Einaudi, 1953). "The serial story replaces and, at the same time, encourages the day dreams of the man in the street; it is really a dream dreamt with one's eyes open. . . . In this case it can be said that, among the people, fancy is the result of a (social) inferiority complex that gives birth to lengthy fantasies built around the idea of revenge, or the punishment of those guilty of inflicting the evils suffered, etc."; ibid., p. 108.

11. Eugène Sue, preface to *Atar-Gull*. See Bory, *Eugène Sue. . .* , p. 102.

12. See E. Faral, *Les arts poetiques du XIIe et du XIIIe siècle* (Paris: Vrin, 1958). It is not by chance that the writings of these theorists are being dug up by the structuralists.

13. See Chapter 4 of this book.

14. On the structural definition of Kitsch, see Umberto Eco, "La struttura del cattivo gusto," in *Apocalittici e Integrati* (Milan: Bompiani, 1964).

15. Marx and Engels, chapter 8, p. 2.

16. "The expressions that Rodolphe uses in his conversation with Clémence, 'to make attractive,' 'use one's natural taste,' 'direct the intrigue,' 'make use of one's penchants towards cunning and dissimulation,' 'sublimate imperious and inexorable instincts to generous impulses,' etc.; these expressions, like the instincts that are by preference attributed to women, betray the secret source of Rodolfe's wisdom: Fourier's doctrine"; ibid., p. 5.

17. It should be mentioned that it is difficult to make Sue's strange theories on prison reform and penal reform in general fit into this scheme of things. Here we are witnessing a free improvisation by the author on the theme of 'reform' and an elaboration of his own political and humanitarian ideals outside the context of the novel itself; the flights of fancy that break up the action of the 'melodrama' develop quite independent themes. Yet even here the mechanism of arousing tension coupled with immediate reassurance is still

active. It is a provocation to demand the abolition of the death penalty, but in its place the punishment of being blinded is suggested (the culprit would have before him years of sheer, unrelieved introspection in which to repent and find his true self); it is a provocation to write that prisons harm far more than they cure and that to herd together scores of criminals in one big room, in a state of enforced idleness, can only make the wicked worse and even corrupt the good; but the reader's anxiety is allayed by the proposal of segregation in individual cells as an alternative (analogous to blinding as an alternative to the death penalty).

18. "Presentation" to *Les Mystères.* . . .

CHAPTER SIX

Narrative Structures in Fleming

In 1953 Ian Fleming published *Casino Royale,* the first novel in the 007 series. Being a first work, it is subject to the then current literary influence, and in the fifties, a period which had abandoned the traditional detective story in favor of the hard-boiled novel, it was impossible to ignore the presence of Mickey Spillane.

To Spillane *Casino Royale* owes, beyond doubt, at least two characteristic elements. First, the girl Vesper Lynd, who arouses the confident love of Bond, is in the end revealed as an enemy agent. In a novel by Spillane the hero would have killed her, whereas in Fleming's the woman has the grace to commit suicide; but Bond's reaction has the Spillane characteristic of transforming love into hatred and tenderness into ferocity: "The bitch is dead, now," Bond telephones to his London office, and so ends his romance.

Second, Bond is obsessed by an image: that of a Japanese expert in codes whom he killed in cold blood on the thirty-sixth floor of the RCA building at Rockefeller Center with a bullet shot from a window of the fortieth floor of the skyscraper opposite. By an analogy that is surely not accidental, Mike Hammer seems to be haunted by the memory of a small Japanese he killed in the jungle during the war, though with greater emotive participation (Bond's homicide, authorized officially by the double zero, is more ascetic and bureaucratic). The memory of the Japanese is the beginning of the undoubted nervous disorders of Mike Hammer (his sadomasochism and his suspected impotence); the memory of his first homicide could have been the origin of the neurosis of James Bond,

"Le strutture narrative in Fleming," in *Il caso Bond,* ed. O. Del Buono and U. Eco (Milan: Bompiani, 1965). R. A. Downie, trans., in *The Bond Affair* (London: MacDonald, 1966). This chapter is an extensively revised version of the translation.

[144]

except that, within the ambit of *Casino Royale,* either the character or his author solves the problem by nontherapeutic means: Fleming excludes neurosis from the narrative possibilities. This decision was to influence the structure of the following eleven novels by Fleming and presumably forms the basis for their success.

After helping to blow up two Bulgarians who had tried to get rid of him, after suffering torture in the form of a cruel abuse of his testicles, after enjoying the elimination of Le Chiffre by a Soviet agent, having received from him a cut on the hand, cold-bloodedly carved while he was conscious, and after risking his love life, Bond, relaxing during his well-earned convalescence in a hospital bed, confides a chilling doubt to his French colleague, Mathis. Have they been fighting for a just cause? Le Chiffre, who had financed Communist spies among the French workers— was he not "serving a wonderful purpose, a really vital purpose, perhaps the best and highest purpose of all"? The difference between good and evil—is it really something neat, recognizable, as the hagiography of counterespionage would like us to believe? At this point Bond is ripe for the crisis, for the salutary recognition of universal ambiguity, and he sets off along the route traversed by the protagonist of le Carré. But at the very moment he questions himself about the appearance of the devil and, sympathizing with the Enemy, is inclined to recognize him as a "lost brother," Bond is treated to a salve from Mathis: "When you get back to London you will find there are other Le Chiffres seeking to destroy you and your friends and your country. M will tell you about them. And now that you have seen a really evil man, you will know how evil they can be and you will go after them to destroy them in order to protect yourself and the people you love. You know what they look like now and what they can do to people. . . . Surround yourself with human beings, my dear James. They are easier to fight for than principles. . . . But don't let me down and become human yourself. We would lose such a wonderful machine."

With this lapidary phrase Fleming defines the character of James Bond for the novels to come. From *Casino Royale* there remains the scar on his cheek, the slightly cruel smile, the taste for good food, and a number of subsidiary characteristics minutely documented in the course of this first volume; but, persuaded by Mathis's words, Bond is to abandon the treacherous life of moral meditation and of psychological anger, with all the neurotic dangers that they entail. Bond ceases to be a subject for psychiatry and remains at the most a physiological object (except for a return to psychic diseases in the last, untypical novel in the series, *The Man with the Golden Gun*), a magnificent machine, as the author and the public, as well as Mathis, wish. From that moment Bond does not meditate upon truth and justice, upon life and death, except in rare moments of boredom, usually in the bar of an airport but always in the form of a casual daydream, never allowing himself to be infected by doubt (at least in the novels; he does indulge in such intimate luxuries in the short stories).

From the psychological point of view, the conversion has taken place quite suddenly, on the basis of four conventional phrases pronounced by Mathis, but the conversion should not be justified on a psychological level. In the last pages of *Casino Royale,* Fleming, in fact, renounces all psychology as the motive of narrative and decides to transfer characters and situations to the level of an objective structural strategy. Without knowing it Fleming makes a choice familiar to many contemporary disciplines: he passes from the psychological method to the formalistic one.

In *Casino Royale* there are already all the elements for the building of a machine that functions basically on a set of precise units governed by rigorous combinational rules. The presence of those rules explains and determines the success of the '007 saga'—a success which, singularly, has been due both to the mass consensus and to the appreciation of more sophisticated readers. I intend here to examine in detail this narrative machine in order to identify the reasons for its success. It is my plan to devise a descriptive table of the narrative structure in the works of Ian Fleming while evaluating for each structural element the probable incidence upon the reader's sensitivity. I shall try, therefore, to distinguish such a narrative structure at five levels:

(1) the opposition of characters and of values;
(2) play situations and the story as a 'game';
(3) a Manichean ideology;
(4) literary techniques;
(5) literature as collage.

My enquiry covers the range of the following novels listed in order of publication (the date of composition is presumably a year earlier in each case):

Casino Royale (1953);
Live and Let Die (1954);
Moonraker (1955);
Diamonds are Forever (1956);
From Russia, With Love (1957);
Dr. No (1958);
Goldfinger (1959);
Thunderball (1961);
On Her Majesty's Secret Service (1963);
You Only Live Twice (1964).

I shall refer also to the stories in *For Your Eyes Only* (1960) and to *The Man with the Golden Gun* (1965), but shall not take into consideration *The Spy Who Loved Me* (1962), which seems quite untypical.

6.1.   The opposition of characters and of values

The novels of Fleming seem to be built on a series of oppositions which allow a limited number of permutations and interactions. These dichotomies constitute invariant features around which minor couples rotate as free variants. I have singled out fourteen couples, four of which are opposing characters, the others being opposing values, variously personified by the four basic characters:

    (1) Bond-M;
    (2) Bond-Villain;
    (3) Villain-Woman;
    (4) Woman-Bond;
    (5) Free World–Soviet Union;
    (6) Great Britain–Non-Anglo-Saxon Countries;
    (7) Duty-Sacrifice;
    (8) Cupidity-Ideals;
    (9) Love-Death;
    (10) Chance-Planning;
    (11) Luxury-Discomfort;
    (12) Excess-Moderation;
    (13) Perversion-Innocence;
    (14) Loyalty-Disloyalty.

These pairs do not represent 'vague' elements but 'simple' ones that are immediate and universal, and, if we consider the range of each pair, we see that the variants allowed in fact include all the narrative devices of Fleming.

Bond-M is a dominated-dominant relationship which characterizes from the beginning the limits and possibilities of the character of Bond and which sets events moving. Psychological and psychoanalytical interpretations of Bond's attitude toward M have been discussed in particular by Kingsley Amis. The fact is that, even in terms of pure fictional functions, M represents to Bond the one who has a global view of the events, hence his superiority over the 'hero' who depends upon him and who sets out on his various missions in conditions of inferiority to the omniscient chief. Frequently, his chief sends Bond into adventures the upshot of which he had discounted from the start. Bond is thus often the victim of a trick—and it does not matter whether things happen to him beyond the cool calculations of M. The tutelage under which M holds Bond—obliged against his will to visit a doctor, to undergo a nature cure (*Thunderball*), to change his gun (*Dr. No*)—makes so much the more insidious and imperious his chief's authority. We can, therefore, see that M represents certain other values such as Duty, Country, and Method (as an element of programming contrasting with Bond's own inclination to rely on improvisation). If Bond is the hero, hence in possession of exceptional qualities, M represents Measure, accepted perhaps as a national virtue. But Bond is not so exceptional as a hasty reading of the books (or the spectacular interpretation which films give of the books) might make one think. Fleming always affirmed that he had thought of Bond as an absolutely ordinary person, and it is in contrast with M that the real stature of 007 emerges, endowed with physical attributes, with courage and fast reflexes, but possessing neither these nor other qualities in excess. It is, rather, a certain moral force, an obstinate fidelity to the job—at the command of M, always present as a warning—that allows him to overcome superhuman ordeals without exercising any superhuman faculty.

The Bond-M relationship presupposes a psychological ambivalence, a reciprocal love-hate. At the beginning of *The Man with the Golden Gun,* Bond, emerging from a lengthy amnesia and having been conditioned by the Soviets, tries a kind of ritual parricide by shooting at M with a cyanide pistol; the gesture loosens a longstanding series of narrative tensions which are aggravated every time M and Bond find themselves face to face.

Started by M on the road to Duty (at all costs), Bond enters into conflict with the Villain. The opposition brings into play diverse values, some of which are only variants of the basic couples listed above. Bond represents Beauty and Virility as opposed to the Villain, who often appears monstrous and sexually impotent. The monstrosity of the Villain is a constant point, but to emphasize it we must here introduce a methodological notion which will also apply in examining the other couples. Among the variants we must consider also the existence of vicarious characters whose functions are understood only if they are seen as 'variations' of one of the principal personages, some of whose characteristics they carry on. The vicarious roles function usually for the Woman and for the Villain; one can see as variations of M certain collaborators of Bond—for example, Mathis in *Casino Royale,* who preaches Duty in the appropriate M manner (albeit with a cynical and Gallic air).

As to the characteristics of the Villain, let us consider them in order. In *Casino Royale* Le Chiffre is pallid and smooth, with a crop of red hair, an almost feminine mouth, false teeth of expensive quality, small ears with large lobes, and hairy hands. He never smiles. In *Live and Let Die* Mr. Big, a Haitian, has a head that resembles a football, twice the normal size and almost spherical. "The skin was grey-black, taut and shining like the face of a week-old corpse in the river. It was hairless, except for some grey-brown fluff above the ears. There were no eyebrows and no eyelashes and the eyes were extraordinarily far apart so that one could not focus on them both, but only on one at a time. . . . They were animal eyes, not human, and they seemed to blaze." His gums are pale pink.

In *Diamonds Are Forever* the Villain appears in three different, vicarious roles. Two are Jack and Seraffimo Spang, the first of whom has a humped back and red hair ("Bond did not remember having seen a red-haired hunchback before"), eyes which might have been borrowed from a taxidermist, big ears with rather exaggerated lobes, dry red lips, and an almost total absence of neck. Seraffimo has a face the color of ivory, black puckered eyebrows, a bush of shaggy hair, and jutting, ruthless jaws; if it is added that Seraffimo used to pass his days in a Spectreville of the Old West dressed in black leather chaps embellished with silver spurs, pistols with ivory butts, a black belt and ammunition—also that he used to drive a train of 1870 vintage furnished with a Victorian carriage —the picture is complete. The third vicarious figure is Señor Winter, who travels with a label on his suitcase which reads "My blood group is F" and who is really a killer in the pay of the Spangs. Señor Winter is a gross and sweating individual, with a wart on his hand, a placid visage, and protruding eyes.

In *Moonraker* Hugo Drax is six feet tall, with "exceptionally broad" shoulders, a large and square head, and red hair. The right half of his face is shiny and wrinkled from unsuccessful plastic surgery, the right eye different from and larger than the left and "painfully bloodshot." He has heavy moustaches, whiskers to the lobes of his ears, and patches of hair on his cheekbones: the moustaches concealed with scant success a prognathous upper jaw and a marked protrusion of his upper teeth. The backs of his hands are covered with reddish hair. Altogether he evokes the idea of a ringmaster at the circus.

In *From Russia, With Love,* the Villain generates three vicarious figures. Red Grant, the professional murderer in the pay of Smersh, has short, sandy-colored eyelashes; colorless, opaque blue eyes; a small, cruel mouth; innumerable freckles on his milk-white skin; and deep, wide pores. Colonel Grubozaboyschikov, head of Smersh, has a narrow and sharp face; round eyes like two polished marbles, weighed down by two flabby pouches; a broad, grim mouth; and a shaven skull. Finally, Rosa Klebb, with the humid, pallid lip stained with nicotine, the raucous voice, flat and devoid of emotion, is five-feet-four, with no curves, dumpy arms, short neck, too sturdy ankles, and grey hair gathered in a tight "obscene" bun. She has shiny, yellow-brown eyes, wears thick glasses, and has a sharp nose with large nostrils that is powdered white. "The wet trap of a mouth, that went on opening and shutting as if it was operated by wire under the chin" completes the appearance of a sexually neuter person.

In *From Russia, With Love,* there occurs a variant that is discernible only in a few other novels. There enters also upon the scene a strongly drawn being who has many of the moral qualities of the Villain, but uses them in the end for good, or at least fights on the side of Bond. An example is Darko Kerim, the Turkish agent in *From Russia, With Love.* Analogous to him are Tiger Tanaka, the head of the Japanese secret service in *You Only Live Twice,* Draco in *On Her Majesty's Secret Service,* Enrico Colombo in "Risico" (a story in *For Your Eyes Only*), and—partially—Quarrel in *Dr. No.* They are at the same time representative of the Villain and of M, and we shall call them "ambiguous representatives'. With these Bond always stands in a kind of competitive alliance: he likes them and hates them at the same time, he uses them and admires them, he dominates them and is their slave.

In *Dr. No* the Villain, besides his great height, is characterized by the lack of hands, which are replaced by two metal pincers. His shaved head has the appearance of a reversed raindrop; his skin is clear, without wrinkles; the cheekbones are as smooth as fine ivory; his eyebrows are dark as though painted on; his eyes are without eyelashes and look "like the mouths of two small revolvers"; his nose is thin and ends very close to his mouth, which shows only cruelty and authority.

In *Goldfinger* the eponymous character is a textbook monster—that is, he is characterized by a lack of proportion: "He was short, not more than five feet tall, and on top of the thick body and blunt, peasant legs was set, almost directly into the shoulders, a huge and it seemed exactly round head. It was as if Goldfinger had been put together with bits of other people's bodies. Nothing seemed to belong." His vicarious figure is that of the Korean, Oddjob, who, with fingers like spatulas and fingertips like solid bone, could smash the wooden balustrade of a staircase with a karate blow.

In *Thunderball* there appears for the first time Ernst Starvo Blofeld, who crops up again in *On Her Majesty's Secret Service* and in *You Only Live Twice,* where in the end he dies. As his vicarious incarnations we have in *Thunderball* Count Lippe and Emilio Largo: both are handsome and personable, however vulgar and cruel, and their monstrosity is purely mental. In *On Her Majesty's Secret Service* there appear Irma Blunt, the *longamanus* of Blofeld, a distant reincarnation of Rosa Klebb, and a series of Villains in outline who perish tragically, killed by an avalanche or by a train. In *You Only Live Twice,* the primary role is resumed by Blofeld, already described in *Thunderball:* a child-like gaze from eyes that resemble two deep pools, surrounded "like the eyes of Mussolini" by clear whites, eyes having the symmetry and silken black lashes that recall the eyes of a doll; a mouth like a badly healed wound under a heavy squat nose; altogether an expression of hypocrisy, tyranny, and cruelty, on a Shakespearean level. Blofeld weighs twenty stone. As we learn in *On Her Majesty's Secret Service,* he lacks earlobes. His hair is a wiry, black crewcut.

To make more constant the Bond-Villain relationship, there is also a racial quality common to all Villains, along with other characteristics. The Villain is born in an ethnic area that stretches from Central Europe to the Slav countries and to the Mediterranean basin: usually he is of mixed blood and his origins are complex and obscure. He is asexual or homosexual, or at any rate is not sexually normal. He has exceptional inventive and organizational qualities which help him acquire immense wealth and by means of which he usually works to help Russia: to this end he conceives a plan of fantastic character and dimensions, worked out to the smallest detail, intended to create serious difficulties either for England or for the Free World in general. Gathered in the figure of the Villain, in fact, the negative values which we have distinguished in some pairs of opposites, the Soviet Union and other non-Anglo-Saxon countries (the racial convention blames particularly the Jews, the Germans, the Slavs, and the Italians, always depicted as halfbreeds), Cupidity elevated to the dignity of paranoia, Planning as technological methodology, satrapic Luxury, physical and psychical Excess, physical and moral Perversion, radical Disloyalty.

Le Chiffre, who organizes the subversive movement in France, comes from a mixture of Mediterranean and Prussian or Polish strains and has Jewish blood revealed by small ears with large lobes. A gambler not basically disloyal, he still betrays his own bosses and tries to recover by criminal means money lost in gambling. He is a masochist (at least so the Secret Service dossier proclaims). He has bought a great chain of brothels, but has lost his patrimony by his exalted manner of living.

Mr. Big is a black who enjoys with Solitaire an ambiguous relationship of exploitation (he has not yet acquired her favors). He helps the Soviet by means of his powerful criminal organization founded on the voodoo cult, finds and sells in the United States treasure hidden in the seventeenth century, controls various rackets, and is prepared to ruin the American economy by introducing, through the black market, large quantities of rare coins.

Hugo Drax displays indefinite nationality—he is English by adoption —but in fact he is German. He holds control of columbite, a material indispensable to the construction of reactors, and gives to the British crown the means of building a most powerful rocket. He plans, however, first to make the rocket fall, when tested atomically on London, and then to flee to Russia (equation: Communist-Nazi). He frequents clubs of high class and is passionately fond of bridge, but only enjoys cheating.

His hysteria does not permit one to suspect any sexual activity worthy of note.

Of the secondary characters in *From Russia, With Love,* the chief are from the Soviet Union and, in working for the Communist cause, enjoy comforts and power: Rosa Klebb, sexually neuter, "might enjoy the act physically, but the instrument was of no importance"; Red Grant, a were-wolf who kills for pleasure, lives splendidly at the expense of the Soviet government in a villa with a swimming pool. The science-fiction plot consists of the plan to lure Bond into a complicated trap, using for bait a woman and an instrument for coding and decoding ciphers, and then to kill and to checkmate the English counterspy.

Dr. No is a Chinese-German halfbreed who works for Russia. He shows no definite sexual tendencies (having in his power Honeychile, he plans to have her torn to pieces by the crabs of Crab Key). He has a flourishing guano industry and plans to cause guided missiles launched by the Americans to deviate from their course. In the past he has built up his fortune by robbing the criminal organization of which he had been elected cashier. He lives, on his island, in a palace of fabulous pomp.

Goldfinger has a probable Baltic origin, but also has Jewish blood. He lives splendidly from commerce and from smuggling gold, by means of which he finances Communist movements in Europe. He plans the theft of gold from Fort Knox (not its radioactivation, as the film indicates) and, to overcome the final barrier, sets up an atomic attack on a NATO installation and tries to poison the water of Fort Knox. He does not have a sexual relationship with the woman he dominates, but limits himself to the acquisition of gold. He cheats at cards by using expensive devices such as binoculars and radios; he cheats to make money, even though he is fabulously rich and always travels with a stock of gold in his luggage.

Blofeld is of a Polish father and a Greek mother. He exploits his position as a telegraph clerk to start in Poland a flourishing trade in secret information and becomes chief of the most extensive independent organization for espionage, blackmail, rapine, and extortion. Indeed, with Blofeld Russia ceases to be the constant enemy—because of the general international relaxation of tension—and the part of the malevolent organization assumed by SPECTRE has all the characteristics of SMERSH, including the employment of Slav-Latin-German elements, the use of torture, the elimination of traitors, and the sworn enmity to all the powers of the Free World. Of the science-fiction plans of Blofeld, that of *Thunderball* is to steal from NATO two atomic bombs and with these to blackmail England and America; that of *On Her Majesty's Secret Service* envisages the training in a mountain clinic of girls with suitable allergies to condition them to spread a mortal virus intended to ruin the agriculture and livestock of the United Kingdom; and in *You Only Live Twice,* Blofeld, affected by a murderous mania, organizes a fantastic suicidal garden near the coast of Japan, which attracts legions of heirs of the Kamikaze who are bent on poisoning themselves with exotic, refined, and lethal plants, thus doing grave and complex harm to the human patrimony of Japanese democracy. Blofeld's tendency toward satrapic pomp shows itself in the kind of life he leads in the mountain of Piz Gloria and, more particularly, on the island of Kyashu, where he lives in medieval tyranny and passes through his *hortus deliciarum* clad in metal armor. Previously Blofeld showed himself to be ambitious of honors (he aspired to be known as the Count of Blenville), a master of planning, an organizing genius, as treacherous as needs be, and sexually impotent—he lived in marriage with Irma Blofeld, also asexual and hence repulsive. To quote Tiger Tanaka, Blofeld "is a devil who has taken human form."

Only the evil characters of *Diamonds Are Forever* have no connections with Russia. In a certain sense the international gangsterism of the Spangs appears to be an earlier version of Spectre. For the rest, Jack and Seraffimo possess all the characteristics of the canon.

To the typical qualities of the Villain are opposed the Bond characteristics, particularly Loyalty to the Service, Anglo-Saxon Moderation opposed to the excess of the halfbreeds, the selection of Discomfort and the acceptance of Sacrifice opposed to the ostentatious Luxury of the enemy, the genial improvisation (Chance) opposed to the cold Planning which it defeats, the sense of an Ideal opposed to Cupidity (Bond in various cases wins from the Villain in gambling, but as a rule returns the enormous winnings to the Service or to the girl of the moment, as occurred with Jill Masterson). Some oppositions function not only in the Bond-Villain relationship but also in the behavior of Bond. Thus Bond is normally loyal but does not disdain overcoming a cheating enemy by a deceitful trick and blackmailing him (see *Moonraker* or *Goldfinger*). Even Excess and Moderation, Chance and Planning are opposed in the acts and decisions of Bond. Duty and Sacrifice appear as elements of internal debate each time Bond knows he must prevent the plan of the Villain at the risk of his life, and in those cases the patriotic ideal (Great Britain and the Free World) takes the upper hand. He calls also on the racist need to show the superiority of the Briton. Also opposed in Bond are Luxury (the choice of good food, care in dressing, preference for sumptuous hotels, love of the gambling table, invention of cocktails, and so on) and Discomfort (Bond is always ready to abandon the easy life—even when it appears in the guise of a Woman who offers herself—to face a new aspect of Discomfort, the acutest point of which is torture).

We have discussed the Bond-Villain dichotomy at length because in fact it embodies all the characteristics of the opposition between Eros and Thanatos, the principle of pleasure and the principle of reality, culminating in the moment of torture (in *Casino Royale* explicitly theorized as a sort of erotic relationship between the torturer and the tortured). This opposition is perfected in the relationship between the Villain and the Woman; Vesper is tyrannized and blackmailed by the Soviets, and therefore by Le Chiffre; Solitaire is the slave of Mr. Big; Tiffany Case is dominated by the Spangs; Tatiana is the slave of Rosa Klebb and of the Soviet government in general; Jill and Tilly Masterson are dominated, to different degrees, by Goldfinger, and Pussy Galore works under his orders; Domino Vitali is subservient to the wishes of Blofeld through the physical relationship with the vicarious figure of Emilio Largo; the English girls of Piz Gloria are under the hypnotic control of Blofeld and the virginal surveillance of Irma Blunt; Honeychile, wandering pure and untroubled on the shores of his cursed island, has a purely symbolic relationship with the power of Dr. No, except that at the end Dr. No offers her naked body to the crabs (she has been dominated by the Villain through the vicarious effort of the brutal Mander and has justly punished Mander by causing a scorpion to kill him, anticipating the revenge of No—who had recourse to crabs); and, finally, Kissy Suzuki lives on her island in the shade of the cursed castle of Blofeld, suffering a purely allegorical domination shared by the whole population of the place. In an intermediate position is Gala Brand, who is an agent of the Service but who becomes the secretary of Hugo Drax and establishes a relationship of submission to him. In most cases the Villain-Woman relationship culminates in the torture the woman undergoes along with Bond; here the Love-Death pair functions also, in the sense of a more intimate erotic union of the two through their common ordeal.

Dominated by the Villain, however, Fleming's woman has already been previously conditioned to domination, life for her having assumed the role of the villain. The general scheme is (i) the girl is beautiful and good; (ii) she has been made frigid and unhappy by severe trials suffered in adolescence; (iii) this has conditioned her to the service of the Villain; (iv) through meeting Bond she appreciates her positive human chances; (v) Bond possesses her but in the end loses her. This curriculum is common to Vesper, Solitaire, Tiffany, Tatiana, Honeychile, and Domino; rather vague as for Gala; equally shared by the three vicarious women of Goldfinger (Jill, Tilly, and Pussy—the first two have had a sad past, but only the third has been violated by her uncle; Bond possessed the first and the third; the second is killed by the Villain; the first is tortured with gold paint; the second and third are Lesbians, and Bond redeems only the third; and so on); more diffuse and uncertain for the group of girls on Piz Gloria (each has had an unhappy past, but Bond in fact possesses only one of them; similarly, he marries Tracy, whose past was unhappy because of a series of unions, dominated by her father, Draco, and who was killed in the end by Blofeld, who realizes at this point his domination and who ends by Death the relationship of Love which she entertained with Bond); Kissy Suzuki's unhappiness is the result of a Hollywoodian experience which has made her chary of life and of men.

In every case Bond loses the woman, either by her own will or by that of another (in the case of Gala, it is the woman who marries somebody else, although unwillingly) and either at the end of the novel or at the beginning of the following one (as happened with Tiffany Case). Thus, in the moment in which the Woman solves the opposition to the Villain by entering with Bond into a purifying-purified, saving-saved relationship, she returns to the domination of the negative. Every woman displays an internal combat between the couple Perversion-Purity (sometimes external, as in the relationship of Rosa Klebb and Tatiana) which makes her similar to the Richardsonian persecuted virgin. The bearer of purity, notwithstanding and despite her perversion, eager to alternate lust with torture, she would appear likely to resolve the contrast between the privileged race and the non-Anglo-Saxon halfbreed, since she often belongs to an ethnically inferior breed; but insofar as the erotic relationship always ends with a form of death, real or symbolic, Bond resumes willy-nilly his purity as an Anglo-Saxon bachelor. The race remains uncontaminated.

6.2. Play situations and the story as a 'game'

The various pairs of oppositions (of which we have considered only a few possible variants) seem like the elements of an *ars combinatoria* with fairly elementary rules. It is clear that in the engagement of the two poles of each couple there are, in the course of the novel, alternative solutions: the reader does not know at which point of the story the Villain defeats Bond or Bond defeats the Villain, and so on. But toward the end of the book the algebra has to follow a prearranged pattern: as in the Chinese game that 007 and Tanaka play at the beginning of *You Only Live Twice,* hand beats fist, fist beats two fingers, two fingers beat hand. M beats Bond, Bond beats the Villain, the Villain beats Woman, even if at first Bond beats Woman; the Free World beats the Soviet Union, England beats the Impure Countries, Death beats Love, Moderation beats Excess, and so on.

This interpretation of the story in terms of a game is not accidental. The books of Fleming are dominated by situations that we call 'play situations'. First are several archetypal situations such as the Journey and the Meal; the Journey may be by Machine (and here occurs a rich symbolism of the automobile, typical of our century), by Train (another archetype, this of obsolescent type), by Airplane, or by Ship. But a meal, a pursuit by machine, or a mad race by train always takes the form of a game. Bond decides the choice of foods as though they formed the pieces of a puzzle, prepares for the meal with the same scrupulous attention as that with which he prepares for a game of bridge (see the convergence, in a means-end connection, of the two elements in *Moonraker*), and he intends the meal as a play. Similarly, train and machine are the elements of a wager made against an adversary: before the journey is finished, one of the two has finished his moves and given checkmate.

At this point it is useless to record the occurrence of the play situations, in the true and proper sense of conventional games of chance, in each book. Bond always gambles and wins, against the Villain or some vicarious figure. The detail with which these games are described is the subject of further consideration in section 6.4, which deals with literary technique; here it must be said that, if these games occupy a prominent space, it is because they form a reduced and formalized model of the more general play situation that is the novel. The novel, given the rules of combination of oppositional couples, is fixed as a sequence of 'moves' inspired by the code and constituted according to a perfectly prearranged scheme. The invariable scheme is the following:

A. M moves and gives a task to Bond;
B. Villain moves and appears to Bond (perhaps in vicarious forms);
C. Bond moves and gives a first check to Villain or Villain gives first check to Bond;
D. Woman moves and shows herself to Bond;
E. Bond takes Woman (possesses her or begins her seduction);
F. Villain captures Bond (with or without Woman, or at different moments);
G. Villain tortures Bond (with or without Woman);
H. Bond beats Villain (kills him, or kills his representative or helps at their killing);
I. Bond, convalescing, enjoys Woman, whom he then loses.

The scheme is invariable in the sense that all the elements are always present in every novel (so that it might be affirmed that the fundamental rule of the game is "Bond moves and mates in eight moves"). That the moves always be in the same sequence is not imperative. A minute detailing of the ten novels under consideration would yield several examples of a set scheme we might call ABCDEFGHI (for example, *Dr. No*), but often there are inversions and variations. Sometimes Bond meets the Villain at the beginning of the volume and gives him a first check, and only later receives his instructions from M. For example, *Goldfinger* presents a different scheme, BCDEACDFGDHEHI, where it is possible to notice repeated moves: two encounters and three games played with the Villain, two seductions and three encounters with women, a first flight of the Villain after his defeat and his ensuing death, and so on. In *From*

Russia, With Love, the company of Villains increases—through the presence of the ambiguous representative Kerim, in conflict with a secondary Villain, Krilenku, and the two mortal duels of Bond with Red Grant and with Rosa Klebb, who was arrested only after having grievously wounded Bond—so that the scheme, highly complicated, is BBBBDA(BBC)EFGH (I). There is a long prologue in Russia with the parade of the Villain figures and the first connection between Tatiana and Rosa Klebb, the sending of Bond to Turkey, a long interlude in which Kerim and Krilenku appear and the latter is defeated, the seduction of Tatiana, the flight by train with the torture suffered by the murdered Kerim, the victory over Red Grant, the second round with Rosa Klebb, who, while being defeated, inflicts serious injury upon Bond. In the train and during his convalescence, Bond enjoys love interludes with Tatiana before the final separation.

Even the basic concept of torture undergoes variations, being sometimes a direct injustice, sometimes a kind of succession or course of horrors that Bond must undergo, either by the explicit will of the Villain (*Dr. No*) or by accident during an escape from the Villain, but always as a consequence of the moves of the Villain (for example, a tragic escape in the snow, pursuit, avalanche, and hurried flight through the Swiss countryside in *On Her Majesty's Secret Service*).

Occurring alongside the sequence of fundamental moves are numerous side issues which enrich the narrative by unforeseen events, without, however, altering the basic scheme. For a graphic representation of this process, we may summarize the plot of one novel—*Diamonds Are Forever*—by placing on the left the sequence of the fundamental moves, on the right the multiplicity of side issues:

	Long curious prologue which introduces one to diamond smuggling in South Africa
Move A. M sends Bond to America as a sham smuggler	
Move B. Villains (the Spangs) appear indirectly in the description of them given to Bond	
Move D. Woman (Tiffany Case) meets Bond in the role of go-between	
	Detailed journey by air, in the background two vicarious Villains; play situations; imperceptible duel between hunters and prey

Move B. First appearance in the plane of vicarious Villain Winter (Blood Group F)

Move B. Meeting with Jack Spang

Meeting with Felix Leiter, who brings Bond up to date about the Spangs

Move E. Bond begins the seduction of Tiffany

Long interval at Saratoga at the races; to help Leiter Bond in fact "damages" the Spangs

Move C. Bond gives a first check to the Villain

Appearance of vicarious Villains in the mud bath and punishment of the treacherous jockey, anticipating symbolically the torturing of Bond; the whole Saratoga episode represents a play situation in miniature; Bond decides to go to Las Vegas; detailed description of the district

Move B. Appearance of Seraffimo Spang

Another long and detailed play situation; play with Tiffany as croupier gambling at table, indirect amorous skirmish with the woman, indirect gamble with Seraffimo; Bond wins money

Move C. Bond gives a second check to Villain

Next evening, long shooting match between cars; association of Bond and Ernie Cureo

Move F. Spang captures Bond

Long description of Spectre and the train-playing of Spang

Move G. Spang has Bond tortured

With the aid of Tiffany, Bond begins a fantastic flight by railway

	trolley through the desert followed by the locomotive-plaything driven by Seraffimo; play situation
Move H. Bond defeats Seraffimo, who crashes into the mountain on the loco-motive	
	Rest with his friend Leiter, de-parture by ship, long amorous con-valescence with Tiffany, exchanges of coded telegrams
Move E. Bond finally possesses Tiffany	
Move B. Villain reappears in the form of Winter	
	Play situation on board ship; mor-tal gamble played by infinitesimal moves between the two killers and Bond; play situation becomes sym-bolized on reduced scale in the lottery on the course of the ship; the two killers capture Tiffany; acrobatic action by Bond to reach the cabin and kill the killers
Move H. Bond overcomes vicari-ous Villains finally	
	Meditations on death in the pres-ence of the two corpses; return home
Move I. Bond knows he can en-joy well-earned repose with Tiffany, and yet ...	
	... deviations of the plot in South Africa, where Bond destroys the last link of the chain
Move H. Bond defeats for the third time the Villain in the person of Jack Spang	

For each of the ten novels it would be possible to trace a general plan. The collateral inventions are rich enough to form the muscles of the separate skeletons of narrative; they constitute one of the great attrac-tions of Fleming's work, but they do not testify, at least not obviously, to his powers of invention. As we shall see later, it is easy to trace the collateral inventions to definite literary sources, and hence these act as familiar reference marks to romanesque situations acceptable to readers. The true and original story remains immutable, and suspense is stabilized curiously on the basis of a sequence of events that are entirely pre-determined. The story of each book by Fleming, by and large, may be summarized as follows: Bond is sent to a given place to avert a 'science-fiction' plan by a monstrous individual of uncertain origin and definitely not English who, making use of his organizational or productive activity, not only earns money, but helps the cause of the enemies of the West. In facing this monstrous being, Bond meets a woman who is dominated by him and frees her from her past, establishing with her an erotic relation-ship interrupted by capture by the Villain and by torture. But Bond de-feats the Villain, who dies horribly, and rests from his great efforts in the arms of the woman, though he is destined to lose her. One might wonder how, within such limits, it is possible for the inventive writer of fiction to function, since he must respond to a demand for the sensational and the unforeseeable. In fact, in every detective story and in every hard-boiled novel, there is no basic variation, but rather the repetition of a habitual scheme in which the reader can recognize something he has already seen and of which he has grown fond. Under the guise of a machine that produces information, the criminal novel produces redundancy; pretend-ing to rouse the reader, it in fact reconfirms him in a sort of imaginative laziness and creates escape by narrating, not the Unknown, but the Already Known. In the pre-Fleming detective story, however, the immu-table scheme is formed by the personality of the detective and of his colleagues, while within this scheme are unravelled unexpected events (and most unexpected of all is the figure of the culprit). On the contrary, in the novels of Fleming, the scheme even dominates the very chain of events. Moreover, the identity of the culprit, his characteristics, and his plans are always apparent from the beginning. The reader finds himself immersed in a game of which he knows the pieces and the rules—and perhaps the outcome—and draws pleasure simply from following the minimal variations by which the victor realizes his objective.

We might compare a novel by Fleming to a game of football in which we know beforehand the place, the numbers and personalities of the players, the rules of the game, and the fact that everything will take place within the area of the great pitch—except that in a game of football we do not know until the very end who will win. It would be more accurate to compare a novel by Fleming to a game of basketball played by the Harlem Globetrotters against a local team. We know with absolute confidence that the Globetrotters will win: the pleasure lies in watching the trained virtuosity with which they defer the final moment, with what ingenious deviations they reconfirm the foregone conclusion, with what trickeries they make rings round their opponents. The novels of Fleming exploit in exemplary measure that element of foregone play which is typical of the escape machine geared for the entertainment of the masses. Perfect in their mechanism, such machines represent the narrative structure which works upon a material which does not aspire to express any ideology. It is true that such structures inevitably entail ideological positions, but these do not derive so much from the structured contents as from the way of structuring them.

6.3. A Manichean ideology

The novels of Fleming have been variously accused of McCarthyism, Fascism, the cult of excess and violence, racism, and so on. It is difficult, after the analysis we have carried out, to maintain that Fleming is not inclined to consider the British superior to all Oriental or Mediterranean races or that Fleming does not profess to heartfelt anti-Communism. Yet it is significant that he ceased to identify the wicked with Russia as soon as the international situation rendered Russia less menacing according to the general opinion. It is significant also that, while he is introducing the gang of Mr. Big, Fleming is profuse in his acknowledgment of the new African nations and of their contribution to contemporary civilization (Negro gangsterism would represent a proof of the industrial efficiency attained by the developing countries); when the Villain is supposed to have Jewish blood, Fleming is always fairly unexplicit; he never shows more than a cautious, middle-class chauvinism. Thus arises the suspicion that our author does not characterize his creations in such and such a manner as a result of an ideological opinion but purely for rhetorical purposes. By 'rhetoric' I mean an art of persuasion which relies on *endoxa,* that is, on the common opinions shared by the majority of readers.

Fleming is, in other words, cynically building an effective narrative apparatus. To do so he decides to rely upon the most secure and universal principles and puts into play precisely those archetypal elements that have proved successful in fairy tales. Let us recall for a moment the pairs of oppositional characters: M is the King and Bond is the Knight entrusted with a mission; Bond is the Knight and the Villain is the Dragon; that Lady and Villain stand for Beauty and the Beast; Bond restores the Lady to the fullness of spirit and to her senses—he is the Prince who rescues Sleeping Beauty; between the Free World and the Soviet Union, England and the non-Anglo-Saxon countries is realized the primitive epic relationship between the Privileged Race and the Lower Race, between White and Black, Good and Bad. Fleming is a racist in the sense that any artist is one if, to represent the devil, he depicts him with oblique eyes; in the sense that a nurse is one who, wishing to frighten children with the bogeyman, suggests that he is black. It is singular that Fleming should be anti-Communist with the same lack of discrimination as he is anti-Nazi and anti-German. It isn't that in one case he is reactionary and in the other democratic. He is simply Manichean for operative reasons: he sees the world as made up of good and evil forces in conflict.

Fleming seeks elementary oppositions; to personify primitive and universal forces, he has recourse to popular standards. In a time of international tensions, popular notions of 'wicked Communism' exist beside those of the unpunished Nazi criminal. Fleming uses them both in a sweeping, uncritical manner.

At the most, he tempers his choice with irony, but the irony is completely masked and is revealed only through incredible exaggeration. In *From Russia, With Love,* the Soviet men are so monstrous, so improbably evil that it seems impossible to take them seriously. And yet, in his brief preface, Fleming insists that all the narrated atrocities are absolutely true. He has chosen the path of fable, and fable must be taken as truthful if it is not to become a satirical fairy tale. The author seems almost to write his books for a two-fold reading public, those who take them as gospel truth and those who see their humor. In order to work as ambiguous texts, however, they must appear authentic, credible, ingenious, and plainly aggressive. A man who chooses to write in this way is neither a Fascist nor a racist; he is only a cynic, an expert in tale engineering.

If Fleming is a reactionary at all, it is not because he identifies the figure of 'evil' with a Russian or a Jew. He is reactionary because he makes use of stock figures. The very use of such figures (the Manichean dichotomy, seeing things in black and white) is always dogmatic and intolerant—in short, reactionary—whereas he who avoids set figures, who recognizes nuances and distinctions and who admits contradictions is democratic. Fleming is conservative as, basically, the fable—any fable —is conservative; his is the static, inherent, dogmatic conservatism of fairy tales and myths, which transmit an elementary wisdom, constructed and communicated by a simple play of light and shade, by indisputable archetypes which do not permit critical distinction. If Fleming is a 'Fascist', he is so because of his inability to pass from mythology to reason.

The very names of Fleming's protagonists suggest the mythological nature of the stories by fixing in an image or in a pun the character from the start, without any possibility of conversion or change. (One cannot be called Snow White and not be white as snow, in face and in spirit.) The wicked man lives by gambling? He will be called Le Chiffre. He is working for the Reds? He will be called Red—and Grant if he works for money, duly granted. A Korean professional killer by unusual means will be Oddjob. One obsessed with gold is Auric Goldfinger. A wicked man is called No. Perhaps the half-lacerated face of Hugo Drax will be conjured up by the incisive onomatopoeia of his name. Beautiful, transparent, telepathic Solitaire evokes the coldness of the diamond. Chic and interested in diamonds, Tiffany Case recalls the leading jewellers in New York and the beauty case of the mannequin. Ingenuity is suggested by the very name of Honeychile; sensual shamelessness, by that of Pussy Galore. A pawn in a dark game? Such is Domino. A tender Japanese lover, quintessence of the Orient? Such is Kissy Suzuki. (Would it be accidental that she recalls the name of the most popular exponent of Zen spirituality?) We pass over women of less interest such as Mary Goodnight or Miss Trueblood. And if the name Bond has been chosen, as Fleming affirms, almost by chance, to give the character an absolutely common appearance, then it would be by chance, but also by guidance, that this model of style and success evokes the luxuries of Bond Street or treasury bonds.

By now it is clear how the novels of Fleming have attained such a wide success: they build up a network of elementary associations to achieve something original and profound. Fleming also pleases the sophisticated readers who here distinguish, with a feeling of aesthetic pleasure, the purity of the primitive epic impudently and maliciously translated into current terms and who applaud in Fleming the cultured man, whom they recognize as one of themselves, naturally the most clever and broadminded.

Such praise Fleming might merit if he did not develop a second facet much more cunning: the game of stylistic oppositions, by virtue of which the sophisticated reader, detecting the fairy-tale mechanism, feels himself a malicious accomplice of the author, only to become a victim, for he is led on to detect stylistic inventions where there is, on the contrary—as will be shown—a clever montage of *déjà vu*.

6.4. Literary techniques

Fleming 'writes well', in the most banal but honest meaning of the term. He has a rhythm, a polish, a certain sensuous feeling for words. That is not to say that Fleming is an artist; yet he writes with art.

Translation may betray him. The beginning of the Italian version of *Goldfinger*—"James Bond stava seduto nella sala d'aspetto dell'aeroporto di Miami. Aveva già bevuto due bourbon doppi ed ora rifletteva sulla vita e sulla morte" (James Bond was seated in the departure lounge of Miami Airport. He had already drunk two double bourbons and was now thinking about life and death)—is not the same as "James Bond, with two double bourbons inside him, sat in the final departure lounge of Miami Airport and thought about life and death." In the English phrase there is only one sentence, an elegant display of *concinnitas*. There is nothing more to say. Fleming maintains this standard.

He tells stories that are violent and unlikely. But there are ways and ways of doing so. In *One Lonely Night* Mickey Spillane describes a massacre carried out by Mike Hammer:

> They heard my scream and the awful roar of the gun and the slugs stuttering and whining and it was the last they heard. They went down as they tried to run and felt their legs going out from under them. I saw the general's head jerk and shudder before he slid to the floor, rolling over and over. The guy from the subway tried to stop the bullets with his hand but just didn't seem able to make it and joined the general on the floor.

When Fleming describes the death of Le Chiffre in *Casino Royale,* we meet a technique that is undoubtedly more subtle:

> There was a sharp "phut," no louder than a bubble of air escaping from a tube of toothpaste. No other noise at all, and suddenly Le Chiffre had grown another eye, a third eye on a level with the other two, right where the thick nose started to jut out below the forehead. It was a small black eye, without eyelashes or eyebrows. For a second the three eyes looked out across the room and then the whole face seemed to slip and go down on one knee. The two outer eyes turned trembling up towards the ceiling.

There is more shame, more reticence, more respect than in the uneducated outburst of Spillane; but there is also a more baroque feeling for the image, a total adaptation of the image without emotional comment, and a use of words that designate things with accuracy. It is not that Fleming renounces explosions of Grand Guignol; he even excels in them and scatters them through his novels. But when he orchestrates the macabre on a wide screen, even here he reveals much more literary venom than Spillane possesses.

Consider the death of Mr. Big in *Live and Let Die.* Bond and Solitaire, tied by a long rope to the bandit's ship, have been dragged behind in order to be torn to pieces on the coral rocks in the bay. In the end the ship, shrewdly mined by Bond a few hours earlier, blows up, and the two victims, now safe, witness the miserable end of Mr. Big, shipwrecked and devoured by barracuda:

> It was a large head and a veil of blood streamed down over the face from a wound in the great bald skull. . . . Bond could see the teeth showing in a rictus of agony and frenzied endeavour. Blood half veiled the eyes that Bond knew would be bulging in their sockets. He could almost hear the great diseased heart thumping under the grey-black skin. . . . The Big Man came on. His shoulders were naked, his clothes stripped off him by the explosion, Bond supposed, but the black silk tie had remained and it showed round the thick neck and streamed behind the head like a Chinaman's pigtail. A splash of water cleared some blood away from the eyes. They were wide open, staring madly towards Bond. They held no

appeal for help, only a fixed glare of physical exertion. Even as Bond looked into them, now only ten yards away, they suddenly shut and the great face contorted in a grimace of pain. "Aaarh," said the distorted mouth. Both arms stopped flailing the water and the head went under and came up again. A cloud of blood welled up and darkened the sea. Two six-foot thin brown shadows backed out of the cloud and then dashed back into it. The body in the water jerked sideways. Half of the Big Man's left arm came out of the water. It had no hand, no wrist, no wrist-watch. But the great turnip head, the drawn-back mouth full of white teeth almost splitting it in half, was still alive. . . . The head floated back to the surface. The mouth was closed. The yellow eyes seemed still to look at Bond. Then the shark's snout came right out of the water and it drove in towards the head, the lower curved jaw open so that light glinted on the teeth. There was a horrible grunting scrunch and a great swirl of water. Then silence.

This parade of the terrifying has precedents in the eighteenth and nineteenth centuries: the final carnage, preceded by torture and painful imprisonment (preferably with a virgin), is pure Gothic. The passage quoted here is abridged; Mr. Big suffers even more agonies. In the same manner Lewis's Monk was dying for several days with his own lacerated body lying on a steep cliff. But the Gothic terrors of Fleming are described with a physical precision, a detailing by images, and for the most part by images of things. The absence of the watch on the wrist bitten off by the shark is not just an example of macabre sarcasm; it is an emphasis on the essential by the inessential, typical of the *école du regard.*

And here let us introduce a further opposition which affects not so much the structure of the plot as that of Fleming's style: the distinction between a narrative incorporating wicked and violent acts and a narrative that proceeds by trifling acts seen with disillusioned eyes.

What is surprising in Fleming is the minute and leisurely concentration with which he pursues for page after page descriptions of articles, landscapes, and events apparently inessential to the course of the story and, conversely, the feverish brevity with which he covers in a few paragraphs the most unexpected and improbable actions. A typical example is to be found in *Goldfinger,* with two long pages dedicated to a casual meditation on a Mexican murder, fifteen pages dedicated to a game of golf, and twenty-five pages occupied with a long car trip across France as against the four or five pages which cover the arrival at Fort Knox of a false hospital train and the *coup de théâtre* which culminates in the failure of Goldfinger's plan and in the death of Tilly Masterson.

In *Thunderball* a quarter of the volume is occupied by descriptions of the naturalist cures Bond undergoes in a clinic, though the events that occur there do not justify lingering over the details of diets, massage, and Turkish baths. The most disconcerting passage is perhaps that in which Domino Vitali, after having told Bond her life-story in the bar of the

Casino, monopolizes five pages to describe, with great detail, the box of Player's cigarettes. This is something quite different from the thirty pages employed in *Moonraker* to describe the preparations and the development of the bridge party with Sir Hugo Drax; here at least suspense is set up, in a definitely masterly manner, even for those who do not know the rules of bridge. The passage in *Thunderball,* on the contrary, is an interruption, and it does not seem necessary to characterize the dreaming spirit of Domino by depicting in such an abundance of nuances her tendency to a purposeless 'phenomenology'.

It is also 'purposeless' to introduce diamond smuggling in South Africa in *Diamonds Are Forever* by opening with the description of a scorpion, as though seen through a magnifying glass, enlarged to the size of some prehistoric monster, as the protagonist in a story of life and death at animal level, interrupted by the sudden appearance of a human being who crushes the scorpion. Then the action of the book begins, as though what has gone before represents only the titles, cleverly presented, of a film which then proceeds in a different manner.

And even more typical of this technique of the aimless glance is the beginning of *From Russia, With Love,* where we have a whole page of virtuosity exercised upon the body, death-like in its immobility, of a man lying by the side of a swimming pool being explored pore by pore, hair by hair, by a blue and green dragonfly. As soon as the author has infused the scene with a subtle sense of death, the man moves and frightens away the dragonfly. The man moves because he is alive and is about to be massaged. The fact that lying on the ground he seems dead has no relevance to the purpose of the narrative that follows.

Fleming abounds in such passages of high technical skill which makes us see what he is describing, with a relish for the inessential, and which the narrative mechanism of the plot not only does not require but actually rejects. When the story reaches its fundamental action (the basic "moves" enumerated in an earlier section), the technique of the aimless glance is decisively abandoned. The moments of descriptive reflection, particularly attractive because they are sustained by polished and effective language, seem to sustain the poles of Luxury and Planning, whereas those of rash action express the moments of Discomfort and of Chance.

Thus the opposition of the two techniques (or the technique of this opposition of styles) is not accidental. If Fleming's technique were to interrupt the suspense of a vital action, such as frogmen swimming towards a mortal challenge, to linger over descriptions of submarine fauna and coral formations, it would be like the ingenuous technique of Salgari, who is capable of abandoning his heroes when they stumble over a great root of Sequoia during their pursuit in order to describe the origins, properties, and distribution of the Sequoia on the North American continent.

In Fleming the digression, instead of resembling a passage from an encyclopaedia badly rendered, takes on a twofold shape: first, it is rarely a description of the unusual—such as occurs in Salgari and in Verne— but a description of the already known; second, it occurs not as encyclopaedic information but as literary suggestion, displayed in order to get a sort of literary promotion. Let us examine these two points, because they reveal the secret of Fleming's stylistic technique.

Fleming does not describe the Sequoia that the reader has never had a chance to see. He describes a game of canasta, an ordinary motor car, the control panel of an airplane, a railway carriage, the menu of a restaurant, the box of a brand of cigarettes available at any tobacconist's. Fleming describes in a few words an assault on Fort Knox because he knows that none of his readers will ever have occasion to rob Fort Knox; he expands in explaining the gusto with which a steering wheel or a golf club can be gripped because these are acts that each of us has accomplished, may accomplish, or would like to accomplish. Fleming takes time to convey the familiar with photographic accuracy because it is with the familiar that he can solicit our capacity for identification. We identify not with the one who steals an atom bomb but with the one who steers a luxurious motor launch; not with the one who explodes a rocket but with the one who accomplishes a lengthy ski descent; not with the one who smuggles diamonds but with the one who orders a dinner in a restaurant in Paris. Our credulity is solicited, blandished, directed to the region of possible and desirable things. Here the narration is realistic, the attention to detail intense; for the rest, so far as the unlikely is concerned, a few pages and an implicit wink of the eye suffice. No one has to believe them.

And, again, the pleasure of reading is given not by the incredible and the unknown but by the obvious and the usual. It is undeniable that Fleming, in exploiting the obvious, uses a verbal strategy of a rare kind, but this strategy makes us fond of redundancy, not of information. The language performs the same function as do the plots. The greatest pleasure arises not from excitement but from relief.

The minute descriptions constitute, not encyclopaedic information, but literary evocation. Indubitably, if an underwater swimmer swims towards his death and I glimpse above him a milky and calm sea and vague shapes of phosphorescent fish which skim by him, his act is inscribed within the framework of an ambiguous and eternal indifferent Nature which evokes a kind of profound and moral conflict. Usually Journalism, when a diver is devoured by a shark, says that, and it is enough. If someone embellishes this death with three pages of description of coral, is not that Literature?

This technique—sometimes identified as Midcult or as Kitsch—here finds one of its most efficacious manifestations—we might say the least irritating, as a result of the ease and skill with which its operation is conducted, if it were not that this artifice forces one to praise in the works of Fleming not the shrewd elaboration of the different stories but a literary phenomenon.

The play of Midcult in Fleming sometimes shows through (even if none the less efficacious). Bond enters Tiffany's cabin and shoots the two killers. He kills them, comforts the frightened girl, and gets ready to leave.

> At last, an age of sleep, with her dear body dovetailed against his and his arms around her forever.
>
> Forever?
>
> As he walked slowly across the cabin to the bathroom, Bond met the blank eyes of the body on the floor.
>
> And the eyes of the man whose blood-group had been F spoke to him and said, "Mister, nothing is forever. Only death is permanent. Nothing is forever except what you did to me."

The brief phrases, in frequent short lines like verse, the indication of the man through the leitmotiv of his blood-group, the biblical figure of speech of the eyes which 'talk'; the rapid solemn meditation on the fact— obvious enough—that the dead remain so. . . . The whole outfit of a 'universal' fake which Dwight MacDonald had already distinguished in the later Hemingway. And, notwithstanding this, Fleming would still be justified in evoking the spectre of the dead man in a manner so synthetically literary if the improvised meditation upon the eternal fulfilled the slightest function in the development of the plot. What will he do now, now that he has been caressed by a shudder for the irreversible, this James Bond? He does absolutely nothing. He steps over the corpse and goes to bed with Tiffany.

6.5.   Literature as collage

Hence Fleming composes elementary and violent plots, played against fabulous opposition, with a technique of novels 'for the masses'. Frequently he describes women and scenery, marine depths and motorcars with a literary technique of reportage, bordering closely upon Kitsch and sometimes failing badly. He blends his narrative elements with an unstable montage, alternating Grand Guignol and *nouveau roman,* with such broadmindedness in the choice of material as to be numbered, for good or for ill, if not among the inventors, at least among the cleverest exploiters of an experimental technique. It is very difficult when reading these novels, after their initial diverting impact has passed, to perceive to what extent Fleming simulates literature by pretending to write literature and to what extent he creates literary fireworks with cynical, mocking relish by montage.

Fleming is more literate than he gives one to understand. He begins chapter 19 of *Casino Royale* with "You are about to awake when you dream that you are dreaming." It is a familiar idea, but it is also a phrase of Novalis. The long meeting of diabolical Russians who are planning the damnation of Bond in the opening chapter of *From Russia, With Love* (and Bond enters the scene unaware, only in the second part) reminds one of *Faust*'s prologue in the Hell.

We might think that such influences, part of the reading of well-bred gentlemen, may have worked in the mind of the author without emerging into consciousness. Probably Fleming remained bound to a nineteenth-century world, of which his militaristic and nationalistic ideology, his racialist colonialism, and his Victorian isolationism are all hereditary traits. His love of traveling, by grand hotels and luxury trains, is completely of *la belle époque*. The very archetype of the train, of the journey on the Orient Express (where love and death await him), derives from Tolstoy by way of Dekobra to Cendrars. His women, as has been said, are Richardsonian Clarissas who correspond to the archetype brought to light by Fiedler (see *Love and Death in the American Novel*).

But what is more, there is the taste for the exotic, which is not contemporary, even if the islands of Dream are reached by jet. In *You Only Live Twice,* we have a garden of tortures which is very closely related to that of Mirbeau in which the plants are described in a detailed inventory that implies something like the *Traité des poisons* by Orfila, reached possibly by way of the meditation of Huysmans in *Là-bas*. But *You Only Live Twice,* in its exotic exaltation (three-quarters of the book is dedicated to an almost mystical initiation to the Orient), in its habit of quoting from ancient poets recalls also the morbid curiosity with which Judith Gauthier, in 1869, introduced the reader to the discovery of China in *Le dragon impérial*. And if the comparison appears farfetched—well, then, let us remember that Ko-Li-Tsin, Gauthier's revolutionary poet, escapes from the prisons of Peking by clinging to a kite and that Bond escapes from the infamous castle of Blofeld by clinging to a balloon (which carries him a long way over the sea, where, already unconscious, he is collected by the gentle hands of Kissy Suzuki). It is true that Bond hung on to the balloon remembering having seen Douglas Fairbanks do so, but Fleming is undoubtedly more cultured than his character is. It is not a matter of seeking out analogies and of suggesting that there is in the ambiguous and evil atmosphere of Piz Gloria an echo of Mann's magic mountain: sanatoria are in the mountains and in the mountains it is cold. It is not a question of seeing in Honeychile, who appears to Bond from the foam of the sea, Anadiomene, the bird-like girl of Joyce: two bare legs bathed by the waves are the same everywhere. But sometimes the analogies do not only concern the psychological atmosphere. They are structural analogies. Thus it happens that "Quantum of Solace," one of the stories in *For Your Eyes Only,* presents Bond sitting upon a chintz sofa of the governor of the Bahamas and listening to the governor tell, after a lengthy and rambling preamble, in an atmosphere of rarefied discomfort, the long and apparently inconsistent story of an adulterous woman and a vindictive husband, a story without blood and without dramatic action, a story of personal and private actions, after the telling of which Bond feels himself strangely upset and inclined to see his own dangerous activities as infinitely less romantic and intense than the events of certain private and commonplace lives. Now, the structure of this tale, the technique of description and the introduction of characters, the disproportion between the preamble and the story, the inconsistency of the story, and the effect it produces—all recall strangely the habitual course of many stories by Barbey d'Aurevilly. And we may also recall that the idea of a human body covered with gold appears in Dmitri Merezkowskij (except that in this case the culprit is not Goldfinger but Leonardo da Vinci).

It may be that Fleming had not pursued such varied and sophisticated reading, and in that case one must only assume that, bound by education and psychological make-up to the world of today, he copied solutions without being aware of them, reinventing devices that he had smelled in the air. But the most likely theory is that, with the same effective cynicism with which he constructed his plots according to archetypal oppositions, he decided that the paths of invention, for the readers of our century, can return to those of the great nineteenth-century *feuilleton,* that as against the homely normality—I do not say of Hercule Poirot but, rather, of Sam Spade and Michael Shayne, priests of an urbane and foreseeable violence—he revised the fantasy and the technique that had made Rocambole and Rouletabille, Fantomas and Fu Manchu famous. Perhaps he has gone further, to the cultured roots of truculent romanticism, and thence to their more morbid affiliations. An anthology of characters and situations treated in his novels would appear like a chapter of Mario Praz' *The Romantic Agony.*

To begin with his evil characters, the red gleams of the looks and the pallid lips recall the archetype of the baroque Giovan Battista Marino's Satan, from whom sprang up (through Milton) the romantic generation of *les ténébreux:*

> In his eyes were sadness lodged and death
> Light flashed turbid and vermillion.
> The oblique looks and twisted glares
> Were like comets, and like a lamp his lashes
> And from the nostrils and pallid lips. . . .

Only that in Fleming an unconscious dissociation is performed, and the characteristics of the fine dark one, fascinating and cruel, sensual and ruthless, are subdivided between the Villain and Bond.

Between these two characters are distributed the traits of the Schedoni of Ann Radcliffe and of Ambrosio of Lewis, of the Corsair and of the Giaour of Byron; to love and suffer is the fate that pursues Bond as it did René of Chateaubriand: "everything in him turned fatal, even happiness itself. . . ." But it is the Villain that, like René, is "cast into the world like a great disaster, his pernicious influence extended to the beings that surrounded him."

The Villain, who combines the charm of a great controller of men with great wickedness, is the Vampire, and Blofeld has almost all the characteristics of the Vampire of Merimée ("Who could escape the charm of his glance? . . . His mouth is bleeding and smiles like that of a man drugged and tormented by odious love"). The philosophy of Blofeld, especially as preached in the poisoned garden of *You Only Live Twice,* is that of the Divine Marquis in his pure state, perhaps transferred into English by Maturin in *Melmoth.* And the exposition of the pleasure that Red Grant derives from murder is a minor treatise on sadism—except that both Red Grant and Blofeld (at least when in the last book he commits evil not for profit but from pure cruelty) are presented as pathological cases. This is natural enough: the times demand compliance; Freud and Kraft-Ebbing have not lived in vain.

It is pointless to linger over the taste for torture except to recall the pages of the *Journaux Intimes* in which Baudelaire comments on their erotic potentiality; it is pointless perhaps to compare finally the model of Goldfinger, Blofeld, Mr. Big, or Dr. No with that of various *Übermensch* produced by the *feuilleton* literature. But it cannot be denied that of all such even Bond 'wears' several characteristics, and it will be opportune to compare the various descriptions of the hero—the ruthless smile, the cruel, handsome face, the scar on his cheek, the lock of hair that falls rebelliously over his brow, the taste for display—with this description of a Byronic hero concocted by Paul Féval in *Les mystères de Londres:*

> He was a man of some thirty years at least in appearance, tall in stature, elegant and aristocratic. . . . As to his face, he offered a notable type of good looks: his brow was high, wide without lines, but crossed from top to bottom by a light scar that was almost imperceptible. . . . It was not possible to see his eyes; but, under his lowered eyelids, their power could be divined. . . . Girls saw him in dreams with thoughtful eye, brow ravaged, the nose of an eagle, and a smile that was devilish, but divine. . . . He was a man entirely sensual, capable at the same time of good and of evil; generous by nature, frankly enthusiastic by nature, but selfish on occasion;

cold by design, capable of selling the universe for a quarter of gold at his pleasure. . . . All Europe has admired his oriental magnificence; the universe, after all, knew that he spent four million every season. . . .

The parallel is disturbing, but does not need philological verification: the prototype is scattered in hundreds of pages of a literature at first and second hand, and, after all, a whole vein of British decadence could offer Fleming the glorification of the fallen angel, of the monstrous torturer, of the *vice anglais*. Wilde, accessible to any educated gentleman, was ready to suggest the head of John the Baptist, upon a plate, as a model for the great grey head of Mr. Big floating on the water. As for Solitaire, who withheld herself from him though exciting him, it is Fleming himself who uses, as the title of a chapter, the name of "allumeuse": her prototype reappears time and again in d'Aurevilly, in the princess d'Este of Péladan, in the Clara of Mirbeau, and in the Madone des Sleepings of Dekobra.

On the other hand, Fleming cannot accept for woman the decadent archetype of *la belle dame sans merci,* which agrees little with the modern idea of femininity, and he mixes it up with the model of the persecuted virgin. And it seems that he has taken into account the suggestions given one hundred years ago by Louis Reybaud to the future writers of a good *feuilleton:* "Take, sir, a young woman, unhappy and persecuted; add to it a brutal tyrant. . . ." But Fleming probably did not need those recipes; he had enough wit to discover it by himself.

However, we are not here concerned with a psychological interpretation of Fleming as individual but with an analysis of the structure of his text, the relationship between the literary inheritance and the crude chronicle, between nineteenth-century tradition and science fiction, between adventurous excitement and hypnosis, fused together to produce an unstable patchwork, a tongue-in-cheek *bricolage,* which often hides its ready-made nature by presenting itself as literary invention. To the extent to which it permits a disenchanted reading, the work of Fleming represents a successful means of leisure, the result of skillful craftsmanship. To the extent that it provides to anyone the thrill of poetic emotion, it is the last *avatar* of Kitsch; to the extent that it provokes elementary psychological reactions in which ironic detachment is absent, it is only a more subtle, but not less mystifying, example of soap opera.

Since the decoding of a message cannot be established by its author, but depends on the concrete circumstances of reception, it is difficult to guess what Fleming is or will be for his readers. When an act of communication provokes a response in public opinion, the definitive verification will take place not within the ambit of the book but in that of the society that reads it.

Part Three   Open/Closed

CHAPTER SEVEN

Peirce and the Semiotic Foundations of Openness: Signs as Texts and Texts as Signs

7.1. The analysis of meaning

An intensional semantics is concerned with the analysis of the content of a given expression. This kind of study has assumed in the last two decades two forms, complementary and/or alternative to each other: the *interpretative* analysis with the format of a compositional spectrum of markers and the *generative* analysis in form of predicates and arguments. While the former approach seems to be exclusively concerned with the meaning of elementary lexical entries, the latter seems to fit the needs of a *textual analysis* which considers both the semantic and the pragmatic aspect of discourses.

I think, however, that such a clear-cut opposition should not be established. As it is proposed in Chapter 8 of this book, *a sememe is in itself an inchoative text, whereas a text is an expanded sememe.* The author who has more clearly advocated such an assumption (implicitly as well as explicitly) is Charles Sanders Peirce. Some elements of Peirce's thought can be reexamined in the light of such theoretical perspectives: Peirce's theory of interpretant cannot but lead to a form of meaning analysis which fits both the requirements of an interpretative and a generative

A shorter version of this chapter was presented at the Christian Gauss Seminars, Princeton University, November 1976. The main lines of the research were previously advanced in papers presented at the Charles Sanders Peirce Symposium, Johns Hopkins University, Baltimore, 1975 ("Peirce's Notion of Interpretant," *MLN* 91, no. 6), and the C. S. Peirce Bicentennial International Congress, Amsterdam, 1976. This chapter reproduces, with minor revisions and additions, "Peirce and Contemporary Semantics," *VS* 15 (1976).

semantics and only from Peirce's point of view can many problems of contemporary text theories be satisfactorily solved.

According to the principles of compositional analysis, a semiotic expression (be it a verbal item or any type of physical utterance) conveys, according to linguistic conventions, an organized and analyzable content, formed by the aggregation (or hierarchy) of semantic features. These features constitute a system, either closed or open, and belong to different contents of different expressions in different arrangements. Compositional analysis should describe and define a virtually infinite number of contents by means of a possibly finite ensemble of features, but this exigency of economy gives rise to many aporias.

If the features constitute a finite set of metasemiotic constructions, then their mode of describing a virtually infinite amount of contents sounds rather disappointing. By such features as 'human', 'animate', 'masculine', or 'adult' (see Chomsky), one can distinguish a bishop from a hippopotamus, but not a hippopotamus from a rhinoceros. If, on the contrary, one elaborates more analytical metasemiotic features such as 'not-married' or 'seal' (as it happens in the interpretative perspective of Katz and Fodor), one is obliged to foresee an incredible number of other features such as 'lion', 'bishop', or 'with two eyes', therefore losing universality and running the risk that the set of metasemiotic features contains as many items as the language to be analyzed.

Moreover, it is hard to establish which kind of hierarchy these features should be accorded to. A simple relation of embedding from genus to species can help only to a certain extent. It is, for example, obviously important to know that a schooner is a sailing ship, that a sailing ship is a vessel, a vessel a boat, and a boat a vehicle (marine), but this kind of classification does not distinguish a schooner from a brigantine, since it disregards other features such as the form of the sails and the number of the masts. Provided this requirement is satisfied, it remains to be known what purposes a brigantine or a schooner serves.

As a further criticism we can add that a compositional analysis in terms of universal features does not say satisfactorily in which linguistic environments the item can be inserted without producing ambiguity. There are rules of subcategorization, establishing the immediate syntactic compatibility of a given item, and there are selectional rules establishing some immediate semantic compatibility, but these instructions do not go beyond the normal format of a dictionary. Some scholars have proposed a semantic representation with the format of an *encyclopedia*, and this solution seems to be the only one capable of conveying the whole information entailed by a given term; but the encyclopedic representation excludes the possibility of establishing a finite set of metasemiotic features and makes the analysis potentially infinite.

7.1.2.   Other approaches have tried to overcome these difficulties by representing the items of a lexicon as predicates with n arguments. Bierwisch, for instance, represents *father* as "X parent of Y + Male X + (Animate Y + Adult X + Animate Y)" and *kill* as "X_s cause (X_d change to ($-$ Alive X_d) + Animate X_d)." This kind of representation not only takes into account the immediate semantic markers (in form of a dictionary), but also characterizes the item through the relations it can have, within the framework of a proposition, with other items. In this perspective single semantic items are viewed as already inserted in a possible co-text.

Generative semantics has improved the use of predicate calculus, but shifting from the representation of single terms to the logical structure of the propositions (McCawley, Lakoff, and others). Only Fillmore has tried, with his case grammar, to unify both interpretive-compositional and generative perspective. Fillmore remarks that the verbs *ascend* and *lift* are both motion verbs and are both used to describe a motion upward, but *lift* requires conceptually two objects (the one moving upward, the other causing the motion), whereas *ascend* is a one-argument predicate. This remark leads one to recognize that arguments, in natural languages, can be identified with *roles* (similar to the *actants* in Greimas' structural semantics); for any predicate there is an Agent, a Counteragent, an Object, a Result, an Instrument, a Source, a Goal, an Experiencer, and so on. This kind of analysis solves very well the problem of the classification of features, following a sort of logic of action. Moreover, it satisfies the encyclopedic requirement and transforms a purely classificatory representation into an operational schema: the composition of the meaning of a predicate tells us how to act in order to give rise to the denoted action or in order to isolate it within a context. *To walk,* for instance, should mean that there is a human agent, using ground as a counteragent, moving his body in order to displace it (as a result) from a spacial source to a spacial goal, by using legs as instrument, and so on.

However, some objections can be raised. (i) Whereas the roles can be recognized as a set of innate universals expressed by a fixed inventory of linguistic expressions, the linguistic features which fill in these roles are again potentially infinite (how many kinds of instrument can be foreseen?). (ii) The proposal of such a 'case grammar' seems to work apropos of predicates, but requires some additions as far as the representation of arguments is concerned. Using a knife as instrument, I can kill someone, but what about the semantic representation of *knife*? It seems that, more than a predicate argument structure, it could be useful in this case to employ such categories as *who produces* it, *with what material,* according to *what formal rule* and for *what purpose.* This kind of representation recalls the four Aristotelian causes (Efficient, Formal, Material, and Final); but the representation of an 'object' could also be transformed into the representation of the action required to produce this object (therefore: not *knife* but *to make a knife*). (iii) A complete semantic theory should also take into account syncategorematic terms such as preposition and adverb (*for, to, below, while,* and so on). According to the research of many scholars (Leech, Apresjan, and others), it seems that this is possible, but we are far from recognizing that those researches are to be considered both satisfactory and definitive (for all these problems see Eco, 1976). I think that an exploration into Peirce's theory of interpretant can strongly help to improve all these approaches.

7.1.3.   There is, in any case, a sort of gap between contemporary compositional analysis and Peirce's semiotic account of interpretants. Contemporary analyses are concerned mainly with a semantics of verbal languages, whereas Peirce was dealing with a general semiotics concerning all types of sign. I have elsewhere demonstrated that Peirce offers the theoretical opportunity of extending the problem of compositional analysis to every semiotic phenomenon (Eco, 1976), including images and gestures.

Nevertheless, in order to maintain a certain parallelism between the two poles of our inquiry, I shall limit the subject of sections 7.2 and 7.3 to Peircean proposals and examples concerning *verbal* language, even though this methodological decision obliges me to underestimate the important relationship between symbols, icons, and indices. Someone could object that this limitation is imposed by the very nature of my subject matter: Peirce has said that only symbols (not icons and indices) are interpretable. "Pragmaticism fails to furnish any translation of meaning of a proper name or other designation of an individual object" (5.429); qualities have "no perfect identities, but only likenesses, or partial identities" (1.418). Only symbols seem to be instances of genuine Thirdness (since they can be interpreted), whereas icons are qualitatively degenerate and indices are reactionally degenerate, both depending on something else without any mediation (the icon from a quality, the index from an object) (2.92 and 5.73). Moreover, "it is not all signs that have logical interpretants, but only intellectual concepts and the like" (5.482).

I think, however, that the context of Peirce's thought happily contradicts these statements.[1] It is difficult to assume, as Peirce does in 1.422 and 1.447, that qualities are always general without asserting that they can and should be in some way defined and interpreted. And as far as icons are concerned, it should be remembered that the possibility of making deductions by observing those icons which are called diagrams depends on the fact that diagrams can be interpreted and do arouse interpretants in the mind of their interpreters.[2]

7.1.4.   A sign-function correlates a given expression to a given content. This content has been defined by a given culture irrespective of whether a given state of the world corresponds to it. 'Unicorn' is a sign as well as is 'dog'. The act of mentioning, or of referring to, them is made possible by some indexical devices, and 'dog' can be referred to an individually existent object, whereas 'unicorn' cannot. The same happens with the image of a dog and the image of a unicorn. Those which Peirce called iconic signs are also expressions related to a content; if they possess the properties of (or are similar to) something, this something is not the object or the state of the world that could be referred to, but rather a structured and analytically organized content. The image of a unicorn is not similar to a 'real' unicorn; neither is recognized because of our experience of 'real' unicorns, but has the same features displayed by the definition of a unicorn elaborated by a given culture within a specific content system. The same can be demonstrated apropos of indexical devices (see Eco, 1976).

The self-sufficiency of the universe of content, provided by a given culture, explains why signs can be used in order to lie. We have a sign-function when something can be used in order to lie (and therefore to elaborate ideologies, works of art, and so on). What Peirce calls signs (which to somebody stand for something else in some respect or capacity) are such just because I can use a representamen in order to send back to a fictitious state of the world. Even an index can be falsified in order to signify an event which is not detectable and, in fact, has never caused its supposed representamen. Signs can be used in order to lie, for they send back to objects or states of the world only *vicariously.* In fact, they send immediately back to a certain content. I am thus asserting that the relationship between *signifiant* and *signifié* (or between *sign-vehicle* and *significatum,* or between *sign* and *meaning*) is autonomous in itself and does not require the presence of the referred object as an element of its definition. Therefore it is possible to elaborate a theory of signification on the grounds of a purely intensional semantics. I am not saying that an extensional semantics is devoid of any function; on the contrary, it controls the correspondence between a sign-function and a given state of the world, when signs are used in order to mention something. But I am stressing the fact that an extensional semantics can be elaborated (and that processes of reference or mention can be established) only because an intensional semantics is possible as a self-sufficient cultural construct (that is, a code or a system of codes).

Can we say that the texts of Peirce entitle us to accept this perspective? Obviously, in the Peircean framework, when signs are applied to concrete experiences or *haecceitates,* they are related to the indicated objects.

But it is not by chance that in 1.540 Peirce established a difference between sign and representamen; when he says that he uses the words 'sign' and 'representamen' differently, he means that the sign is the concrete, *token* element (the utterance) used in the concrete process of communication and reference, whereas the representamen is the *type* to which a coding convention assigns a certain content by means of certain interpretants. "By sign I mean anything that conveys any definite notion of an object in any way, as such conveyers of thought are familiarly known to us. Now I start with this familiar idea and make the best analysis I can of what is essential to a sign, and I define a *representamen* as being whatever that analysis applies to. . . . In particular all signs convey notions to *human minds;* but I know no reason why every representamen should do so." I read this passage as the proposal of a difference between a theory of signification and a theory of communication. Representamens are type-expressions conventionally correlated to a type-content by a given culture, irrespective of the fact that they can be used in order to communicate effectively something to somebody.

Peirce continually oscillates between these points of view, but never makes their difference explicit. Therefore when dealing with interpretants the object remains as an abstract hypothesis which gives a sort of pragmatic legitimacy to the fact that we are using signs; and when on the contrary dealing with objects, the interpretant acts in the background as an unnoticed but highly effective mediation which permits us to understand signs and to apply them to such and such concrete experience.

7.2. Interpretant, ground, meaning, object

7.2.1. Let me examine some basic definitions of interpretant. In 1.339 the definition looks rather mentalistic: "A sign stands *for* something *to* the idea which it produces, or modifies. . . . That for which it stands is called its *object,* that which it conveys, its *meaning;* and the idea to which it gives rise, its *interpretant.*" But in 2.228 (probably some years later, according to Hartshorne and Weiss, who, without identifying the date of the first fragment, list it among the texts of 1895 and give the second one as written in 1897) Peirce specifies: "A sign, or representamen, is something which stands to somebody for something in some respect or capacity. It addresses somebody, that is, it creates in the mind of that person an equivalent sign, or perhaps a more developed sign. That sign which it creates I call the *interpretant* of the first sign. The sign stands for something, its *object.* It stands for that object, not in all respects, but in reference to a sort of idea, which I have sometimes called the *ground* of the representation." As everybody realizes, in the second fragment the interpretant is no longer an idea but another sign. If there is an idea, it is the idea of that second sign, which should have its own representamen independently of that idea. Moreover, the idea here intervenes in order to reduce the *haecceitates* of the given object: this object is only such insofar as it is thought under a certain profile. It is thought of as an abstraction and a model of a possible biased experience.

It is absurd to maintain that Peirce intended by object a given concrete thing. This would be possible, at most, when considering the expression 'that dog' (and in this case only the object is a *hecceity,* 5.434). But according to Peirce even 'to go', 'up', and 'whenever' are representamens. Obviously, for a realist such as Peirce, even these expressions are referred to concrete experiences; and also from the point of view of a theory of signification oppositions such as 'up' vs. 'down' or 'to go' vs. 'to come' are established as elements of the content insofar as they reflect and legitimize our concrete experience of space and time relations. But according to Peirce 'to go' is an expression that has no identity other than the agreement between its several manifestations; therefore its object is only the natural existence of a law, and an idea is a thing even though it has not the mode of existence of a hecceity (3.460). As for an expression such as 'Hamlet was insane', Peirce says that its object is only an imaginary world (therefore the object is determined by the sign), whereas a command such as 'Ground arms!' has as its proper object either the subsequent action of the soldiers or "the Universe of things desired by the Commanding Captain at that moment" (5.178). The fact that in this passage Peirce mixes up the response of the soldiers and the intention of the captain by defining both as objects shows that there is something ambiguous in his definition of object. In fact, the first case represents an *interpretation* of the sign, as we shall see later. But in either case it is clear that the object is not necessarily a thing or a state of the world but a rule, a law, a prescription: it appears as the operational description of a set of possible experiences.

As a matter of fact, Peirce speaks of two kinds of objects (4.536, in 1906). There is a *dynamic* object, which "by some means contrives to determine the sign to its representation," and there is an *immediate* object, which is "the object as the sign itself represents it, and whose Being is thus dependent upon the Representation of it in the Sign."

7.2.2. To understand the relationship between representamen (or sign), object, meaning, and interpretant, we should examine the concept of ground. In 2.418 the object is more accurately defined as a correlate of the sign (the sign 'man' can be correlated to the sign 'homme' as its object), and the third element of the correlation, along with the interpretant, is not the meaning, but the ground. A sign refers to a ground "through its object, or the common characters of those objects." The interpretant is very significantly defined as "all the facts known about its object."

In 1.551 (1867) there is a clue capable of explaining why the term 'ground' may have been sometimes substituted with meaning, and vice versa. The proposition 'this stove is black' assigns to the word stove a 'general attribute'. This kind of attribute is elsewhere called a 'quality', and as such it should be a mere Firstness. But a quality, even though being in itself a pure monad, is something general when we are 'reflecting upon' it (4.226). In a Scotist line of thought, it is an individual—a monad—insofar as it is a quality of the thing, but it is universal—an abstraction—insofar as it is caught by the intellect. A quality is a 'general idea' and an 'imputed character' (1.559); it is an *intelligibile*.[3] Being a 'general attribute' (1.551), it is, among the possible general attributes of the object, the one which has been selected in order to focus the object *in some respects*. This expression is explicitly formulated later (for instance, in 2.228, thirty years later), but it is implicit in 1867 (1.553) when it is said that the interpretant represents the relate 'as standing for' the correlate. The ground is an attribute of the object as far as it (the object) has been *selected* in a certain way and only some of its attributes have been made *pertinent,* thus constituting the Immediate Object of the sign. The ground being only one among the possible predicates of the object (the stove could also be perceived and described as hot, big, dirty, and so on), it is a 'common character' and a 'connotation' (1.559; here connotation being opposed to denotation as meaning is opposed to denotatum). We shall see later that the meaning seems to be something more complex than *one* imputed character or attribute; it is 'a sort of skeleton diagram', an 'outline sketch' of the object considering "what modifications the hypothetical state of things would require to be made in that picture" (2.227). In can therefore be suggested at this point that the ground is only a *meaning component;* in fact, symbols which determine their *grounds* of imputed qualities, that is, terms, are 'sums of marks' (1.559). The purport of such a statement will be more clear in section 7.2.5. For the moment it is sufficient to recognize that both ground and meaning are of the nature of an idea: signs stand for their objects, "not in all respects, but in reference to a sort of idea, which we have sometimes called the *ground* of the representamen," and 'idea' is not meant in a Platonic sense, but rather "in that sense in which we say that one man catches another man's idea" (2.228). The ground is what can be comprehended and transmitted of a given object under a certain profile: it is the content of an expression and appears to be identical with meaning (or a basic component of it).

7.2.3. It remains for us to ascertain in which sense a ground (as a meaning) differs from an interpretant. In 1.338 (as well as in other passages) the interpretant is the idea to which the sign gives rise in the mind of the interpreter (even if the real presence of an interpreter is not required). For this reason the problem of interpretants is studied, more than in the framework of Speculative Grammar, in that of Speculative Rhetoric, which deals with the relationship between signs and interpreters. But we have seen that a ground is an idea in the sense in which an idea is caught during the communicative intercourse between two interpreters. Therefore it should be said that there is no profound difference between the meaning (as a sum of grounds) and the interpretant, a meaning being capable of being described only by means of interpretants. The interpretant is a way to represent, by means of another sign (*man* equals *homme*), what the representamen in fact *selects* of a given object (its ground).

The difficulty disappears, in any case, if one considers that the notion of ground serves to distinguish the Dynamic Object (the object in itself such as it "by some means contrives to determine the sign to its representation," 4.536) from the Immediate Object, whereas the interpretant serves to establish the relationship between representamen and Immediate Object. The Immediate Object is the way in which the Dynamic Object is focused, this 'way' being nothing else but the ground or meaning. In fact the Immediate Object is "the object as the sign itself represents it and whose Being is thus dependent upon the Representation of it in the sign" (4.536). The Dynamic Object motivates the sign, but the sign through the ground institutes the Immediate Object, which is 'internal' (8.534), an 'Idea' (8.183), a 'mental representation' (5.473). Obviously, in order to describe the Immediate Object of a sign, one cannot but make recourse to the interpretants of that sign.

In this sense the meaning (object of the Speculative Grammar) "is, in its primary acceptation, the translation of a sign into another system of signs" (4.127), and "the meaning of a sign is the sign it has to be trans-

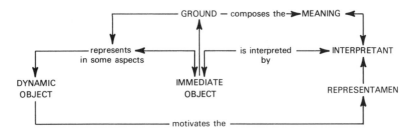

Figure 7.1

lated into" (4.132). So the interpretation by interpretants is the way in which the ground (as immediate object) is manifested as meaning. The interpretant (as object of Speculative Rhetoric) is without doubt "that which the Sign produces in the Quasi-mind that is the Interpreter" (4.536), but, since the presence of the interpreter is not essential to the definition of the interpretant, this latter is "in the first place" to be considered as Immediate Interpretant, that is, "the interpretant as it is revealed in the right understanding of the Sign itself, and is ordinarily called the *meaning* of the sign" (4.536).

Therefore, being distinguished as formal objects of different semiotic approaches and in reference to different points of view, ground, meaning, and interpretant are in fact the same, since it is impossible to define the ground if not as meaning, and it is impossible to define any meaning if not as a series of interpretants. Many passages confirm this opinion: "by the *meaning* of a term . . . we understand the entire general intended interpretant" (5.179); "it seems natural to use the word *meaning* to denote the intended interpretant of a symbol" (5.175); "the complete Immediate Object, or meaning" (2.293).

7.2.4. Nevertheless, we know that the interpretant is, not only the meaning of a term, but also the conclusion of an argument drawn from the premises (1.559). Has the interpretant a broader and more complex sense than meaning? In 4.127, when saying that—in its primary acceptation—the meaning is the translation of a sign into another sign, Peirce says that, in another acceptation "here applicable" (Peirce is dealing with problems of logic of quantity), meaning "is a second assertion from which all that follows from the first assertion equally follows, and *vice versa*. This is as much as to say that the one assertion 'means' the other." The meaning of a proposition, as well as its interpretant, does not exhaust its possibilities of being developed into other assertions and in this sense is "a law, or regularity of indefinite future" (2.293). The meaning of a proposition embraces "every obvious necessary deduction" (5.165).

So the meaning is in some way entailed by the premise, and, in more general terms, meaning is everything that is semantically *implied* by a sign. One could thus say that, according to Peirce, the meaning of a sign *inchoatively* contains all the texts within which that sign can be inserted. A sign is a textual matrix.

7.2.5. At this point, however, the notion of meaning seems to be rather broad. Instead of being applied to single terms, it is applied to premises and arguments. Is there, beyond the meaning of a *dicisign* and of an *argument,* something such as the particular meaning of a *rheme?* The answer to this question depends on the principle that everything which can be said of a dicent and of an argument can be said of the rhemes that constitute them. In other words, the theory of interpretants (and of meaning) concerns, not only arguments, but also single terms, and, in the light of such a theory, the content of a single term becomes something similar to an encyclopedia.

Given the item *sinner,* the fact that it can be interpreted as 'miserable' should be taken into account by the compositional representation of it. Therefore the rheme *sinner* should imply or entail all the possible illative consequences regarding it. The argument "all sinners are miserable, John is a sinner, therefore he is miserable" is nothing else but the natural and necessary development of the inchoative possibilities of the rheme and the only way to make evident its interpretants. Obviously, also the opposite is true, that is, any argument is nothing else than the analytical assertion of the interpretants to be assigned to a given item (from arguments dicisigns and rhemes can be derived) (3.440). In 2.293 it is said that a symbol *denotes* an individual and *signifies* a character, this character being a general meaning (it should be remembered that the ground of a sign is its connotation and its 'imputed character', 1.559). The distinction between denoting and signifying depends on the distinction between extension and intension, *breadth* and *depth,* or—in contemporary terms—denotation and meaning, or *referring to* and *meaning somewhat.* The concept of depth is linked with the one of information which is the 'measure of predication' and "the sum of synthetical propositions in which the symbol is subject or predicate" (2.418). All these concepts concern, not only propositions and arguments, but also rhemes or terms.

"A *Rheme* is a Sign which, for its Interpretant, is a sign of a qualitative Possibility" (it isolates a ground), "that is, is understood as representing such and such kind of possible Object. Any Rheme, perhaps, will afford some information; but it is not interpreted as doing so" (2.250). In other texts Peirce seems to be less insecure. Not only "the signification of a term is all the qualities which are indicated by it" (2.431), but terms appear as a set of marks (or features, or relations, or characters; see 2.776) ruled, as well as are propositions, by the principle of *nota notae est nota rei ipsius* (3.166). "The marks already known to be predicable of the term include the entire depth of another term not previously known to be so included, thus increasing the *comprehensive distinctness* of the former term" (2.364). A term can have both necessary and accidental marks, the necessary being either strict or proper (2.396), and these marks constitute the *substantial depth* of a term, that is, "the real concrete form which belongs to everything of which a term is predicable with absolute truth" (*substantial breadth* being "the aggregate of real substances of which alone a term is predicable with absolute truth")

(2.414). In this sense the depth of a term, or its intension, is the sum of intensional or semantic marks that characterizes its content. Those marks are general units (*nominantur singularia sed universalia significantur,* 2.433, from John of Salisbury's *Metalogicon*). Therefore they are those *imputed characters* called 'ground'.

This set of features (or marks) is destined to grow along with the growing of our knowledge of the objects; the rheme attracts, so to speak, as a lodestone, all the new marks that the process of knowledge attributes to it: "every symbol is a living thing, in a very strict sense that is no mere figure of speech. The body of the symbol changes slowly, but its meaning inevitably grows, incorporates new elements and throws off old ones" (2.222). All this seems to suggest that the term is in itself an encyclopedia containing every character it can acquire in every new general proposition. But all this is something more than a mere suggestion.

Peirce clearly stresses many times the fact that any term is in itself an inchoative proposition (any rheme is potentially the dicent in which it can be subsequently inserted), and it is so in a way which recalls the contemporary semantic concept of a term as a predicate with n arguments. The meaning of logical terms is a *rudimentary assertion* (2.342) in the same way in which a proposition is a rudimentary argumentation (2.344): this is the basic principle of interpretation, that is, the reason why every sign produces its own interpretants. A term is a rudimentary proposition because it is *the blank form of a proposition:* "by *rheme,* or *predicate*, will here be meant a blank form of proposition which might have resulted by striking out certain parts of a proposition, and leaving a *blank* in the place of each, the part stricken out being such that if each blank were filled with a proper name, a proposition (however nonsensical) would thereby be recomposed" (4.560). In 2.379, even though speaking of the forms of propositions, Peirce shows that, given the verb *to marry*, it can be semantically represented as '—marries—to—', which is the same as saying that, in order to represent generatively the syntactic nature of *to marry,* one should write '$m(x,y,z)$' (see also 3.64). This procedure, duly developed, implies that the semantic representation of a term concerns phenomena of entailment and of semantic "presupposition." In terms which recall Carnap's *meaning postulates,* Peirce says that $h_i \longrightarrow\!\!\!\!\!< d_i$ "means that on the occasion i, if the idea h is definitively forced upon the mind, then on the same occasion the idea d is definitively forced upon the mind" (2.356). This is the principle of *nota notae* of traditional logic, but in the same pages Peirce insists on the possibility of an intensional logic to be opposed to the ordinary logic of general classes of things. He separates the problem of *propositions in extension* from that of *propositions in comprehension*, therefore elaborating twelve types of propositions in which the subject is a class of things but the predicate is a group of marks (2.520,521). One could object that the method of *blanks* is applicable only to verbs or predicates concerning actions, according to Peirce's logic of relatives. In fact, in Aristotle the word 'rhema' means only 'verb'. However, Peirce identifies many times rheme with *term:* "any symbol which can be a direct constituent of a proposition is called term" (2.238). There are also syncategorematic terms, whereas "any term fit to be subject of a proposition may be termed *onoma"* (2.331). In any case, a common noun is a 'rhematic symbol' (2.261). In 8.337 we are told that class names and proper names are also rhemes. The choice of the term 'rhema' could be due to the fact that Peirce maintained that even nouns are reified verbs (3.440 and 8.337). To settle definitely the question, "a rheme is any sign that is not true nor false, like almost any single word except 'yes' and 'not' " (8.337).

In many instances Peirce makes recourse to the *blank* form when dealing with adjectives and nouns; in 1.363 the method is applied to *lover* and *servant*, and in 4.438 there is the following example of rheme: 'every man is the son of—', which constitutes a perfect example of semantic representation of the item 'father' viewed from the standpoint of a logic of relatives. The affinity of such a perspective with the one of a case grammar based on a logic of action will become more clear in section 7.3.1. It is obvious that, from such a point of view, "proper nouns stand, but the demarcation of common nouns from verbs becomes indefensible," and "meaning of nouns in his logic of relatives, like that of verbs, lies in possible action" (Feibleman, 1946: 106–107, with reference to the passage which will be examined in the following section).

7.2.6. The best examples of how a term can be resolved into a network of marks (this network constituting its meaning) are given in 1.615 and 2.330, with the definition of the words 'hard' and 'lithium'. In 1.615 we we are told that "so long as the stone remains hard, every essay to scratch it by the moderate pressure of a knife will surely fail. To call the stone hard is to predict that no matter how often you try the experiment, it will fail every time." In 2.330 it is said that "if you look into a textbook of chemistry for a definition of *lithium* you may be told that it is that element whose atomic weight is 7 very nearly. But if the author has a more logical mind he will tell you that if you search among minerals that are vitreous, translucent, grey or white, very hard, brittle, and insoluble, for one which imparts a crimson tinge to an unluminous flame, this mineral being triturated with lime or witherite rats-bane, and then fused, can be partly dissolved in muriatic acid; and if this solution be evaporated, and the residue be extracted with sulphuric acid, and duly purified, it can be converted by ordinary methods into a chloride, which being obtained in the solid state, fused, and electrolyzed with half a dozen powerful cells will yield a globule of a pinkish silvery metal that will float on gasolene; and the material of *that* is a specimen of lithium."

This definition sounds strikingly similar to an analysis in terms of semantic marks organized according to a case grammar of some sort. What makes the analogy hard to establish is the fact that Peirce's definition contains an impressive amount of characters, which are difficult to organize into a structure of arguments and predicates or of different actions and *actants*. Peirce shows how a representation in the form of an encyclopedia should be, but he does not say how it could be formally elaborated. One of the reasons for such a complexity is that in this definition there is not a sharp distinction between the marks that should be basically attributed to the meaning and those that can be further interpreted as included or entailed by the basic ones, according to the principle of *nota notae*. Had Peirce said that lithium is an alkaline metal, some of its properties could have been considered as semantically entailed by the first character. But Peirce was not giving an example of 'economic' definition; on the contrary, he was showing how a term entails the globality of information about it. A satisfactory translation of this definition into a formal semantic representation should distinguish those two levels of interpretation.

Another aspect of the definition is that it constitutes, in spite of its encyclopedic complexity, only a section of the possible global encyclopedia of *lithium*. The Immediate Object established by the definition puts the corresponding Dynamic Object in focus only *in some respects,* that is, it takes into account only what is required in order to insert the term within a strictly chemical-physical proposition or argumentation. This means that the regulative model of an encyclopedia foresees many 'paths' or many complementary disjunctions of the entire semantic spectrum. The marks imputed here should have been labeled as concerning a technical universe of discourse. Lithium is a vitreous, translucent mineral which sometimes appears as a globule of pinkish silvery metal; if the universe of discourse had been an imaginary one (for instance, a fairy tale), then those marks would have been differently focused and organized along with others which do not appear in the above representation. For instance, lithium is known as the lightest solid element at ordinary temperature, and this character of 'lightness' should have been considered in another context. Peirce was conscious of this problem, and the solution that his whole philosophical system provides for concerns some crucial problems of contemporary semantics, namely, (i) whether the marks are universal and finite in number or not, and (ii) what size the encyclopedical representation should assume in order to be both satisfactory and reasonably reduced.

7.2.7.   In the light of the Peircean notion of interpretant, one no longer needs a finite set of metasemiotic construction. Any sign interpreting another sign, the basic condition of semiosis is its being interwoven with signs sending back to signs, in an *infinite regression*. In such a theoretical landscape any interpretant of a given sign, being in its turn and under other circumstances a sign, becomes temporarily a metasemiotic construction acting (for that occasion only) as *explicans* of the interpreted *explicatum* and being in its turn intrepreted by another interpretant. "The object of representation can be nothing but a representation of which the first representation is the interpretant. But an endless series of representations, each representing the one behind it, may be conceived to have an absolute object as its limit. The meaning of a representation can be nothing but a representation. In fact, it is nothing but the representation itself conceived as stripped of irrelevant clothing. But this clothing never can be completely stripped off; it is only changed for something more diaphanous. So there is an infinite regression here. Finally, the interpretant is nothing but another representation to which the torch of truth is handled along; and as representation, it has its interpretant again. Lo, another infinite series" (1.339).

This infinite series could, however, make the semantic encyclopedia unattainable and the work of semantic analysis continuously baffled by its own need of completedness. But there is a logical limit, and the encyclopedia cannot be infinite; this limit is just the *universe of discourse*. The list of the twelve *propositions in comprehension* (2.520) quoted above presupposes a limited universe of marks. "An unlimited universe would comprise the whole realm of the logically possible. . . . Our discourse seldom relates to this universe: we are either thinking of the physical possible, or of the historical existent, or of the world of some romance, or of some other limited universe. . . . A universe of things is unlimited in which every combination of characters, short of the whole universe of characters, occurs in some object. . . . In like manner the universe of characters is unlimited in case every aggregate of things short of the whole universe of things possesses in common one of the characters of the universe of characters. . . . In our ordinary discourse, on the other hand, not only are both universes limited, but, further than that, we have nothing to do with individual objects or simple marks: so that we have simply the two distinct universes of thing and marks related to one another, in general, in a perfectly indeterminate manner" (2.519,520; also 6.401).[4]

The notion of universe of discourse, along with the one of 'possible world' (2.236), links any semantic representation to contextual selections (see Eco, 1976, 2.11) and opens interesting perspectives on contemporary *text grammars*.

7.2.8. There is, however, a question. The fact that lithium is vitreous, translucent, hard, brittle, and so on seems to be without any doubt a matter of predication in terms of general qualities (or marks or characters). But what about the fact that *"if* triturated with lime and if refused *then* partly dissolving in muriatic acid"? To be grey is a quality, to react in a given way to a given excitement is a sort of behavior or a sequence of facts confirming a hypothesis. Obviously, this sequence of facts 'interprets' the first sign, but this would only mean that—even though characters are interpretants—not all interpretants are mere characters. Nevertheless, also "a portrait with the name of the original below is a proposition" (5.569). This statement involves a double consequence: on one hand, an icon is basically a ground, a quality, a Firstness; on the other hand, what we commonly call icons (for instance, paintings) are not mere icons but, rather, hypoicons or *iconic signs,* that is, complex interpretants of the name below them, and only in this way can they act as a subject-term in a proposition. Moreover, suppose that a painting represents the fall of Constantinople: it is undeniable that it should be interpreted and that it could arouse many possible inferences in the mind of its possible interpreter.

To generate a further question, it should be remembered that in some cases also the Dynamic Object of a sign can act as its interpretant. The most typical case is the command *Ground arms!* which has as its proper object either the subsequent action of the soldiers or "the Universe of things desired by the Commanding Captain at that moment" (5.178): a very ambiguous definition, since the response of the soldiers seems to be at the same time both the interpretant and the object of the sign. Undoubtedly, many subsequent behavioral responses, verbal answers, images interpreting a caption, and *vice versa* are interpretants.[5] Are they characters?

To solve this point one should state that (i) even qualities are always as complex as sequences of facts, and (ii) even sequences of facts are capable of being generalized as marks.

7.2.9. Now, Peirce says with absolute clarity that, even though marks are qualities, they are not mere Firstnesses; they are general and there is no 'redness' which is not the result of a perceptual construction, not a pure perception, but a *percept* (the percept "is a construction," and the perceptual fact is "the intellect's description of the evidence of sense," 2.141). But, in order to have this intellectual construction, one passes from a mere percept (a Rheme) to a Perceptual Judgment of which such a fact is the Immediate Interpretant (5.568). And a perceptual judgment is "a judgment asserting in a propositional form what a character of a percept directly present to the mind is" (5.54). To say that something is red does not mean that we have *seen* it; we have received an image, but the assertion that this something has the attribute of being red is already a judgment. Thus every mark never being a mere Firstness, and being always and already inserted into a correlation as a fact, its predication is always an experience of thirdness (5.182, 5.157, 5.150, 5.183).[6] In this sense there is no substantial difference between saying that lithium is green and saying that lithium "dissolves when triturated." In the former case we have something similar to a dicisign, in the latter something similar to an argument, but both 'signs' interpret the rheme *lithium*. There is no methodological difference between characters and other sorts of interpretants from the point of view of the description of the meaning of a term. The attribution of a mark is only a perceptual judgment, but "perceptual judgments are to be regarded as an extreme case of abductive inference" (5.153).

On the other hand, the very fact that some soldiers, in different circumstances, accomplish a given regular action every time *Ground arms!* is uttered by an officer means that this behavior is already subsumed under a concept, has become an abstraction, a law, a regularity. In order to be inserted into this relation, the behavior of the soldiers has become, just as the quality of redness, something general, insofar as it is intended as a character.

7.3.   Final interpretant and dynamic object

7.3.1.   What remains to be asked is how, in the philosophy of a thinker who calls himself a Scotist realist, there can be something such as an infinite semiotic regression, the object which has determined the sign never being apparently determined by it, if not in the phantasmatic form of Immediate Object. This can be explained only from the point of view of speculative rhetoric and in the light of the pragmatic notion of final interpretant; and only at that point will it be possible to understand why Peircean semantics assumes a rudimentary format of a case grammar.

How can a sign express a Dynamic Object, belonging to the Outer World (5.45), since "from the nature of things" it cannot express it (8.314)? How can a sign express the Dynamic Object ("the Object as it is," 8.183, an object "independent of itself," 1.538), since "it can only be a sign of that object in so far as that object is itself of the nature of a sign or thought" (1.538)? How can one link a sign to an object, since in order to recognize an object one needs a previous experience of it (8.181), and the sign does not furnish any acquaintance or recognition of the object (2.231)? The answer is already given at the end of the definition of *lithium:* "the peculiarity of this definition—or rather this precept that is more serviceable than a definition—is that it tells you what the word *lithium* denotes by prescribing what you are to *do* in order to gain a perceptual acquaintance with the object of the word" (2.330). The meaning of a symbol lies in the class of actions designed to bring about certain perceptible effects (Goudge, 1950: 155).

"The idea of meaning is such as to involve some reference to a purpose" (5.166). All this can become clearer if one thinks that the so-called Scotist realism of Peirce cannot be viewed but in the perspective of his pragmaticism. Reality is more a Result than a mere Datum. And in order to understand clearly what the meaning of a sign is destined to produce as Result, one must consider the notion of Final Interpretant.

7.3.2. By producing series of immediate responses (energetic interpretants), a sign establishes step by step a *habit,* a regularity of behavior in the interpreter or user of that sign. A habit being "a tendency . . . to behave in a similar way under similar circumstances in the future" (5.487), the final interpretant of a sign is, as a result, this habit (5.491). This is the same as to say that the correspondence between meaning and representamen has assumed the format of a law; but this also means that to understand a sign is to learn what to do in order to produce a concrete situation in which one can obtain the perceptual experience of the object the sign refers to.

But the category of 'habit' has a double sense, a behavioral (or psychological) sense and a cosmological one. A habit is a cosmological regularity: even the laws of nature are the results of habit taking (6.97), and "all things have a tendency to take habits" (1.409). If a law is an active force (a Secondness), order and legislation are a Thirdness (1.337): to take a habit is to establish or assume an ordered and regulated way of being. Therefore, coming back to the definition of lithium, the final interpretation of it stops at the production of a habit in a double sense: there is the human habit to understand the sign as an operational precept, and there is the cosmological habit according to which there will always be lithium every time nature behaves in a certain way. The final interpretant expresses the same law governing the Dynamic Object by prescribing both the way in which to experience the perception of it and the way in which it works and is perceptible.

7.3.3. At this point we can understand what kind of hierarchy rules the disposition of interpretants in this tentative model of semantic representation: it is an ordered and purposeful sequence of possible operations. Marks are organized not according to some 'logical' embedding in terms of genuses and species but, rather, according to the essential operations to be performed by an agent, using a certain instrument upon a certain object in order to overcome the resistence of a counterobject and thus to attain a certain goal.

In this way the apparent opposition between the intensional semantics of infinite semiosic regression and the extensional semantics of reference to Dynamic Objects is solved. It is true that signs cannot give us a direct acquaintance with objects, since they can only prescribe to us what to do in order to realize this acquaintance. Signs have a direct connection with Dynamic Objects only insofar as objects determine the formation of a sign; on the other hand, signs only 'know' Immediate Objects, that is, meanings. There is a difference between the *object of which a sign is a sign* and the *object of a sign:* the former is the Dynamic Object, a state of the outer world; the latter is a semiotic construction and should be recognized as a mere object of the inner world, except that, in order to describe this 'inner' object, one should make recourse to interpretants, that is, to other signs taken as representamen, therefore experiencing other objects of the outer world.

The Dynamic Object is—semiotically speaking—at our disposal only as a set of interpretants organized according to a compositional spectrum operationally structured. But while being, from a semiotic point of view, the possible object of a concrete experience, it is, from an ontological point of view, the concrete object of a possible experience.

All these remarks oblige us to revisit the notion of interpretant, not only as a category of Peirce's theory of meaning, but as a more central category of a general semiotics dealing, not only with semantics, but also with pragmatics. General semiotics should be conceived as a theory of all species of signs, concerned both with the structure of semiotic codes and with the inferential labor of text interpretation.

7.4.   Unlimited semiosis: A pragmatic perspective

7.4.1.   One could say that, sending back from one representation to another, Peirce is in fact betraying his 'medieval' realism: he cannot show how a sign can be referred to an object, and he dissolves the concrete relationships of indication into an infinite network of signs sending back to signs, as in a finite but unlimited universe of ghostly semiological appearances.

On the contrary, I believe that, with the doctrine of interpretants and the notion of unlimited semiosis, Peirce has reached the highest level of his realism. Except that this is not an ontological but a pragmatic realism. Let me first consider the philosophy of unlimited semiosis in the light of the requirements of present semiotics and then turn back to the interpretants as viewed in the light of Peirce's pragmaticism. We will see that in both cases the suggestions Peirce gives us are in the line of a pragmatic and realistic theory of intersubjective 'truth'.

The so-called Peircean medieval realism, with its taste for individual and concrete *realia,* should not be overestimated and should be always dialectically set against his pragmaticism. In this perspective Peirce was interested not only in objects as ontological sets of properties, but also in objects as occasions and results of active experience. To discover an object means to discover the way by which we operate upon the world producing objects or producing practical uses of them.

A sign can produce an emotional and an energetical interpretant. If we consider a musical piece, the emotional interpretant is our normal reaction to the charming power of music, but this emotional reaction may elicit a sort of muscular or mental effort. This kind of response is the energetic interpretant. But an energetic response does not need to be interpreted; rather, it produces (I guess, by further repetitions) a change of habit. This means that, after having received a series of signs and having variously interpreted them, our way of acting within the world is either transitorily or permanently changed. This new attitude, this pragmatic issue, is the final interpretant. At this point the unlimited semiosis stops (and this stopping is not final in a chronological sense, since our daily life is interwoven with those habit mutations). The exchange of signs produces modifications of the experience. The missing link between semiosis and physical reality as practical action has been found. The theory of interpretants is not an idealistic one.

Moreover, cosmologically speaking, even nature has habits and these are laws or regularities. The medieval realism of Peirce can be summarized by the statement "general principles are really operative in nature" (5.101). Since there are general principles, the ultimate meaning (or the final interpretant) of a sign can be conceived as the general rule permitting us to test or to produce that habit. Therefore the habit produced by a sign is both a behavioral attitude to act in some regular way and the rule or prescription of that action. Remember the definition of *lithium*. It is both the physical rule governing the production of it and the disposition we should acquire in order to produce an experience of it. The objectivity of such a pragmatic law is given by the fact that it is intersubjectively testable. Here is the opposition between James' Pragmatism and Peirce's Pragmaticism: there are general tendencies and there are operational rules allowing all of us to test them. Therefore habit is the 'final' interpreted definition of an operational rule.

It is extremely interesting to detect that such a conception is applicable even to iconic signs. In 5.483 Peirce explains the criterion of similitude between triangles and says that similarity is nothing else but a rule of construction: "to predicate any such concept of a real or imaginary object is equivalent to declaring that a certain operation, corresponding to the concept, if performed upon that object, would (certainly, or probably, or possibly, according to the mode of predication) be followed by a result of a definite general prescription." But to have understood a sign as a rule through the series of its interpretants means to have acquired the habit to act according to the prescription given by the sign:

"the conclusion (if it comes to a definite conclusion), is that under given conditions, the interpreter will have formed the habit of acting in a given way whenever he may desire a given kind of result. The real and living logical conclusion *is* that habit: the verbal formulation merely expresses it. I do not deny that a concept, proposition, or argument may be a logical interpretant. I only insist that it cannot be the final logical interpretant, for the reason that it is itself a sign of that very kind that has itself a logical interpretant. The habit alone, which though it may be a sign in some other way, is not a sign in that way in which that sign of which it is the logical interpretant is the sign. The habit conjoined with the motive and the conditions has the action for its energetic interpretant; but the action cannot be a logical interpretant, because it lacks generality." Thus, through pragmaticism, Peirce has joined his Scotist realism: the action is the place in which the *haecceitas* ends the game of semiosis.

But Peirce is not only a contradictory thinker, he is a dialectical one, and more so than he is usually believed to be. The final interpretant is not final in a chronological sense. Semiosis dies at every moment. But, as soon as it dies, it arises again like the Phoenix. Individual action lacks generality, but uniformly repeated actions can be described in general terms. Just at the end of the above quotation, Peirce adds: "But how otherwise can a habit be described than by a description of the kind of action to which it gives rise, with the specification of the conditions and the motive?" Thus the repeated action responding to a given sign becomes in its turn a new sign, the representamen of a law interpreting the former sign and giving rise to new processes of interpretation.

In this sense Peirce verifies the behavioristic hypothesis in semiotics, to the extent that it can be useful: if one hears a strange sound in an unknown language and detects that, *every time* it is uttered, its receiver reacts with a facial expression of rage, one can legitimately infer that that word is a nasty one; the conventional behavior of the receiver becomes an interpretant of the meaning of the word. I do not know what it precisely means but I can begin to list it among insults, therefore acquiring a first definition by hyperonimy. In this dialectical opposition between semiosis and concrete action, Peirce displays what he calls his 'conditional idealism' (5.494): any sufficient inquiry in principle can lead to a sort of objective agreement on the concrete results of semiosis. The final interpretant is at the same time a result and a rule.

The system of systems of codes, which could look like an irrealistic and idealistic cultural world separate from the concrete events, leads men to act upon the world; and this action continuously converts itself into new signs, giving rise to new semiotic systems. The Peircean notion of interpretant takes into account, not only the synchronic structure of semiotic systems, but also the diachronic destructurization and restructurization of those systems.

7.4.2. There is a reason why many semantic theorists of our century have given up studying meaning by translating this notion into the one of referent. The reason is that, if one wants to keep the content of an expression separate from its possible object, one risks falling into a mentalistic or psychologistic theory. The content of the expression should then be what 'travels' within the head of an interpreter receiving a given expression. Since we cannot check such an event, certain theorists preferred to give up on meaning. The only alternatives were either to substitute it with the corresponding state of the world (a rigid extensional interpretation of signs) or to reduce it to the behavior elicited by the sign (according to Morris' second phase, 1946); but, since there are expressions that possess a meaning which cannot be detected through observable behavior, the behavioristic test seems to me rather disappointing. The recent developments in structural and compositional semantics have elaborated a purely metalinguistic description of the content, as a network of oppositional units which are selectively and hierarchically organized to form the compositional spectrum of a given item. But the problem posed by these theories, as we have seen in 7.1.1, is always a methodological one and brings into question the status of the meaning components. Are they theoretical constructs? Are they representing a finite set? Are the components of a verbal item verbal expression too? The notion of interpretant solves all these problems.

If a representamen sends back to a given content unit and if this unit is formed by minor and more elementary units, all of these cannot be approached but by means of mediatory signs.

Within the framework of a general semiotic theory, which is considering not only verbal expression but any kind of signification, along with the relationship between different systems, the compositional analysis of a verbal term should not consider as its interpretants only linguistic terms. Among the interpretants of the word 'red' are also images of red objects or a red cue as the specific space within the gradated continuum of the chromatic spectrum. Among the interpretants of the word 'dog' are all the images of dog displayed by encyclopedias, zoological treatises, and all the comic strips in which that word has been associated to these images, and vice versa. Among the interpretants of the military command *Ground arms!* are, at the same time, the correspondent trumpet signal and the responding behavior of the group of soldiers. A semantic theory can analyze the content of an expression in various ways: by finding out the equivalent expression in another semiotic substance (the image of a dog vs. the word 'dog'); by finding out all the equivalent expressions in the same semiotic system (synonymy); by showing the possibility of mutual translation between different codes within the same semiotic substance (translation from one language to another); by substituting an expression with a more analytical definition; by associating to an expression all the emotional connotations conventionally recognized by a given culture and therefore specifically coded ('lion' connotatively meaning 'fierceness' and 'ferocity'). But no semantic analysis can be complete without analyzing verbal expressions by means of visual, objectal, and behavioral interpretants, and vice versa.

This list of possible components corresponds to the various types of interpretants proposed by Peirce. I am still not convinced that (as somebody has suggested) the classification 'immediate, dynamical and final' corresponds to the one 'emotional, energetic and logical'. I think that Peirce has foreseen many types of interpretants, but has failed to organize them in a correct categorical analysis just because he did not directly think of their possible classification as means of content analysis.

But it is not so important to outline a complete casuistry of interpretants; it is more useful and far more urgent to show how this notion saves the category of content (and of meaning) from being an ungraspable platonic abstraction or an undetectable mental event. Once the interpretant is equated with any coded intentional property of the content, since these properties cannot be isolated but under the form of the other signs (that is, other representamens), the elements of the content become something physically testable. A given culture displays, in any of its activities, accepted correlations between representamens (or expressions), each becoming in turn the interpretant of the other. In order to understand how an explicit correlation of expressions makes the content analyzable, think of the Rosetta Stone, carrying the simultaneous translation of a hieroglyphic text in Demotic and in Greek. The content of the first Egyptian text has become testable because of the mediation of the Greek one, this latter being in its turn interpretable, not only because there existed public lexicons equating given words with given contents, but also because these contents were already largely analyzed by the Western culture. Egyptian became understandable insofar as it was interpreted by Greek, and Greek was understandable insofar as it was already interpreted, not only by other languages, but also by the correspondence between Greek words and many images, facts, and behaviors, as well as by the continued work of mutual definition performed by the Greek language reflecting upon itself by means of treatises, poems, letters, and so on. Notice that, according to Peirce, interpretants are not only what I have equated to the semantic elementary components; as a matter of fact, the notion of interpretant is richer than that. Even the inferential labor elicited by a sentence or by a book is to be considered an interpretation of the first semiotic stimulus. If I interpret Peirce correctly, the entirety of Stendhal's text *Le rouge et le noir* should be considered an interpretation of the proposition 'Napoleon died in 1821'.

And, in fact, it happens that only by fully realizing the drama of a young Frenchman suffering from the paralysis of Restoration can one really understand what it means that Napoleon irreversibly died in 1821. After reading Stendhal's novel one enriches that statement by a further series of possible connotative contents. And, if that statement has an object, even the immediate object of the expression becomes more 'dense' because of that particular interpretation. *Le rouge et le noir* is an interpretant of the above statement for at least two reasons: first, because of its internal structure, that is, by its contextual references to the situation of France after the death of Napoleon; second, because of the many testable critical statements which have presented Stendhal's novels as a *Bildungsroman* telling the story of an impossible and frustrated Bonapartist dream. Therefore the book is recognized as the interpretant of the statements by force of concrete and testable correlations, just as we know that a given portrait interprets the content of the word 'Napoleon' because of the label put on the framework by the author, accepted by the museums, and reproduced as a caption in innumerable books on art history.

Obviously, in order to make the interpretant a fruitful notion, one must first of all free it from any psychological misunderstanding. I do not say that Peirce did it. On the contrary, insofar as, according to him, even ideas are signs, in various passages the interpretants appear also as mental events. I am only suggesting that from the point of view of the theory of signification, we should perform a sort of surgical operation and retain only a precise aspect of this category. Interpretants are the testable and describable correspondents associated by public agreement to another sign. In this way the analysis of content becomes a cultural operation which works only on physically testable cultural products, that is, other signs and their reciprocal correlations. Therefore the process of unlimited semiosis shows us how signification, by means of continual shiftings which refer a sign back to another sign or string of signs, circumscribes *cultural units* in an asymptotic fashion, without even allowing one to touch them directly, though making them accessible through other units. Thus one is never obliged to replace a cultural unit by means of something which is not a semiotic entity, and no cultural unit has to be explained by some platonic, psychic, or objectal entity. Semiosis explains itself by itself: this continual circularity is the normal condition of signification and even allows communicational processes to use signs in order to mention things and states of the world.

NOTES

1. On this matter Peirce is very contradictory. In 1885 (1.372) "a term is a mere general description, and neither icon nor index possesses generality."

But in 1896 (1.422, 477) qualities "which are Firstnesses as well as icons" are general. In 1902 (2.310) only a Dicisign can be true or false, but in 1893 it is said (2.441) that two icons can form a proposition: The icon of a Chinese and the icon of a woman can be composed together to form a proposition and therefore function as general terms. In 1902 (2.275) an icon, even though being a mere image of the object, "produces an interpretant idea." In 2.278 icons can work as predicates of an assertion. In order to explain this apparent contradiction, it should be said that Peirce distinguishes icons as instances of Firstness (and thus as a component of the process which goes from perception to judgment) from iconic representamens, or *hypoicons*. Hypoicons being a representamen, they are already Thirdnesses and are therefore interpretable. However, the entire matter is not so clear: in 1906 (4.9) it is asserted that "I recognize a logic of icons, and a logic of indices, as well as a logic of symbols."

2. Diagrams are interpretable (1.54). It is true that, whereas symbols *include* their consequences, icons *exhibit* them (2.282); this is 1893. But in 1901 (3.641) it is clearly said that there is not a substantial difference between reasoning by observing diagrams and reasoning by syllogisms. In 1905 (4.347) Peirce says that in graphs "the necessary consequences of these logical relations are at the same time signified, or can, at least, be made evident by transforming the diagram in certain ways." Apropos of section 7.2.5 of this chapter, a further remark is interesting (4.345): "I use the word 'signify' in such a sense that I say that a relative rheme signifies its corresponding relation."

3. Since blackness is not considered in itself, but is known as referred to the stove, it can only be attributed as a general. "We cannot comprehend an agreement of two things" but only "an agreement in some respect" (1.551). The following remarks are suggested by Caprettini (1976).

4. This view is consistent with Peirce's cosmology. There is an ideal world (in which two contradictory propositions are possible) and there is an actual world (in which, given a possible proposition, its contradictory is impossible); the latter is a selection and an arbitrary determination of the former (6.192). The actual universe, in respect to that vast representamen (5.119) which is the entire universe perfused with signs (5.448 n.), is a "universe of discourse," so to speak, reducing all the possible characters to a manageable number.

5. The example *Ground arms!* is repeatedly cited (see, for instance, 8.315). As for a broad acceptation of interpretant, "we may take a sign in so broad a sense that the interpretant of it is not a thought, but an action or an experience, or we may even so enlarge the meaning of a sign that its interpretant is a mere quality of feeling" (8.332).

6. All this between 1901 and 1903. In 1891 (reviewing the *Principles of Psychology* by James) Peirce was more cautious: "In perception the conclusion is not thought but actually seen, so that it is not exactly a judgment, though it is tantamount to one" (8.65). "Perception attains a virtual judgment, it subsumes something under a class, and not only so, but virtually attaches to the proposition the seal of assent" (8.66).

CHAPTER EIGHT

Lector in Fabula: Pragmatic
Strategy in a Metanarrative Text

La logique mène à tout,
à condition d'en sortir.
Alphonse Allais

A. The Text as Expression

Un drame bien parisien
Alphonse Allais

CHAPITRE PREMIER

*Où l'on fait connaissance avec un Monsieur et une Dame qui auraient pu
être heureux, sans leurs éternels malentendus.*

O qu'il ha bien sceu
choisir, le challan!
Rabelais.

A l'époque où commence cette histoire, Raoul et Marguerite (un joli
nom pour les amours) étaient mariés depuis cinq mois environ.
Mariage d'inclination, bien entendu.

Alphonse Allais (1854–1905) published this short story in *Le chat noir* (April 26,
1890). Chapters 4–7 were published in André Breton's *Anthologie de l'humour noir*.
See Appendix 2 for an English translation by Fredric Jameson.

Raoul, un beau soir, en entendant Marguerite chanter la jolie romance du colonel Henry d'Erville:

> L'averse, chère à la grenouille,
> Parfume le bois rajeuni.
> . . . Le bois, il est comme Nini.
> Y sent bon quand y s'débarbouille.

Raoul dis-je, s'était juré que la divine Marguerite (*diva Margarita*) n'appartiendrait jamais à un autre homme qu'à lui-même.

Le ménage eût été le plus heureux de tous les ménages, sans le fichu caractère des deux conjoints.

Pour un oui, pour un non, crac! une assiette cassée, une gifle, un coup de pied dans le cul.

A ces bruits, Amour fuyait éploré, attendant, au coin du grand parc, l'heure toujours proche de la réconciliation.

Alors, des baisers sans nombre, des caresses sans fin, tendres et bien informées, des ardeurs d'enfer.

C'était à croire que ces deux cochons-là se disputaient pour s'offrir l'occasion de se raccommoder.

CHAPITRE II

Simple épisode qui, sans se rattacher directement à l'action, donnera à la clientèle une idée sur la façon de vivre de nos héros.

> *Amour en latin faict amor.*
> *Or donc provient d'amour la mort*
> *Et, par avant, soulcy qui mord,*
> *Deuils, plours, pièges, forfaitz, remord . . .*
> (Blason d'amour.)

Un jour, pourtant, ce fut plus grave que d'habitude.

Un soir, plutôt.

Ils étaient allés au Théâtre d'Application, où l'on jouait, entre autres pièces, *L'Infidèle,* de M. de Porto-Riche.

—Quand tu auras assez vu Grosclaude, grincha Raoul, tu me le diras.

—Et toi, vitupéra Marguerite, quand tu connaîtras mademoiselle Moreno par cœur, tu me passeras la lorgnette.

Inaugurée sur ce ton, la conversation ne pouvait se terminer que par les plus regrettables violences réciproques.

Dans le coupé qui les ramenait, Marguerite prit plaisir à gratter sur l'amour-propre de Raoul comme sur une vieille mandoline hors d'usage.

Aussi, pas plutôt rentrés chez eux, les belligérants prirent leurs positions respectives.

La main levée, l'œil dur, la moustache telle celle des chats furibonds, Raoul marcha sur Marguerite, qui commença, dès lors, à n'en pas mener large.

La pauvrette s'enfuit, furtive et rapide, comme fait la biche en les grands bois.

Raoul allait la rattraper.

Alors, l'éclair génial de la suprême angoisse fulgura le petit cerveau de Marguerite.

Se retournant brusquement, elle se jeta dans les bras de Raoul en s'écriant:

—Je t'en prie, mon petit Raoul, défends-moi!

CHAPITRE III

Où nos amis se réconcilient comme je vous souhaite de vous réconcilier souvent, vous qui faites vos malins.

> *"Hold your tongue, please!"*

. . . .
. . . .

CHAPITRE IV

Comment l'on pourra constater que les gens qui se mêlent de ce qui ne les regarde pas feraient beaucoup mieux de rester tranquilles.

> *C'est épatant ce que le monde deviennent rosse depuis quelque temps!*
> (Paroles de ma concierge dans la matinée de lundi dernier.)

Un matin, Raoul reçut le mot suivant:

"Si vous voulez, une fois par hasard, voir votre femme en belle humeur, aliez donc, jeudi, au bal des Incohérents, au Moulin-Rouge. Elle y sera masquée et déguisée en pirogue congolaise. A bon entendeur, salut!

"UN AMI."

Le même matin, Marguerite reçut le mot suivant:

"Si vous voulez, une fois par hasard, voir votre mari en belle humeur, allez donc, jeudi, au bal des Incohérents, au Moulin-Rouge. Il y sera, masqué et déguisé en templier fin de siècle. A bon entendeuse, salut!

"UNE AMIE."

Ces billets ne tombèrent pas dans l'oreille de deux sourds.

Dissimulant admirablement leurs desseins, quand arriva le fatal jour:

—Ma chère amie, fit Raoul de son air le plus innocent, je vais être forcé de vous quitter jusqu'à demain. Des intérêts de la plus haute importance m'appellent à Dunkerque.

—Ça tombe bien, répondit Marguerite, délicieusement candide, je viens de recevoir un télégramme de ma tante Aspasie, laquelle, fort souffrante, me mande à son chevet.

CHAPITRE V

Où l'on voit la folle jeunesse d'aujourd'hui tournoyer dans les plus chimériques et passagers plaisirs, au lieu de songer à l'éternité.

> *Mai vouéli vièure pamens:*
> *La vido es tant bello!*
> Auguste Marin.

Les échos du *Diable boiteux* ont été unanimes à proclamer que le bal des Incohérents revêtit cette année un éclat inaccoutumé.

Beaucoup d'épaules et pas mal de jambes, sans compter les accessoires.

Deux assistants semblaient ne pas prendre part à la folie générale: un Templier fin de siècle et une Pirogue congolaise, tous deux hermétiquement masqués.

Sur le coup de trois heures du matin, le Templier s'approcha de la Pirogue et l'invita à venir souper avec lui.

Pour toute réponse, la Pirogue appuya sa petite main sur le robuste bras du Templier, et le couple s'éloigna.

CHAPITRE VI

Où la situation s'embrouille.

> *—I say, don't you think the rajah laughs at us?*
> *—Perhaps, sir.*
> Henry O'Mercier.

—Laisse-nous un instant, fit le Templier au garçon du restaurant, nous allons faire notre menu et nous vous sonnerons.

Le garçon se retira et le Templier verrouilla soigneusement la porte du cabinet.

Puis, d'un mouvement brusque, après s'être débarrassé de son casque, il arracha le loup de la Pirogue.

Tous les deux poussèrent, en même temps, un cri de stupeur, en ne se reconnaissant ni l'un ni l'autre.

Lui, ce n'était pas Raoul.

Elle, ce n'était pas Marguerite.

Ils se présentèrent mutuellement leurs excuses, et ne tardèrent pas à lier connaissance à la faveur d'un petit souper, je ne vous dis que ça.

CHAPITRE VII

Dénouement heureux pour tout le monde, sauf pour les autres.

> *Buvons le vermouth grenadine,*
> *Espoir de nos vieux bataillons.*
> George Auriol.

Cette petite mésaventure servit de leçon à Raoul et à Marguerite.

A partir de ce moment, ils ne se disputèrent plus jamais et furent parfaitement heureux.

Ils n'ont pas encore beaucoup d'enfants, mais ça viendra.

B. The Text as Content: Levels of Interpretation

8.1. Introductory remarks

8.1.1. How to read a metatext

To the one-dimensional reader, Allais' *Un drame bien parisien* (hereafter *Drame*) may appear to be a mere literary joke, a disturbing exercise in verbal *trompe-l'oeil*, something half-way between the engravings by Escher and a *pastiche* à la Borges (*ante litteram*). *Just because of this* it must be taken as a text telling its own unfortunate story. Since its misfortune has been carefully planned, *Drame* does not represent a textual failure: it represents a metatextual achievement. *Drame* must be read twice: it asks for both a naive and a critical reading, the latter being the interpretation of the former.[1]

I assume that the reader of the present essay has already read *Drame* without skipping to the present introductory remarks. I suppose that the reader has read *Drame* only *once* at a normal reading speed. Therefore the following pages represent a specimen of a second (or critical) reading. In other words, the present essay is not only an analysis of *Drame* but also an analysis of the naive reading of *Drame*. However, since any critical reading is at the same time the analysis of its own interpretative procedures, the present essay is also an interpretation of a possible critical (or second) reading of *Drame*.

But *Drame* has been assumed to be a metatext. As such it tells at least three stories: (i) the story of what happens to its *dramatis personae;* (ii) the story of what happens to its naive reader; (iii) the story of what happens to itself as a text (this third story being potentially the same as the story of what happens to the critical reader). Thus my present essay is not an analysis of something happening outside *Drame* as a text (the adventures of its readers being spurious data borrowed from a psychological or sociological enquiry about the empirical fate of a textual object): the present essay is nothing else but the story of the adventures of *Drame*'s Model Readers.[2]

8.1.2. A metatextual strategy

When he comes to chapter 6, *Drame*'s reader is completely jammed. My purpose is to explain why.

According to our most commonsensical intuition, chapters 6 and 7 cannot be justified without assuming that the previous chapters were postulating a reader eager to make the following hypotheses: (i) At the end of chapter 4 the reader must suspect that Raoul will go to the ball disguised as a Templar to catch Marguerite in the act—and that the opposite is devised by Marguerite. (ii) During the reading of chapter 5 the reader must suspect that the two maskers attending the ball are Raoul and Marguerite duly disguised (or at most he must confusedly suspect that four individuals are attending the ball). Notice that none has realized that each letter tells how the marital partners will be disguised but does not mention the disguise of the supposed lover: therefore neither Raoul nor Marguerite could decide to assume the disguise of their rivals. On the contrary, many readers (see Appendix 1) implicitly or explicitly assume that each letter is dealing with both disguises ("Raoul receives a letter where it is said that Marguerite, disguised as a Pirogue, will meet her lover, disguised as a Templar," and vice versa). I am therefore assuming that this kind of reading was more or less the one foreseen by Allais when he prepared his textual trap.[3]

The text itself is of an adamantine honesty; it never says anything to make one believe that Raoul or Marguerite plan to go to the ball; it presents the Pirogue and the Templar at the ball without adding anything to make one believe that they are Raoul and Marguerite; it never says that Raoul and Marguerite have lovers. Therefore it is the reader (as an empirical accident independent of the text) who takes the responsibility for every mistake arising during his reading, and it is only the reader who makes mischievous innuendos about the projects of Raoul and Marguerite.

But the text postulates the presumptuous reader as one of its constitutive elements: if not, why is it said in chapter 6 that the two masks cried out in astonishment, neither one recognizing the other? The only one to be astonished should be the reader who has made a wrong hypothesis without being authorized to do so.

The reader, however, has been more than authorized to make such a hypothesis. *Drame* takes into account his possible mistakes because *it has carefully planned and provoked them*. Besides, if the reader's inferences were planned and provoked, why should the text refuse and punish them as a deviancy? Why show so blantantly that they are inconsistent with the "real" story?

The implicit lesson of *Drame* is, in fact, coherently contradictory: Allais is telling us that not only *Drame* but every text is made of two components: the information provided by the author and that added by the Model Reader, the latter being determined by the former—with various rates of freedom and necessity. But, in order to demonstrate this textual theorem, Allais has led the reader to fill up the text with contradictory information, thus cooperating in setting up a story that cannot stand up. The failure of the apparent story of *Drame* is the success of Allais' theoretical assumption and the triumph of his metatextual demonstration.[4]

8.2.   The strategy of discursive structure

8.2.1.   Speech-act strategy

The building up of the Model Reader(s) as a possible interpretative strategy requires some pragmatical devices. *Drame* performs them, in the first instance, as a subtle interplay of perlocutionary and illocutionary signals, displayed all along the discursive surface.

Grammatically speaking, the text is dominated by a first person (the narrator) who at every step reiterates the fact that someone is reporting (tongue in cheek) events that are not necessarily to be believed; in other words, these interventions of the first grammatical person are stipulating a mutual contract of fair distrust: "You do not believe me and I know that you are not believing me; nevertheless, let us accept everything said in this text as if it were true."

Many overcoded expressions are used to make evident such a situation: /à l'époque où commence cette histoire/ is a fictional indicator not dissimilar from /once upon a time/; /un joli nom pour les amours/ sends the reader back to various literary overcoded conventions, operating particularly in the Symbolist period; /Bien entendu/ stresses the fact that the contract concerns a love story (with the whole of its intertextual frames); /Raoul, dis-je . . ./ rivets the presence of the narrator; /c'était à croire que . . ./ entitles the reader to make his own suppositions, to anticipate the conclusions, to go beyond the surface of discursive structures in order to find out and to check narrative schemas, as is usually requested of a reader of fiction.

The text carefully designs its naive reader as the typical consumer of adultery stories such as the market of comédie de boulevard had created. This sort of reader is called into play through a series of allusions to his yearning for satisfactory coups de théâtre. An expression such as /simple épisode qui donnera à la clientèle/ recalls the opening sentences of Tom Jones: "An author ought to consider himself not as a gentleman who gives a private elemosinary treat, but rather as one who keeps a public ordinary at which all persons are welcome for their money. . . ." These customers (or this readership) are members of a paying audience eager to enjoy narrativity according to current recipes. Notice that the epigraph of chapter 1 (quotation from Rabelais) mentions a /challan/, that is, a «customer».

An expression such as /vous qui faites vos malins/ holds up to ridicule the supposed readers, and at the same time recognizes these "smart-alecks" as those who usually expect from a story what the encyclopedia of narrativity has made them eager to expect. It is just for this sort of audience that the text is full of ready-made sentences of the type /la pauvrette s'enfuit, furtive et rapide comme fait la biche en les grands bois/ or /ces billets ne tombèrent pas dans l'oreille de deux sourds/ which reiterate the standard characteristics of the story.

The readership here summoned is the one accustomed to the most credited pieces of discursive stylistical overcoding. For the same reasons it ought to be the one accustomed to the most credited pieces of narrative overcoding.

However, the text does not renounce arousing the suspicions of a possible critical reader. Expressions such as /c'était à croire/, /un jour, *pourtant . . . un soir, plutôt/, /bien entendu/, /comment l'on pourra con-stater/* are so blatantly ironic as to unveil their lies the very moment they assert them.

But all these speech-act strategies become evident only at a second reading. At a first glance the naive reader is lured by the familiar process of narrativity; he suspends his disbeliefs and wonders about the possible course of events. He brackets any extensional comparison and enters the world of *Drame* as if it were his own world.

8.2.2. From discursive to narrative structures

At the level of its discursive structures, *Drame* does not posit particular problems of decoding. The individuals in play are easily recognizable, co-references are plainly evident. The reader understands without pain discursive topics and isotopies. The mode of the discourse being 'classical' and realistic, no particular problem seems to arise. The data of the reader's encyclopedia flow easily into the process of actualization of the content. The world of Raoul and Marguerite looks like the world of the reader (at least of a reader of 1890, or of a reader accepting the competence of a Gay Nineties reader).

The epigraphs seem to introduce some semantic complication (they are, intertextually speaking, rather puzzling), but at a first reading they can be dropped without problems. Otherwise, the text displays a clear strategy of confidential relationship between author and reader, the former being continuously present by conversational signals (*/bien entendu . . . dis-je . . ./*), the latter being pointed out by the author himself by means of direct appeals (*/je vous souhaite . . ./*).

The reader seems to get involved step by step in an Aristotelian process of 'pity', that is, of compassionate participation: *de te fabula narratur*. A perfect device, indeed, in order to arouse 'fear', that is, the expectation of some unanticipated and troubling event.

But this unproblematical nature of discursive level is only apparent. The syntactical mechanism of co-reference is perhaps unambiguous, but the semantic mechanism of co-indexicality is not that simple.

When in chapter 5 a Templar and a Pirogue appear, the reader is supposed to think that they are Raoul and Marguerite (or that at least one of them is either). The co-referential mediation is made by the two letters of chapter 4: since it is said that Raoul is going to the ball disguised as a Templar and there is a Templar attending the ball, then he must be Raoul (the same with Marguerite).

Logically speaking the inference is not correct, but narratively speaking it is such. The reader is resorting to a typical intertextual frame, very common in nineteenth-century narrativity: the topos of the 'pretended unknown'. Popular novels are full of chapters beginning with the description of an unknown character (usually disguised) who, even to the most inattentive reader, clearly appears as one of the previously mentioned heroes of the story. Unfailingly, after this short description, the author gives up his device and takes for granted the fact that the Model Reader has already recognized the unknown figure: "As our readers have certainly realized, the mysterious visitor was Count So-and-So. . . ."

Thus, through the mediation of an inferential walk and by virtue of an intertextual frame, the Model Reader of *Drame* establishes a co-referential link between the names and the pronouns referring to the individuals of chapters 1 to 4 and those referring to the individuals of chapter 5.

Let me stress that such a co-reference is not established on grammatical grounds, but rather on narratological grounds. But this means that the discursive strategy is improved by operations made at the narrative level, while at the same time inferences at this level are implemented by a discursive strategy.

However, the whole of the discursive level has a vicarious function with respect to the narrative level and aims at eliciting processes of expectation and forecasts at the level of the *fabula*. This happens with many fictional texts; what distinguishes *Drame* from its congeners is the fact that in *Drame* the discursive structures, until chapter 6, support two different and mutually irreducible *fabulae*.

In order to recognize a given *fabula* the reader has to identify a narrative topic or a main theme. A narrative topic is nothing but a higher-level *fabula* or an ultimate macroproposition such as can be expressed by a title: *De Bello Gallico* is a satisfactory clue to decide what the corresponding Caesar text is about (see the notion of *discursive topic* in van Dijk, 1977, and the notion of *theme* in Ščeglov and Žolkovskij, 1971). Once a narrative topic has been established (frequently by various tentative abductions and through a trial-and-error process), the reader activates one or more intertextual frames to take his inferential walks and to hazard forecasts apropos of the course of the *fabula*.

At the end of chapter 4 of *Drame,* the reader is, in principle, in the position of singling out two narrative topics (a story of an adultery and a story of a misunderstanding) and may resort to two intertextual frames («adultery» and «misunderstanding»), so as to outline two stories or basic treatments:

Treatment 1: Raoul and Marguerite love each other but are mutually jealous. Each of them receives a letter announcing that his/her partner will meet his/her lover. Both manage to catch the other in the act. The letter(s) was (were) true.

Treatment 2: Raoul and Marguerite love each other, but are mutually jealous. Each of them receives a letter announcing that his/her partner will meet his/her lover. Both manage to catch the other in the act. The letter(s) was (were) lying.

As a mattter of fact, the end of *Drame* does not prove or disprove either hypothesis. Better, it verifies both (and neither). It depends on the type of cooperation implemented by the reader. But the text leads the reader to cooperate in either way.

To do so, *Drame* plots, at the level of discursive structures, a trick concerning the narrative structures whose reasons lie at a more profound level.

It is impossible to explain what happens at the level of the reconstruction of the narrative structures (*fabula*) without resorting to deeper structures, that is, *world structures* (systems of individuals along with their properties and mutual relations) with different imputed truth values. These world structures do not exclude a logic of actions (such as is realized at the level of narrative structures in the format of state changes), these changes being nothing other than possible transformation between world structures. The peculiarity of *Drame* is that it strongly encourages mistakes at the levels of *fabula* while being unequivocal at the level of world structures.

As the discursive structures are duly disambiguated and reduced to a more abstract world structure, one will realize that the text never lies. But at the intermediate level of narrative structures, the text ambiguously entitles one to conceive contradictory world structures.

In order to single out this very peculiar textual strategy, let us begin from an analysis of those aspects of discursive structures that are clearly envisaged to encourage the construction of two alternative *fabulae*.

Two alternative *fabulae* are two narrative isotopies. *Drame* is specially devised to produce contradictory narrative isotopies. It succeeds in doing so by manipulating the reader's attitude to operating semantic disclosures and by establishing two topics—or two fundative questions—at the discursive level.

Drame establishes its discursive topics by reiterating a series of sememes belonging to the same semantic field. The first topic concerns «sex» while the second concerns «logical coherence» or «facts vs. beliefs».

The reader is, however, led to emphasize the first topic so that his quest for a denouement is dominated by the question, Who or where are the unknown intruders that are depriving Raoul and Marguerite of their reciprocal marital rights? (or Where is the sexual menace coming from? —or even, Will Raoul and Marguerite succeed in catching each other in the act?). He will discover too late that the true question is, How many individuals are really involved?

It is evident that the first topic overwhelms the second. The text is very careful to make the first more blatant, but it cannot be said that the second is concealed—it is simply suggested by more sophisticated devices. There is a logic of preference even in activating intertextual frames, and Allais seems to know it very well. In fact, he is unmasking the underlying ideology of his naive reader, so eager to conceive of social life in mere terms of sexual possession. The naive reader is so sensitive to frames concerning sex and marriage (and marriage as a system of sexual duties) because his moral and social sensitivity has been molded by an exaggerated series of *drames bien parisiens,* where a male owns or buys a female as a 'challan' buys or owns a commodity.

It is, however, true that the text does its best to support its reader's ideological biases.

Raoul and Marguerite are married to each other. A /marriage/, to analyze it encyclopedically, is a legal contract, an agreement by which some goods are in common, a parental relationship presupposing and determining other parental relationships, the custom of eating and sleeping together, the possibility of having children legally, a series of social commitments (especially for a bourgeois couple in nineteenth-century Paris), and so on. But in *Drame* it seems rather evident that what really matters is the reciprocal duty of fidelity and its possibility of being jeopardized by adultery.

To blow up this sole property among so many others, chapter 1 surrounds the semantic unit «marriage» with a series of other units uniquely related to sexual matters. Raoul and Marguerite are nice names for lovers; their marriage has been /d'inclination/ and therefore a love affair; Raoul swears that Marguerite will not /belong/ (euphemism) to another man, and so on. Chapter 2 is devoted entirely to jealousy: it could be taken as an interpretation (in Peirce's sense) of the lexeme /jealousy/, as could chapter 4 be taken as an interpretation of /deception/ and of /delation/. Thus co-textual pressures collaborate to isolate, among the possible connotations and denotations of /to be married/ only those connected with mutual possession.

As for the second isotopy, the title, while suggesting frivolity and a 'Parisian' mood, represents an oxymoron and therefore a *contradictio in adiecto:* drama as opposed to comedy. Obviously, the oxymoron 'tames' the contradiction, but it equally suggests that in this story there are things that cannot usually go together.

The title of chapter 1 discloses the notion of 'malentendu', misunderstanding. The last phrase of the same chapter suggests that our two heroes are substantially tricking and fooling themselves.

The epigraph of chapter 2 plays again upon the *coincidentia oppositorum;* false etymologies, paranomasias, phonic similarities and rhymes suggest that everything can become everything else, love and death, biting (aggression) and remorse. For good measure the same epigraph also inserts the hint "piège" (trap).

Chapter 3 has no story, but is absolutely important apropos of the second isotopy. Apparently, the reader is invited to imagine what happens in the privacy of the alcove. The epigraph recalls to the cultivated reader a quotation from Donne: "For God's sake hold your tongue and let me love." More malicious sexual connotations can be added. But from the point of view of isotopy 2, this empty space is an invitation to the reader to write 'ghost' chapters by himself. And he will, as we shall see, after chapter 4. While inviting cooperation in filling up empty narrative spaces, Allais gives, however, an explicit warning: hold your tongue, do not speak too much, you will risk spoiling the coherence of the story. Thus the epigraph contradicts the suggestion given by the empty space.

If chapter 2 is dominated by the theme of infidelity (*L'infidèle*), chapter 4 is dominated by the theme of incoherence (*bal des Incohérents*). The title suggests confusion and intrusion. Explicitly it says that people should not get involved with things that are none of their affair. Implicitly it says: Do not mix yourself up with *my* job!

Additional connotations of incoherence are the *'fin de siècle'* Templar and the very idea of a mask imitating a Congolese pirogue. But in the same chapter the suggestions directing toward isotopy 1 are much too strong: the letters, /*ces billets ne tombèrent pas dans les oreilles de deux sourds*/, dissimulation, false innocence. . . .

Note that in chapters 1-6 jealousy is always aroused by a text: a song in chapter 1, a play in chapter 2, a letter in chapter 4, a newspaper in chapter 5. Nothing is referentially validated, everything is a matter of belief (and of a false one).

We have also seen that throughout the story the author is continuously present through a series of speech acts expressing his own attitude vis-à-vis the events and the characters. These interventions have the function of disturbing the naive identification with the isotopy 1. They stress the metalinguistic presence of the narrator so as to produce effects of defamiliarization or of *Verfremdung* (as in Brecht's epic theater).

8.2.3. *Fabula in fabula*

Were the reader adequately alerted, chapter 2 would function as a reduced model of the whole story, offering him the possibility of detecting the tricking strategy displayed by the author. This chapter could be deleted without compromising the intelligibility of the story. The events here reported do not form part of the *fabula*. However, chapter 2 reproduces, as in a sort of miniature, all the discursive and narrative structures of *Drame*.

After a long and dramatic scene of jealousy (where each of the protagonists only *believes* that his or her partner is lusting after someone else), Raoul pursues Marguerite in order to beat her. At this point Marguerite asks Raoul, clearly her adversary, to help her (obviously against himself).

The *fabula* is rather puzzling, and the reader does not know how to summarize it in terms of actantial roles. In fact, we have many actants: Subject and Object (fight); Sender and Receiver (call for help); Helper and Opponent (rescue). They are embodied in three *roles,* namely, Victim (the She-Hero), Villain, and Helper. But these three roles are manifested by only two *actors,* Raoul and Marguerite, and Raoul plays two irreducibly opposite roles, Helper and Villain.

As a matter of fact, Raoul (the Villain *in reality*) becomes the Helper only insofar as the *propositional attitudes* (wishes or beliefs) of Marguerite are concerned: Marguerite *wants* and/or *believes* Raoul to be her Helper. Her belief acquires a sort of performative value; she does things with words.

To symbolize what happens in this *fabula in fabula,* we can say that,

(i) given h as Helper and $\sim h$ as Villain (or non-Helper),
(ii) given B_m as 'Marguerite believes that', K_m as 'Marguerite knows that', and W_m as 'Marguerite wants that',

the reader (after having discovered that Raoul is the Villain for Marguerite and that she asks him to be her Helper against himself) is led to the following tentative inference:

$$(\forall x) [h(x) \quad \vee \sim h(x)]$$
$$K_m \{[(\exists x) \sim h(x) \cdot (x = Raoul] \cdot W_m [(\exists x\, h(x) \cdot (x = Raoul)]\} \rightarrow B_m$$
possible $[\sim h(x) \cdot h(x)]$.

Therefore Marguerite knows that she wants what is logically (or narratively) impossible. But since she wants it she believes that this contradiction is possible. However, this is not the only inference the reader can make. It is thinkable that Marguerite believes that by wanting something the impossible becomes possible. Or that she wants to make Raoul believe that the impossible is possible, and so on.

In this sense chapter 2 is a *fabula in fabula.* It not only anticipates the maze of objective contradictions through which the entire *fabula* will lead the reader, but also does what the reader himself is expected to do, that is, to transform his expectations (beliefs and desires) into actual states of the *fabula.*

By a careful reading of this chapter, the reader would be able to anticipate the whole course of the story, thus avoiding any mistake. But, as we have said, the theme of misunderstanding and logical incoherence is overwhelmed by the theme of adultery.

It is easy to be wise after the event: the second topic is discovered only at a second reading. Those whom the gods wish to destroy they first drive mad. *Drame* displays its discoursive strategies to madden (or rather blind) its naive reader as far as the strategy of the *fabula* is concerned.

8.3.   The strategy of narrative structure

8.3.1.   Inferential walks and ghost chapters

Taking chapter 2 as a reduced model of *Drame,* one finds in it a clear example which shows the difference between actualizing discoursive structures and actualizing narrative structures.

Raoul pursues Marguerite /*la main levée*/. The reader, resorting to the frame «conjugal quarrel», realizes that Raoul is raising his hand to beat his wife.[5] But, in performing this *semantic disclosure,* the reader is in façt accomplishing a double inferential movement:

(i) he realizes that Raoul wants to beat Marquerite;
(ii) he expects Raoul *actually* to beat Marguerite.

The *discursive inference* (i) is correct. The *narrative* inference (ii) is false, since the further course of the story will disprove it.

At the level of discursive structure the reader is invited to fill up various empty phrastic spaces (texts are lazy machineries that ask someone to do part of their job). At the level of narrative structures, the reader is supposed to make forecasts concerning the future course of the *fabula.*

To do this the reader is supposed to resort to various intertextual frames among which to take his *inferential walks.* Every text, even though not specifically narrative, is in some way making the addressee expect (and foresee) the fulfillment of every unaccomplished sentence: /John will not arrive because . . ./ makes one hazard forecasts about the missing information. Obviously, these expectations are more evidently requested in a narrative text. They are anticipations of the global course of events represented by the *fabula* when it reaches its final state. Frequently, a fictional text not only tolerates but anxiously awaits these inferential walks in order not to be obliged to tell too much.

Frequently, given a series of causally and linearly connected events a . . . . $e,$ a text tells the reader about the event a and, after a while, about the event $e,$ taking for granted that the reader has already anticipated the dependent events b,c,d (of which e is the consequence, according to many intertextual frames). Thus the text implicitly validates a 'ghost chapter', tentatively written by the reader. In other words, the author is sure that the reader has already written by himself a chapter which is not manifested at the level of discursive structures, but which is taken as actualized as far as the narrative sequence is concerned.

What happens, then, in *Drame* at the end of chapter 4? Raoul and Marguerite are informed that their own partners will go to the ball in a good mood. First inference: nobody writes an anonymous letter concerning someone's marital partner if not to make a sexual innuendo. Therefore it is suspected that Raoul and Marguerite will meet their respective lovers. If one meets someone else, then this someone else exists. Notice that the text does not say that Raoul and Marguerite will meet anyone at all. At most—and by an inference—they are supposed to plan to meet someone.

No one has said that the anonymous letters were telling the truth. But at this point the elicited inference is supported by too many intertextual clues: it *usually happens* like this. Furthermore, when Raoul and Marguerite are telling each other that they will be elsewhere the day of the ball, they do it /*dissimulant admirablement leurs desseins*/. Now, /*dissimuler*/ (dissimulate) by semantic disclosure leads one to know that whoever dissimulates does it with respect to a dissimulated object. Since they conceal a project while stating another (nonconcealed) project, this means that the project they utter aloud is false. What is the true one?

The whole universe of intertextuality, from Boccaccio to Shakespeare and further on, is ready to offer us a lot of hints as to satisfactory inferential walks:

When a husband suspects his wife, he will try to catch her in the act (and vice versa). Therefore our characters are planning to attend the ball, each possibly disguised as his/her partner's lover. It does not matter that *neither of them can know the disguise of his/her supposed antagonist* (since each letter speaks only of the partner's disguise). This is a case of naive identification of the reader's knowledge with the character's knowledge, and the text has so cunningly intertwined these pieces of crossed information that it is not reasonably possible to have (at a first reading) an exact picture of the situation. Allais in fact is also playing with the psychology of reading and with the degree of attention that the Model Reader is supposed to display during a naive reading.

Once the yearning for inferential walks has been stirred up, not only does the reader suppose that Raoul and Marguerite will go to the ball, he *makes* them go by writing a ghost chapter between chapters 4 and 5, and during chapter 5 he *makes* them be there. At this point he is unable to distinguish between the possible course of events he has imagined and the events really occurring in the world of the story.

An inferential walk has much to do with a rhetorical entymeme. As such, it starts from a probable premise picked up in the repertory of common opinions, or *endoxa*, as Aristotle said. The endoxa represent the store of intertextual information, and some of them are already mutually correlated in possible general schemas of entymematic chains. Aristotelian *topoi* are nothing but this: overcoded, ready-made paths for inferential walks.

As a matter of fact, the reader makes more (and worse) than an entymeme: he makes a sorites of paralogisms. The letter says that Raoul will attend the ball disguised as a Templar, and the reader obliterates the fact that this piece of information is asserted by a letter and assumes it as matter of fact: Raoul is going to the ball disguised as a Templar. The reader then transforms this contingent proposition (there is a Templar who is Raoul) into a necessary one (for every individual in every possible world, if Templar then Raoul). In chapter 5 the reader finally uses the affirmative particular asserted by the text (there is a Templar) to validate a syllogism in Modus Ponens: if Templar, then Raoul; but Templar, then Raoul.

Unfortunately, the reader is not thinking in logical terms: he is thinking in terms of intertextual frames.

Inferential walks are possible when they are verisimilar: according to *Poetics* (1451b) what has previously happened is more verisimilar than what happens for the first time, since the fact that it happened proves that it was possible. Inferential walks are supported by the repertory of similar events recorded by the intertextual encyclopedia.

Drame's reader enjoys a lot of *topoi* that can help him: he is reading a story taking place during *la belle époque,* when the image of the magnificent 'cocu' dominates the scene. (By the way, M. de Porto-Riche, the author of *L'Infidèle,* the play watched by our heroes, was well known for making in all his plays continual "variations in the same theme, the eternal triangle of the wife, the husband, and the lover" [*Encyclopaedia Britannica*].)

Thus a whole topic entitles our Model Reader to imagine two triangles with the same base and two vertices, so as to form a horned figure, as in Figure 8.1. To frustrate his expectations, the triangle will turn out to be a false square or, better, two parallel lines that never meet, as in Figure 8.2.

Thus *Drame* is a strange sort of betting game. Until chapter 4 it has been like a normal roulette, where you put your stake on the black and

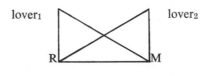

Figure 8.1

Figure 8.2

then red comes. It is a pretty fair game; you play it just in order to check whether your expectations will be verified or not. But you play according to the rules of *that* game. In chapter 6 *Drame* becomes instead a game where you bet, let us say, on 17, and the croupier announces Royal Flush. If you try to react, he asks innocently, "What seventeen? What kind of game did you think you were playing?"

When one imagines a set of individuals (and of relations among them) that the text cannot finally admit, one in fact resorts to opposing to the world of the text a possible world not accessible to it.

8.4. Possible worlds

8.4.1. The notion of possible worlds in text semiotics

The concept of the possible world is indispensable when we wish to speak of inferential walks. Returning to chapter 2 and to the gesture of Raoul, inference (i) concerning the wishes of Raoul deals with the possible world depending on Raoul's propositional attitude; inference (ii) concerning the course of events deals with the possible world of the reader's expectation apropos of the further course of the *fabula*.

We see in chapter 2 that the possible world of Raoul's wishes is contradicted, so to speak, by the 'real' world of the *fabula* (Raoul will not beat Marguerite); and the same happens with the possible world of the reader's expectations. Both worlds are in the last analysis proved to be nonactual by the very fact that the further and the final states of the *fabula* outline a different course of events. Both remain as the sketches of another story, the story that the actual one could have been had things gone differently (that is, had the fictional world, assumed as the 'real' one, been differently organized).

Without the notion of possible worlds, inferential walks could not be distinguished from semantic disclosures, that is, the procedures of actualization of discursive structures. Both activities depend on references to encyclopedic information (various systems of codes and overcoded correlations in the case of semantic disclosure, and intertextual frames in the case of narrative structures), but they are *modally* different.

Semantic disclosures (when, for instance, actualizing the virtual semantic property «human» when a /man/ is named) concern individuals and properties within the world given by the text as the 'actual' one (and usually taken as basically similar to the world of the reader's experience or, better, of the reader's encyclopedia). Inferential walks concern, on the other hand, individuals and properties belonging to different possible worlds imagined by the reader as possible outcomes of the *fabula*.

Our problem is now the following: Is it possible to use the concept of possible worlds in the analysis of the pragmatic process of actualization of narrative structures without assuming it in a merely metaphorical way?

The notion of possible worlds has been elaborated to avoid a whole series of problems connected with intensionality so as to solve them within an extensional framework. To do so, possible-worlds semantics should take into account neither concrete differences in meaning between two expressions nor the code for interpreting a given language: "The semantic theory treats the spaces of entities and possible worlds as bare, undifferentiated sets having no structure whatever, and though the space of moments of time is at least an ordered set, it is common and convenient to impose very few requirements on the ordering relations" (Thomason, 1974:50).

It must be clear that our concern is rather different: we are interested in *concrete* occurrences of semantic disclosures and of inferential walks. From the point of view of a text semiotics, a possible world is not a bare but an *overfurnished* set. In other words, we shall speak not of abstract types of possible worlds that do not contain a list of individuals (Hintikka, 1973:chap. 1), but, on the contrary, of 'pregnant' worlds of which one must know all the acting individuals and their properties.

This assumption is open to a double order of strictures, both expressed by Volli (1978):

(i) The notion of possible worlds is used in many philosophical contexts, sometimes as a mere figure of speech coming from science-fiction novels, sometimes in an extremely metaphysical sense, sometimes as a mere formal calculus dealing with intensional entities as if they were collections of extensional entities, plus an appealing metaphor. Therefore, as a notion in modal logic, it is doubtful; as a philosophical notion it is outdated; and, as a category applicable to natural languages and semiotic systems, it falls under the stricture (ii). Also, from a logical point of view, inasmuch as it depends on the notions of necessity and possibility, it is ruled by a mere *petitio principii*. To say that a proposition *p* is necessary in a given world if it is true in all possible worlds accessible to it does not say anything, since it is frequently said that two or more worlds are mutually accessible (or alternative compossible) when the same necessary propositions hold in all of them. To say that a proposition *p* is possible in a given world, when *p* holds in at least one among its compossible worlds, is even more circular. Moreover, the forms of accessibility (reflexivity, transitivity, symmetry) change according to different modal systems (see Hughes and Cresswell, 1968).

(ii) The notion of possible worlds as used in the context of natural languages is a *substantive* one. If the formal notion at least permits certain calculuses, the substantive one does not; therefore, why use it?

This kind of criticism sounds very convincing, and I am eager to accept it when dealing with a lot of pseudometaphysical questions concerning counterfactuals or the ontological status of what would have happened had things not gone the way they did.

But I cannot avoid some considerations concerning my present research:

(i) It is rather difficult to deal with inferential walks without disposing of some notion of *possible* courses of events.

(ii) A text such as *Drame* seems to suggest that we have to introduce the notion of possible worlds of one's beliefs into the picture in order to explain how *Drame* works (or how it does not work at all).

(iii) If the notion of possible worlds comes from literature, why not bring it back there?

8.4.2.   Some definitions

To avoid a lot of epistemological discussions about the different senses of this notion, let me outline a definition of the possible world, accessibility among worlds, and the identity of a given individual through worlds (transworld identity) which fits the requirement of a semiotic analysis of pragmatic processes in generating and interpreting texts (see mainly Petőfi,1975,1976; Vaina,1976,1977):

(i) a possible world is a *possible state of affairs* expressed by a set of relevant propositions where for every proposition either p or $\sim p$;

(ii) as such it outlines a set of possible *individuals* along with their *properties;*

(iii) since some of these properties or predicates are actions, a possible world is also a *possible course of events;*

(iv) since this course of events is not actual, it must depend on the *propositional attitudes* of somebody; in other words, possible worlds are worlds imagined, believed, wished, and so on.

It has been rather natural for some authors to compare a possible world with a 'complete novel' as an ensemble of statements that cannot be increased without making it inconsistent. A possible world is in effect what such a complete novel describes (Hintikka,1967,1969b). According to Plantinga (1974), "any possible world has its own book: for any possible world W the book on W is the set S of propositions such that p is a member of S if W entails p. . . . Each maximal possible set of propositions is the book on some world" (p. 46).

To say, however, that setting up a possible world is like setting up a text does not imply that setting up a text necessarily means setting up a possible world. If I am telling someone how Columbus discovered America, I am undoubtedly producing a text which refers to what is commonly believed to be the 'real' world. By describing a portion of it, I am taking for granted all the rest of its individuals along with their properties and all the rest of the propositions holding in it.

But something different happens when I set up a fictional possible world such as a fairy tale. When telling the story of Little Red Riding Hood, I furnish a world with a limited number of individuals (mother, girl, grandmother, wolf, hunter, a wood, two houses, a gun) endowed with a limited number of properties holding only for that world; for instance, in this story wolves can speak and human beings have the property of not dying when devoured by wolves.[6]

Within this fictional world (a possible one constructed by the author), human individuals assume propositional attitudes; for instance, Little Red Riding Hood believes that the wolf is trustworthy. This world is a *doxastic* construct of the character (it is immaterial by now how much it overlaps the world of the story). As a doxastic construct it is presented by the author as one of the events of the story. Thus we have two partially different constructs: in the former wolves are not trustworthy, whereas in the latter they are. Since the final state of the story disproves the doxastic world of the character, one must ask to what extent those constructs are mutually comparable and accessible. To answer this question let me make some theoretical assumptions.

8.4.3.   Possible worlds as cultural constructs

First, let me assume that a possible world (hereafter W) is an *ens rationis,* or a *rational construct*. Within its frame the difference between individuals and properties should disappear, individuals being singled out as bundles of properties. Nevertheless, the distinction must be maintained for practical purposes, since no possible world sets up *ex nihilo* all its elements. Hintikka (1973) has shown how one can construct different possible worlds by differently combining four different properties. Given the properties

round   red   not round   not red

shared by four individuals, as shown in Figure 8.3, there can be a W_1 in which x_1 and x_3 exist and in which x_2 and x_4 do not. And there can be

	red	round
x_1	$+$	$+$
x_2	$+$	$-$
x_3	$-$	$+$
x_4	$-$	$-$

Figure 8.3

a W_2 in which only x_2 and x_4 exist, or a third W_3 in which only x_1 exists.

It is clear at this point that individuals in themselves are nothing else but pairs of differently combined properties.

Rescher (1973:331) speaks of a possible world as an *ens rationis,* or as "an approach to possibilia as rational constructs," and proposes a feasible matrix by which one can compose sets of essential and accidental properties thus outlining possible individuals. I would prefer to speak of a 'cultural' construct.

Thus Little Red Riding Hood, within the framework of the story that *creates* her, is a mere spatiotemporal meeting of physical qualities, relations with other characters, actions performed, or passions suffered.[7]

Nevertheless, the text does not list all the possible properties of that girl: by telling us that she is a little girl the text directs our semantic disclosures towards the 'real' world or our world of reference. The same is done with the wolf except for the explicit substitution of the property «nonspeaking» with «able to speak». In this sense a narrative world picks up preexisting sets of properties (and therefore individuals) from the 'real' world, that is, from the world to which the reader is invited to refer as the world of reference.

This happens for both theoretical and practical reasons. No fictional world could be totally autonomous, since it would be impossible for it to outline a maximal and consistent state of affairs by stipulating *ex nihilo* the whole of its individuals and of their properties. As we have seen, it is enough for a story to assert that there exists an (imaginary) individual called Raoul; then, by defining him as a man, the text refers to the normal properties attributed to men in the world of reference. A fictional text abundantly overlaps the world of the reader's encyclopedia. But also, from a theoretical point of view, this overlapping is indispensable, and not only for fictional worlds.

It is quite impossible to build up a complete alternative world or even to describe our 'real' one as completely built up. Even from a strictly formal point of view, it seems hard to produce an exhaustive description of a complete state of affairs, and it is more feasible to resort to a model ensemble or to a partial description, a reduced schema of a possible world which is a part of our 'real' one (Hintikka,1973,1). It is not only a matter of convenience: elsewhere (Eco,1976,2.12,13) I have tried to demonstrate that the Global Semantic Universe or Global Encyclopedia can never be exhaustively outlined, since it is a self-contradictory and continuously evolving system of interrelations. In other words, we are unable to give an exhaustive description even of our world, and its Global Encyclopedia is a mere regulative hypothesis.

Thus all possible worlds, and fictional worlds in particular, pick up many of their individuals as already recognizable as such in the world of reference.

8.4.4. The construction of the world of reference

Within the framework of a constructivistic approach to possible worlds, even a so-called 'actual' or 'real' world of reference must be taken as a possible world, that is, as a cultural construct.

One can say that the fantastic property of not dying when swallowed by a beast does not hold in the 'real' world because it is inconsistent with the second principle of thermodynamics. But to judge this property as 'untrue' or 'impossible', we just refer to a system of notions, that is, to our semantic encyclopedia.

When the medieval reader read in the Bible that Jonah was swallowed by a whale, the reader did not find this fact inconsistent with his own encyclopedia, that is, the various *Specula Mundi* basically founded upon the Bible. Now, his encyclopedia was as much a text as our own (our reasons for judging *our* encyclopedia more reliable are extrasemiotic and extralogical). We can only say that both the story of Jonah and the story of Little Red Riding Hood (taken as pieces of narrativity) respectively overlap *their own* world of reference.[8]

The above assumptions apparently have a metaphysical flavor and sound rather idealistic. But they have a precise operational function in the present framework.

To face the problem of accessibility between worlds and the problem of transworld identity, one has to assume a *constructivistic* approach in which possible worlds are cultural constructs. But since each of these rational constructs overlaps its world of reference, a problem arises: how can rational constructs be compared with something which is *given* (and not constructed) like the world of our experience?

Therefore even the world of reference has to be postulated and dealt with as a cultural construct. In fact, the features characterizing possible worlds as cultural constructs can be adapted to a nonintuitive definition of the world of reference. A possible world is a part of one's conceptual system and depends on conceptual schemas. According to Hintikka

(1969a) possible worlds split into those that fit our propositional attitudes and those which do not. In this sense our commitment to a possible world is an 'ideological' rather than an ontological matter.

I think that by 'ideological' we should understand something which depends on one's own encyclopedia. If a believes that p, says Hintikka, it means that p is the case in all possible worlds compatible with a's beliefs. The beliefs of a can also be a rather trivial matter concerning a very private course of events, but they form part of a larger system of a's beliefs which is a's encyclopedia. If a believes that Jonah could safely be swallowed by a whale, this happens because a's encyclopedia does not contradict this possibility. Living in the Middle Ages a could say that nothing, in the 'real' world of his experience, had ever contradicted this piece of encyclopedic information. Notice that in the Middle Ages a could have been convinced that he had really seen unicorns: his encyclopedia had so molded his perceptual experience that, in the right hour of the day and with appropriate atmospheric and psychological conditions, he could have easily mistaken a deer for a unicorn.

Therefore a's world of reference is an encyclopedic construct. All this can sound rather Kantian, and I do not deny it. Neither does Hintikka: there is not a *Ding an sich* that can be described or even identified outside the framework of a conceptual structure (1969a).

Now, what are the effects upon a theory of possible worlds when this epistemological caution is disregarded?

Possible worlds come to be compared to our own as though we lived in a privileged world of unquestionable and already given individuals and properties, accessibility and transworld identity being only a matter of credibility or conceivability on our part.[9] Accessibility is not a matter of psychological conceivability. To say that one world is accessible to another if the individuals living in the former can conceive of the latter presupposes that one is anthropomorphically putting oneself within a given world taken as the 'actual' one and trying to speculate whether what happens in another world fits the requirements of one's own. This attitude is existentially justified; since our human condition (our *in-der-Welt-sein*) makes us experience our *hic et nunc* and confers on it a preferential status (at the last frontiers of formalization, frequently the *Lebenswelt* is still blackmailing modal logic as well).

But this attitude prevents one from considering even one's own world of reference as a cultural construct. Moreover, it makes it difficult to consider, from the same point of view, the mutual accessibility of two possible worlds W_1 and W_2 equally independent of one's reference world. Fortunately, it has been stated very clearly that 'actual' is an indexical expression and that 'actual world' is every world in which its inhabitants refer to it as the world where they live (see Stalnaker, 1976). But at this point there is no longer an actual world. /Actual/ becomes a linguistic device like /I/ or /this/.

Therefore accessibility as conceivability can be maintained as a mere metaphor, even though a very useful one.

Anyway, conceivability ought not to be confused with compatibility with *one*'s own propositional attitudes. If a propositional attitude is dependent on the assumption of a given encyclopedia, then accessibility (and compatibility) are not a matter of psychology, but one of objective and formal comparison between two cultural constructs. Thus we are only faced with a problem of *transformability among structures*.

We shall see that such an approach accounts both for questions of accessibility among worlds and for transworld identity.

8.5. Textual topics and necessity

8.5.1. Diagnostic properties

In order to go with the notion of possible worlds in textual analysis, one must face the problem of the properties assigned to a given individual: Are there some properties more resistant than others to narcotization? Is there a sort of logical or semantic hierarchy subdividing semantic properties as strictly necessary, sloppily necessary, and merely accidental?

Let us approach it through a textual example.

In chapter 2 Raoul and Marguerite at the end of the play return home in a coupé. By an elementary operation of semantic disclosure the reader understands that a coupé is a carriage. (It is commonly admitted that the proposition «this is a coupé» *entails* «this is a carriage»—as well as «this is a vehicle».)

However, dictionaries also say that a coupé is a "short four-wheeled closed carriage with an inside seat for two and an outside seat on the front for the driver."[10] As such a coupé is frequently confused with a brougham (even though broughams may have two or four wheels and two or four places, and positively have their driver's seat *on the rear*).

There is, however, a reason for which a coupé is somewhat similar to a brougham: both are closed and are 'bourgeois carriages'. As such they may be opposed to a 'proletarian carriage' such as an omnibus, which can have as many as sixteen passengers.

One may thus say that the different properties of broughams and coupés become more or less 'necessary' or 'essential' (this difference will be clarified later) only in respect to discursive and narrative topics: necessity or essentiality is a matter of co-textual comparison. When one compares a coupé with a brougham, the position of the driver's seat becomes *diagnostic* (Nida,1975), whereas that of the top roof does not. When one compares a coupé with a cabriolet, the diagnostic opposition is top roof vs. folding top.

A diagnostic property is one allowing me to single out without ambiguity the class of individuals I am referring to within a given co-textual world (see also Putnam,1970).

In chapter 2 the dominant topic is that our heroes are quarreling. The subtopic is that they are going home. What is implicit (and must be inferred by resorting to common and intertextual frames) is that Raoul and Marguerite, being a decent bourgeois couple, must solve their problems *privately*. What they need is a *closed bourgeois* carriage. The position of the driver's seat is irrelevant. A cabriolet (with its folding top) is excluded, a brougham is not. The translator of *Drame* (see Appendix 2) has translated /coupé/ as «hansom cab»—a carriage which has more or less the same properties as a brougham.

8.5.2.   Entailment as a metalinguistic device

Nevertheless, there is a difference between having four (or two) wheels and being a carriage:

> *This is a coupé but it is not a carriage*

sounds semantically odd, while

> *This is a coupé but it does not have four wheels*

is acceptable.

It seems that there is a difference between *logically* *necessary* properties and *factual* or 'accidental' properties. One can say that, once certain meaning postulates (Carnap,1952) have been accepted, a brougham is *necessarily* a carriage while whether it has two or four wheels is only an *accidental* property (see Figure 8.4).[11]

This difference depends, however, on a linguistic *trompe-l'oeil*. If one wonders why dictionaries never record among the properties of a brougham those of being able to move and being horse-drawn, the obvious answer is that these properties are semantically *included* in the definition of carriage and of vehicle. Without this process of inclusion, a

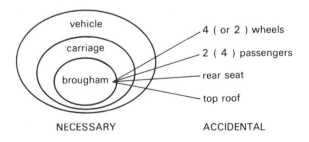

Figure 8.4

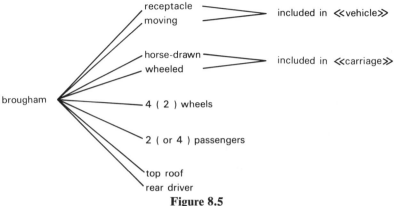

Figure 8.5

'fussy' semantic representation of /brougham/ should assume the format presented in Figure 8.5. In reality this representation should be even more fussy, since also «receptacle», «moving», «horse», and so on, should be dissolved into a network of more analytical definitions.

Fortunately, we have at our disposal *metalinguistic shorthands* by which (to save time and space) we avoid making explicit those properties that the encyclopedia has already recorded under hyperonomical headings (such as «carriage»), so as to make them equally applicable to coaches, chaises, landaus, phetons, berlins, and victorias. This is the phenomenon of unlimited semiosis theorized by Peirce: every sign is interpreted by other signs or strings of signs (definitions and texts), so that every term is a rudimentary assertion, and every proposition a rudimentary argumentation (C.P.2.342–44).

In this way analyzation and procedures of entailment appear only as metalinguistic devices substituting a broader (and potentially infinite) list of factual properties. In a 'fussy' description there will be no difference between necessary and accidental properties, as in the example of meaning postulates proposed by Carnap, where it is a matter of entailment to say that a bachelor is a male adult as well as to say that ravens are black.

It is true that in Carnap's perspective there is still a difference between L-truths and synthetic truths, an L-implication being "meant as explicantum for logical implication or entailment" (Carnap,1947:11) and entailment being intended as a case of analytic truth.

From this point of view, coupés and broughams still seem to be analytically moving structures by virtue of a meaning postulate, while the fact that they were bourgeois vehicles seems to remain a mere factual truth. But on this subject one cannot but agree with Quine's "Two Dogmas of Empiricism" (1951) and his critique of Carnap's views. That a coupé is a carriage is as empirical (dependent on linguistic codes) as the historical notion that it was used by wealthy people (or, to follow Quine, that on Elm Street there is a certain brick house).

The difference between synthetic and analytic depends upon the point of view from which one determines what is the center and what is the periphery of a global and homogeneous system of cultural notions, on which even our capability of organizing concrete experience depends.

At this point the notion of necessary property becomes one of "necessary under some description" (Chisholm,1967:6).

Let us consider once again the relevant properties of the three types of carriage I have mentioned, according to a very simplified compositional analysis (where obviously + means the presence of a certain property, − means its absence, and 0 = undetermined) as shown in Figure 8.6. Properties 1 to 6 are undoubtedly relevant in the co-text of *Drame,* whereas properties 7 and 8 are irrelevant and can be narcotized. But suppose that a coupé is needed by the director of a historical museum of carriages. He wants something that can be precisely distinguished from a brougham (and obviously from an automobile). He looks for properties 3 to 8, especially focusing on properties 7 and 8. What he is not interested in is the ability to move and to contain people: the museum's coupés can have rusty suspensions and damaged spindles.[12]

Let us therefore assume that in detecting properties we are interested in those which are *essential in respect to the textual topic.* We shall thus employ the term 'essential' to indicate those properties which are taken as pertinent in a given universe of discourse. The term 'necessary' will be retained for different purposes (see 8.6.5 and 8.7.2).

8.6. World structures, accessibility, identity

8.6.1. Blowing up (and narcotizing) diagnostic properties as 'essential'
According to the previous chapter, the essentiality of a property is topic-sensitive. Now, we can say that it is the discursive topic which outlines the world structure W_0 as a reduced model of the world of reference,

	receptacle	moving	horse-drawn	wheeled	top roof	2 pass.	4 wheels	front driver
brougham	+	+	+	+	+	0	0	−
hansom	+	+	+	+	+	+	−	+
coupé	+	+	+	+	+	+	+	−
	1	2	3	4	5	6	7	8

Figure 8.6

where the individuals and their properties are selected according to the question governing the textual course. This world structure W_0 cannot be the globality (unattainable) of the world of reference, but just a *profile* of it or *perspective* on it that we take as determinant for the interpretation and the generation of a given text.

Therefore we can say that, if my mother-in-law wonders what might have happened to her son-in-law had he not married her daughter, the obvious answer would be: in her W_0 I and her son-in-law are the same person, but in her counterfactual world W_1 she is dealing with two different persons, one of which is rather imprecise.

If, on the contrary, one wonders what would have happened had the author of the present paper (W_0) never married (W_1), the answer is: probably this paper in W_1 would not contain the present example, but this shift in kinship properties would not seriously affect the procedure of identification: the author of this paper in W_0 will be the same as the author of this paper in W_1.

It has been objected (Volli,1978) that, if a possible world is never complete and overlaps its world of reference, then, when considering the world of reference, one should take into account the entire content of the encyclopedia it represents. Therefore, when considering the W_1 of my mother-in-law's counterfactual, where I exist as borrowed from the 'actual' world, I should consider all the propositions holding in the second one, namely, that the Earth is round, that 17 is a prime number, that Hawaii is in the Pacific, and so on.

This sounds preposterous when compared to the remarks of section 8.5. The above counterfactual depends on a specific discursive topic (my kinship relation with that lady) and this topic has made clear that among my properties only a few must be *blown up* (mainly those of being an adult male and being married to a certain person). All the others are *narcotized* and are potentially *stored* in the encyclopedia this specific topic indirectly trusts. I do not have to speculate whether in W_1 I have two legs as in W_0, since in W_0 it is not requested of me to decide whether I have two legs (I am simply alerted to react should I be outlined in W_1 as a cripple or a *cul-de-jatte*). But this is always a psychological picture of the situation. According to the topic the world structure W_0, reduced in individuals and properties, has been built up so as to compare it to the equally reduced W_1.[13]

8.6.2. Potential variants and supernumeraries

Let me borrow from Rescher (1973) a series of suggestions to outline a simplified model of transworld identity and of accessibility among worlds.

Let us define a possible world as a construct for which are specified the following:

(i)   a family of actual individuals $x_1, x_2, x_3 \ldots$;
(ii) a family of properties $F, C, M \ldots$, attributed to individuals;
(iii) an 'essentiality specification' for every individual, as to whether this property is or is not essential to it;
(iv) relations between properties (for instance, relations of entailment).

Given a W_1 with two individuals x_1 and x_2 and three properties F, C, M, the sign $+$ means that an individual has the corresponding property, the sign $-$ means that it does not, and the parentheses mark the essential properties, as shown in Figure 8.7.

W_1	F	C	M
x_1	(+)	(+)	−
x_2	+	+	(−)

Figure 8.7

Now let us imagine a W_2 in which are individuals with properties as shown in Figure 8.8.

W_2	F	C	M
y_1	(+)	(+)	+
y_2	+	−	(−)
y_3	(+)	(−)	(+)

Figure 8.8

An individual in W_2 is the *potential variant* of its *prototype* individual in W_1 if they differ only in accidental properties (therefore y_1 in W_2 is a variant of x_1 in W_1 and y_2 in W_2 is a variant of x_2 in W_1).

An individual in W_2 is a *supernumerary* in respect to the individuals in W_1 if it differs from them also in essential properties (therefore $y_3 \in W_2$ is supernumerary in respect to W_1).

When a prototype in W_1 has no more than *one* potential variant in W_2, potential variance coincides with so-called transworld identity.

If we come back for a moment to the example given in 8.6.1, where my mother-in-law wonders what might have happened if I had never married her daughter, we see that she refers to a world structure of the sort shown in Figure 8.9, where M is the essential property of being married to her daughter and P is the accidental property of being the author of this paper.

On the contrary, when one wonders what might have happened if the author of this paper had never married, one refers back to a world structure of the sort shown in Figure 8.10.

W_0	M	P
x_1	(+)	+

Figure 8.9

W_0	M	P
x_2	+	(+)

Figure 8.10

It is clear that the x appearing in both worlds is not the same individual. Whichever of the two worlds is taken as a world of reference in respect to the other, the two individuals x_1 and x_2 will appear not as reciprocal variants but as independent supernumeraries. It is clear that in these world structures 'essential' properties are co-textually established insofar as they are textually *diagnostic*.

8.6.3. Transworld identity

The real problem of transworld identity is to single out something as persistent through alternative states of affairs. That is nothing other than the Kantian problem of the constancy of the object. But in making this observation Bonomi (1975:133) remarks that the idea of the object must be linked to the one of its congruence between multiple localizations. Thus transworld identity has to be analyzed from the phenomenological point of view of the Husserlian notion of *Abschattung,* that is, of the different profiles I can assign to the object of my experience. To establish a profile means to outline a textual topic.[14]

Chisholm (1967) proposes a supposed W_0 inhabited by Adam (who lived 930 years) and Noah (who lived 950 years). Then Chisholm wittily begins to outline different worlds in which the two individuals step by step respectively increase and decrease their lifetime to reach a world in which not only Adam lived 950 years and Noah 930 years, but in which Adam is called Noah, and vice versa. Chisholm, once he has arrived at the puzzling question of their identity, skims over the only possible answer, since he does not attempt to establish the essential properties to be taken into account. The answer depends on the question, more exactly on that implicit or explicit question which establishes the discoursive topic. Had the experiment of Chisholm concerned *the first man,* no change in age or name would have altered this essential (or diagnostic) property taken in W_0 as the only point of reference.

8.6.4. Accessibility

Having established these criteria we can now define what we assume as accessibility among worlds.

According to current literature on the subject, accessibility is a dyadic relation $W_i \, R \, W_j$, where W_j is accessible to W_i. To disregard any psychological interpretation of the term /accessibility/ (of the type 'can individuals in W_i conceive of W_j?'), we can say that a W_j is accessible to a W_i when the world structure of W_i can generate (through manipulations of the relations between individuals and properties) the world structure of W_j.

Thus we have different relational possibilities:

  (i) $W_i \, R \, W_j$, but not $W_j \, R \, W_i$: the relation is dyadic but not symmetric;
 (ii) $W_i \, R \, W_j$ and $W_j \, R \, W_i$: the relation is dyadic and symmetric;
(iii) $W_i \, R \, W_j$, $W_j \, R \, W_k$, $W_i \, R \, W_k$: the relation is dyadic and transitive;
 (iv)   the above relation becomes *also* symmetric.

Given two or more worlds these relations can change as to whether

 (a)   the number of individuals and properties is the same in all worlds;
 (b)   the number of individuals increases in at least one world;
 (c)   the number of individuals decreases in at least one world;
 (d)   the properties change;
 (e)   (other possibilities resulting from the combination of the above).

I think that apropos of fictional worlds an interesting typology of this sort can be attempted to distinguish different literary genres (for a first interesting approach see Pavel, 1975). For our present purpose we can consider only certain basic cases.

Let us first examine a case in which (independent of any discrimination among essential and accidental properties) there are in two worlds the same number of individuals and the same properties (see Figure 8.11). It is evident that certain combinatory manipulations can lead the individuals in W_1 to become structurally identical with the individuals in W_2, and vice versa. Therefore in this case $W_1 \, R \, W_2$ and $W_2 \, R \, W_1$.

Let us consider now a second case in which in W_1 there are fewer properties than in W_2 (see Figure 8.12). To make the example more palatable, let us imagine that, according to a previous example borrowed from Hintikka, the properties in W_1 are to be round and red. In W_2 the

W_1	F	C	M		W_2	F	C	M
x_1	+	+	−		y_1	+	−	−
x_2	+	−	+		y_2	−	+	+

Figure 8.11

W_1	round	red
x_1	+	−
x_2	+	+

W_2	round	red	whirling
y_1	+	−	+
y_2	+	+	−

Figure 8.12

same properties are considered plus an additional one, to be a whirling entity.

We can say that in W_3 it is possible to manipulate the world structure in viduals of W_1 inside the world structure of W_2. Individuals x_1 and x_2 can be evaluated in W_2 as shown in Figure 8.13,

$(W_2 \longrightarrow W_1)$	round	red	whirling
y_3	+	−	−
y_4	+	+	−

Figure 8.13

and, from this point of view, y_4 can be said to be structurally identical with y_2, while y_3 appears as a brand new individual.

The opposite is not possible since the world structure of W_1 cannot score the presence or the absence of a property such as whirling. Therefore $W_2 R W_1$, while the symmetrical relation does not hold.

Intuitively, this is the situation outlined by Abbott in *Flatland,* where a being living in a tridimensional world visits a bidimensional one and can conceive of the individuals living there, and manages to describe them, while the individuals of the bidimensional world cannot conceive of the visitor.

Now consider a third case (see Figure 8.14), in which there is also a third world W_3 where the property of whirling is *essential* for every individual and where no individual can both exist and be nonwhirling at the same time (as seems to be the case of the planets of our solar system). We can say that in W_3 it is possible to manipulate the world structure in two ways:

(i) as far as W_1 is concerned, it is possible to proceed as in the previous case $(W_2 R W_1)$ except that the produced individuals can be considered as supernumeraries;

(ii) as far as W_2 is concerned, y_1 in W_2 can be considered a variant of k_1 in W_3 simply by recognizing its property of whirling as essential (at least as far as it does not stop); y_2 in W_2 can be considered a supernumerary.

W_1	round	red	W_2	round	red	whirling	W_3	round	red	whirling
x_1	+	−	y_1	+	−	+	k_1	+	−	(+)
x_2	+	+	y_2	+	+	−	k_2	+	+	(+)

Figure 8.14

Since from the structure of W_3 the other two worlds can be obtained, among these three worlds a dyadic and transitive relation can be recognized: W_1 is accessible to W_2, which in turn is accessible to W_3, while the symmetrical relation does not hold.

8.6.5. Necessary truths and accessibility

A last remark concerns so-called logical or eternal truths that seem to play such an important role in the current literature about possible worlds. I think that logically necessary propositions cannot be ranked as a kind of property. A logical truth such as 'either p or $\sim p$' is the very condition of possibility of the world structures presented above. Suppose there is a W_4 in which the individuals can both have and not have a certain property at the same time. I do not suggest that the possession of a given property can remain undetermined; I simply mean that the signs + and − both have the same value, or none at all.

What I am outlining is obviously neither a possible nor an impossible world. It is the very *impossibility of setting up a world* on the bases of the above criteria. These criteria depend on the principle of identification of mathematical symbols, or on the notion of presence and absence of a property. In the terms we have assumed as primitives, it is impossible to speak of an impossible world.

It would be possible to deal with this ghostly W_4 if we assumed other criteria, as in physics it is possible to assume a different notion of time to speak of certain elementary particles that seem to travel backward in time.

But this is a sort of game that need not be played as far as semiotics of narrative worlds is concerned, at least not insofar as these worlds are produced by human beings speaking to human beings who base their language on the principle of the recognizability and identification of phonemes through possible utterances.

Nevertheless, while the world-structure outlined above seems to fit the requirements of narrative worlds (we shall test this hypothesis in the next section), what has been said apropos of logical truths does not seem to be confirmed by our narrative experience. It is possible to imagine a science-fiction novel in which there are closed causal chains, that is, in which A can cause B, B can cause C, and C can cause A. In this novel an individual can travel backward through time and become his own father, or find another self only a little younger, so that the reader no longer understands *who* is the original character. Let me add that this character can also discover that, while traveling backward, 17 is no longer a prime number. Apparently, worlds where necessary truths do not hold can be imagined and are intuitively possible.

However, this is not true. Such a world is in fact *quoted,* but it is not *constructed,* or—if you want—extensionally *mentioned,* but not intensionally *analyzed.*

To say that 17 is no longer a prime number does not say so much if one does not give the rule to divide it by a number other than itself, displaying the result. And if the principle of identity were denied, the story could not be told, since the author could not name and designate any of the objects of his story, including the two-one individuals.

In fact, such a novel takes for granted a background W_0, with all its logical truths (if any), and simply introduces in its W_1 (accessible to W_0) an individual (a fantastic machine, a spatiotemporal whirl) which has the property of suspending (transitorily) the principle of identity or the principles of mathematics. This property is an *exception operator* like the Magic Donor in fairy tales or God in the theological explanation of miracles.

Although it would be impossible to compare two worlds relying on different logical systems of world construction (since our metasemiotic instrument would be seriously affected), it is not impossible to introduce into a narrative world the still unanalyzed property of being able to suspend a logical law; as a consequence, the science-fiction world W_1 will be one in which two variants of the same prototype in W_0 (or two tokens of the same supernumerary in W_1) are introduced. This affects transworld identity, but does not affect the possibility of constructing such a world by transformation of the world structure W_0.

As a matter of fact, the proper effect of such narrative constructions (be they science-fiction novels or avant-garde texts in which the very notion of self-identity is challenged) is just that of producing a sense of logical uneasiness and of narrative discomfort. So they arouse a sense of suspicion in respect to our common beliefs and affect our disposition to trust the most credited laws of the world of our encyclopedia. They *undermine* the world of our encyclopedia rather than build up another self-sustaining world.

8.7. *Fabula* and possible worlds

8.7.1. The worlds of the *fabula*

Now we can apply the previous theoretical assumption to our notion of *fabula* as the selected aspect of narrative structures-in-process.

Insofar as the *fabula* is carried on by the discursive structure as if it were a series of events constituting the only 'actual' world the reader is concerned with, we can say that a *fabula* encompasses the following:

(i) The possible world W_N imagined and asserted by the author. W_N is an abstraction: it is not the text as a semantico-pragmatic device, since it refers only to the level of *fabula;* it is not a simple state of affairs, since it starts from a given state of affairs s_1 and through lapses of time $t_1 \ldots t_n$ undergoes successive changes of state, so as to reach a final state s_n, each state shifting into the next one through a lapse of time.

Therefore I shall represent a *fabula* W_N as a succession $W_N s_i$ (where $i = 1 \ldots n$), that is, as a succession of *textual states*. A W_N can at most be described as the final state of such a succession $W_N s_n$. Intuitively, we define *Madame Bovary* as a novel telling the story of a bourgeois lady who commits adultery and then dies, and not as the story of a lady quietly living with her husband, as the *fabula* in fact says at its first states.

Notice that these textual states are not possible worlds *in respect to* W_N. They are, rather, actual states of W_N. Once taken that there exists a possible world W_N inhabited by two individuals called Raoul and Marguerite, Raoul going to the theater and Raoul receiving a letter are always the same individual of the same world undergoing two different states, just as the individual who has begun to write this paper is the same individual who is presently continuing to write it, living in the same world even though in two different states of it.

(ii) The possible subworlds W_{Nc} (where $c = $ any of the characters of W_N) that are imagined, believed, wished, and so on, by the characters of the *fabula*. Therefore a given $W_{Nc} s_i$ depicts the possible course of events as imagined (believed, wished, and so on) by a given character within a given state of the *fabula*.

(iii) The possible subworlds W_R that, at every disjunction of probability displayed by the *fabula,* the Model Reader imagines, believes, wishes, and so on, and that further states of the *fabula* in W_N must either approve or disapprove.

A W_{Rc} can also be outlined where the reader imagines, believes, wishes, and so on, that a given character believes, imagines, wishes certain things.

To conclude, one can say that the *fabula* is a possible world W_N which encompasses its successive states. It also encompasses the possible worlds W_{Nc} of the characters of the *fabula*, representing beliefs, wishes, and projects of its characters.

The strategy of discoursive structures step by step elicits the setting up on the part of the reader of possible worlds W_R which picture future possible states of W_N. Since characters, W_{Nc} and the reader's W_R can also be disproved by the states of the *fabula,* these worlds are not necessarily accessible to the world of the *fabula,* as will be shown in section 8.8.

8.7.2. S-necessary properties

The opening macroproposition of *Drame* is /Some time before 1890 there was in Paris a man called Raoul/. Resorting to our encyclopedia, we single out Paris as an individual of W_0 and 1890 as one of its past actual states (/1984/ would be instead a possible state of W_0). But what about Raoul? So far we have no elements to single him out except the fact that he was one of the men living in Paris around 1890.

Fortunately, it is also stated that he was married to Marguerite. This is enough to single out Raoul without mistaking him for another individual (as far as the *fabula* is concerned).

Raoul is that individual who in a world W_N (overlapping W_0) in a state s_1 has the property of being the one and only husband of Marguerite. Using an appropriate symbolization to assign him an *iota operator* of individual identification, we can say that

$$(\exists x) [\text{Man}(x) \cdot \text{Marry } (x,z,W_N,s_0 < s_1)] \cdot (\forall y) [\text{Man}(y) \cdot \text{Marry } (y,z, W_N,s_0 < s_1) \cdot (z = \imath x_2)] \rightarrow (y = \imath x_1) \cdot (\imath x_1 = \text{Raoul}),$$

that is, there is at least one individual x who is a man and who in the world under consideration married another individual z in a state temporally preceding the initial state of W_N; and for every individual y who shares the same properties, provided that the individual z he has married is a previously identified individual, this y cannot but be our individual, who happens to be called Raoul.

This formula sounds strange since, in order to identify Raoul, one needs the previous identification of that x_2 who is not constructed but is taken for granted.

In fact, the identification of Raoul cannot be separated from the symmetrical identification of Marguerite:

$$(\exists x) [\text{Woman}(x) \cdot \text{Marry } (x,z,W_N,s_0 < s_1)] \cdot (\forall y) [\text{Woman}(y) \cdot \text{Marry } (y,z,W_N,s_0 < s_1) \cdot (z = \imath x_1)] \rightarrow (y = \imath x_2) \cdot (\imath x_2 = \text{Marguerite}).$$

Raoul cannot be identified without Marguerite, nor can Marguerite without Raoul. This is not the way we single out individuals in the world of our experience, but this is the way followed by a narrative text in setting up its supernumeraries.

Imagine a text saying the following:

> *There is John. And there is John.*

We would refuse it as a story. Nothing says whether there are one or two Johns. A story might begin, but certainly not continue, this way. Suppose, on the contrary, that the story says the following:

*A certain evening in Casablanca a man with a white jacket was sitting
at Rick's bar. At the same time a man with a blonde woman was leaving
Lisbon.*

The first man is singled out as the one who stands in a specific relation
to a given bar (that stands in a specific relation to Casablanca) in an s_1
taken as the starting state of the story. The second one is singled out by
his relation to a woman and to another city. The specification that the
two relationships hold *at the same time* is enough to make us sure that
we are dealing with two different individuals. Specifications of this kind
characterize different kinds of narrativity: for instance, the *roman-feuilleton* gave a lot of incomplete descriptions which made a certain individual
not immediately identifiable, later to provide the surprise of revealing
that he is a well-known character of the story (topos of the 'false
unknown').

The relation between Raoul and Marguerite or that between the man
with the white jacket and Rick's bar is a dyadic and symmetric relation
xRy where x cannot be without $y,$ and vice versa.

However, this relation between the man in the white jacket, Rick's
bar, and Casablanca is dyadic, transitive but not symmetric. The man
and the bar are singled out by their mutual relation; the bar is also singled
out by its being related to Casablanca. Transitively the man is identified
also by his relation to Casablanca. But Casablanca, as an individual of
W_0 is not necessarily identified by its relation to the bar (or to the man).
So we can say that we have symmetric relations holding between supernumeraries and nonsymmetric relations holding between a supernumerary and a variant of a prototype in W_0. When there are complex inter-
twinings of relations, they are transitive.

I call these relations *S-necessary* or *structurally necessary properties.*
They hold only within the framework of a fictional world and are the
essential requisite for the identification of a supernumerary in any W_N.

Once identified as the husband of Marguerite, Raoul can no longer be
separated from his symmetrical counterpart. The story can very well assume later that he has divorced, but he remains the one who at s_1 was
the husband of Marguerite.

8.7.3. S-necessary and essential properties
Raoul is a man and Marguerite is a woman. These are essential properties, recognized also by the plot, and the *fabula* carries them on. S-necessary properties cannot deny essential ones since S-necessary properties
are also semantically bound. This means that the relation of necessity
holding between Raoul and Marguerite (rSm) appears in the *fabula* as
semantically bound *qua* the relation of marriage (rMm). Were Marguerite a man, too, since (according at least to the meaning postulates

holding in the nineteenth century) /marriage/ is to be analyzed as a relation between two human beings of opposite sex, rMm could not hold (or /marriage/ would have to be intended as a mere figure of speech introduced at the discoursive level).

Thus S-necessary properties, once established as a link producing the syntax of the *fabula,* are also submitted to the requirements of their semantic nature. Therefore they can belong to different semantic categories such as

relations of graduated antonymy (x is smaller than y);
relations of complementarity (x is a male as opposed to y who is a female);
relations of directional opposition (x is at the left of y), and many others, comprehending members of nonbinary oppositions (see Leech, 1974; Lyons,1977).

In any case, all these semantic relations in the *fabula* are structurally linked by S-necessity, and this relation is *symmetrical* in the sense that the narrative function of one element is established by the presence of another (or of many others).

Accidental properties do not interest the *fabula.* The fact that Raoul took a coupé is accidental and, as far as the *fabula* is concerned, our two heroes could have returned home walking.

Notice that, if Marguerite had forgotten or lost her purse in the coupé and the *fabula* had been focused upon the quest for the mysterious coupé, we would have a story like *Le fiacre n. 13, Le chapeau de paille d'Italie,* or "The Purloined Letter," in which the coupé could be a *precise* individual to be singled out through procedures of identification based upon S-necessity.

By S-necessity, supernumeraries in a fictional world are as necessary to each other as two distinctive features are to distinguish a given phoneme from another. To quote a dialogue from Calvino's *Invisible Cities,* when Marco Polo tells Kublai Khan about bridges:

"But which is the stone that supports the bridge? . . ."
"The bridge is not supported by one stone or another. . . . but by the line of the arch they form."
". . . Why do you speak to me of the stones? It is only the arch that matters to me."
". . . Without stones there is no arch."[15]

It is only because of this S-necessary relation that two or more characters in a *fabula* can be taken as the *actors* embodying different roles. Narrative functions à la Propp (Villain, Helper, Victim, Hero, and so on) can exist only by a mutual relation of S-necessity. Fagin is not the Villain of *Clarissa,* just as Lovelace is not the Villain of *Oliver Twist.* Meeting outside *their* stories Fagin and Lovelace might be a very pleasant couple of good guys, and maybe the one could become the Donor of the other.

They *might.* As a matter of fact, they *cannot.* Without a Clarissa on whom to press his attention, Lovelace is lost. Better, he is *unborn.*

To summarize the remarks of paragraphs 8.7.2 and 8.7.3 one can thus say the following:

In a W_N individuals are identified through their structurally necessary properties (hereafter S-necessary properties). These are symmetrical relations of strict textual interdependence. They may or may not be identical with those properties recognized as essential; in any case, they cannot deny them. Accidental properties do not belong to the world of the *fabula* and are taken into account only by the discoursive structures.

8.8. Accessibility among narrative worlds

8.8.1. Relation of accessibility between W_0 and W_N

The comparison of W_N to W_0 can assume different forms in different periods and according to different decisions on the part of the reader:

(i)   He can compare every $W_N s_1$ to W_0 looking for the versimilitude of the different states of affairs taken as synchronic.

(ii) He can compare W_N to different W_0 (I can read the *Divine Comedy* referring to the encyclopedia of a reader of the Middle Ages or to my own).

(iii) According to different literary genres the W_N suggests the right reference world: a historical novel asks for a reference to the W_0 of historical encyclopedia; a fairy tale wants the comparison with the world of our direct experience just to make us feel the pleasure of the Incredible; a rich typology of genres is possible from this point of view (Pavel,1975).

Suppose, however, that the reader has established his reference world W_0. In the case of *Drame* it should be a portion of the nineteenth-century Parisian milieu.

Let us consider a world structure W_0 in which Raoul and Marguerite do not exist; rather, M. de Porto-Riche (1849–1930) and the Théâtre d'Application (in the figure p and t) do exist.

Let us compare it to a world structure W_N where Raoul (r) and Marguerite (m) exist as supernumeraries.

Then let us consider a third world structure $W_0 \rightarrow W_N$ showing the way in which W_N can be constructed starting from W_0 (relation of accessibility).

Among the properties we consider the following: to be a male (M), to be a female (F), to be a playwright (P), and a relational property rMm that means that Raoul and Marguerite stand in a symmetrical relation of marriage. Note that a 'similar' property is formally scored also among the properties of W_0, since it is fully acceptable there that an individual be in *converse* relation with another.

S-necessary properties are represented in W_N between square brackets.

The world structure of W_0, this not being a *fabula,* ignores S-necessary properties. $W_0 \to W_N$ can consider properties which are S-necessary in W_N as normal relations (in this case a relation of converseness between husband and wife) that can be scored either as essential or as accidental.

In W_0 there are two individuals that are accepted in W_N as variants (as a matter of fact, because of the elementarity of the world structures, they are identical). From W_0 is constructible a W_N which contains them.

In W_0, r and m are not considered. They exist in W_N as supernumeraries in respect to W_0. It is not impossible from W_0 to shift to W_N so as to set up W_N as a possible world, accessible from W_0, where these supernumeraries have as essential the property of being reciprocally related. Notice that the relation of S-necessity holds as such only within the fictional world. From W_0 such a relation can be constructed at most as an essential property. I mean that in psychological terms an inhabitant of W_0 can conceive of a possible course of events in which in Paris there lived two persons to be essentially defined as linked by a kinship relationship. No more and no less.

Therefore $W_0\ R\ W_N$. From the reference world we can produce the narrative one, and the narrative world is accessible to the world of reference.

However, this relation is not symmetrical, since, in the world structure of W_N, the rule holds that an individual cannot be identified as such without its S-necessary property. The category of S-necessary property does not make sense in worlds different from the fictional one. Therefore to produce from W_N another world lacking this formative rule is like trying to produce from our world a world in which 17 is not a prime number or in which a is not a (see 8.6.5). In other words, we must deal

W_0	M	F	P	xRy
p	(+)	(−)	(+)	0
t	(−)	(−)	(−)	0

W_N	M	F	P	rMm
p	(+)	(−)	(+)	0
t	(−)	(−)	(−)	0
r	(+)	(−)	(−)	[+]
m	(−)	(+)	(−)	[+]

$W_0 \to W_N$	M	F	P	rMm
p	(+)	(−)	(+)	0
t	(−)	(−)	(+)	0
r	(+)	(−)	−	(+)
m	(−)	(+)	(−)	(+)

Figure 8.15

with W_N as if in it the notion of supernumerary individual dissolved into the property of being necessarily and symmetrically related to another given individual. In W_N a supernumerary is the set of the x's that satisfy the condition of being related symmetrically to another given individual.

The fact that such a set has one and only one member makes the identification of a supernumerary possible.

Since this is all these objects are, it is clear that, in another world in which this relation is not considered a necessary condition for the construction of the world structure, they cannot be constructed.

Therefore it cannot be said that $W_N \ R \ W_0$.

The above demonstration can be taken as a mere game, since no one seems interested in the question whether, from the inside of a fictional world, our world W_0 can be reached (the hypothesis of a fictional text in which a character tries to deal with W_0, as in Pirandello's *Six Characters in Search of an Author,* represents a case of *trompe-l'oeil:* even the author takes part in Pirandello's W_N, a world that encompasses many W_{Nc}).

However, a psychological experiment may be useful.

Consider Dumas' *The Three Musketeers.* There (W_N) we have certain individuals also belonging to W_0 (such as Richelieu and probably d'Artagnan) who retain their essential properties as far as the historical frame is concerned. Richelieu is a French Cardinal, the prime minister of Louis XIII, and so on. Then there are some supernumeraries, among which Athos and Lady de Winter. Besides their essential properties they have the relational property of having been husband and wife (and the *fabula* strictly depends on this interidentification).

Now let us imagine Athos wondering how things might have been were he not the husband of Milady. In this case, from W_N, Athos would not be able to conceive of a variant of himself. He is Athos only insofar as he is the husband of Milady. Split from this relation he would disappear. Athos knows this rule very well and cannot conceive of a world in which both 'Athos exists' and 'Athos does not exist' would be equally nonsensical, since the definition of Athos is nothing but 'this x who is related to Milady'.

Obviously, this is a rather metaphysical game: Athos can have propositional attitudes as an individual of W_N in a W_{Nc} about the course of future events in W_N, but he cannot have propositional attitudes concerning a W_N set up totally differently. But this is exactly what I am trying to say. The world of a *fabula* cannot be otherwise. Were it otherwise, Athos would be somebody else living in another W_N.[16]

The fact is that we are not so interested in speculating about our world from the point of view of a novel, but are, rather, eager to do the opposite, to analyze the world of a novel from our point of view (as happens particularly when applying to novels the criteria of a strictly realistic aesthetics). Thus our previous experiment seems to be preposterous.

But frequently we do use a fictional possible world to judge our own—for instance, when saying with Aristotle that poetry is more philosophical than life, since in poetry nothing happens by chance as happens in life (history), and in poetry everything appears strictly necessary (*Poetics*, 1451b,1452a). So do we when, for instance, we observe that a certain fictional character is more 'true' than its 'real' prototype or that fiction is more 'rational' than life and its characters more 'universally' or 'typically' real than their illusory empirical prototypes. Probably Don Quixote did so.[17]

To conclude: The world of the *fabula* W_N is accessible to W_0, but this relation is not symmetric.

8.8.2. Relations of accessibility among the subworlds of the characters and the states of the *fabula*

The comparison between a W_N (with the globality of its states) and a W_0 is always synchronic. Our reference world can be compared to the entire course of events represented by the whole *fabula* or can be compared step by step to its states, each of them taken as a possible state of affairs. On the contrary, a given possible subworld imagined by a character at a given state of the *fabula* (let it be $W_{Nc}s_n$) can be compared either to a previous or to a further state of the *fabula,* that is, to a $W_N s_1$ or to a $W_N s_3$.

A character can imagine or believe or wish either in the course of discursive structures or in the course of the *fabula*. Let us call the first series of propositional attitudes 'events of the plot'—intending by 'plot' the whole series of events which take place in the course of the discursive development, but which are not strictly essential to the development of the *fabula*. The plot is thus a series of micropropositions which carry on the basic macronarrative propositions to be abduced by the reader when trying to single out the *fabula*. So the fact that in chapter 2 Raoul wants to beat Marguerite concerns the plot, but is unessential to the course of the *fabula*.

Normally, propositional attitudes displayed in the course of the plot concern both essential and accidental properties of the individuals in play, whereas the propositional attitudes displayed in the course of the *fabula* basically concern S-necessary properties.

In the course of the plot, characters set up various imaginary courses of events: one believes that a given person will arrive, whereas this person in fact does not; one thinks that a given person is lying while he or she is telling the truth; and so on. These propositional attitudes are set up by the plot to outline the psychology of the different characters and are frequently rapidly disproved (maybe in the course of the same short sequence of sentences). Frequently, these attitudes produce possible worlds which are inaccessible to the world such as is outlined by the plot. However, these rules of accessibility being the same as those assumed in 8.6.4, when the W_1 of a given character's beliefs scores more properties than are considered by the W_0 of discursive events, the character can readjust his own wrong belief by doing as suggested by Figures 8.12 and 8.13 in 8.6.4. The character readjusts his own beliefs and accepts the world as it is outlined by the plot. He, so to speak, throws away his wrong belief as soon as he recognizes that the (fictional) reality is different.

The question becomes even simpler when there is no difference in properties between the real (fictional) world and the world of one character's beliefs.

In chapter 2 Marguerite outlines a W_1 of her beliefs when thinking that Raoul (who has the property of being essentially related to her by marriage also has the property of coveting Mlle. Moreno. Then she discovers (let us suppose) that it was untrue. The transformation between the two worlds (where C = to covet Moreno) takes place as shown in Figure 8.16. Raoul in Marguerite's world is a variant of Raoul in the world of the plot. In the plot, therefore, relations between worlds follow the same rules as in the world of our common experience (see 8.3.6).

W_1	rMm	C		W_2	rMm	C
r	$(+)$	$+$		r	$(+)$	$-$

Figure 8.16

But there are cases in which the propositional attitudes of the characters make up part of the *fabula* itself. When Oedipus believes that he has nothing to do with the death of Laius, we are facing a belief that has two characteristics: (i) it is indispensable to the development of the *fabula;* (ii) it concerns an S-necessary relation (Oedipus is fictionally nothing else but that individual who has killed his father and married his mother without knowing it). Obviously, to be indispensable to the course of the *fabula* and to be S-necessary are two facets of the same fictional phenomenon.

At a certain point of the story, Oedipus believes that there are at large four individuals: Oedipus (e), who has killed an unknown wayfarer (u) a long time ago; and Laius (l), who has been murdered by an unknown murderer (m).

In the world W_{Nc} of his belief, Oedipus thinks that some properties hold, all S-necessary to identify the characters in play, namely,

eMu: the relation making Oedipus the murderer, and the unknown wayfarer the victim;

mMl: the relation making a given person the murderer, and Laius the
victim.

But the final state of the *fabula* is less complicated. There are only
two individuals, Oedipus and Laius, since the murderer and the unknown
wayfarer were none other than Oedipus and Laius. Only one property is
taken into account by this world structure:

eMl: the relation making Oedipus the murderer and Laius the victim.

To make the individuals distinguishable, let us add an essential property $L =$ to be living. In Oedipus' world the murderer is supposed to
live since he is the culprit to be discovered. At this point the two world
structures take the format shown in Figure 8.17.

It is easy to understand that (according to 8.8.1) these two worlds
are inaccessible to each other, since their world structures are not isomorphic. It is not that one world has more individuals than the other;
it is the fact that these individuals are identified by *different* S-necessary
properties.

In his doxastic world Oedipus believes he has been the murderer of an
unknown wayfarer. In the world of the *fabula,* he is identified as the
murderer of Laius. Obviously, these world structures could have been
complicated by also introducing the property of being the son of Laius
(holding only in W_N) and the one of having married the former wife of
Laius (holding in both). Since these S-necessary relations are semantically bound (see 8.7.3), in W_N it is entailed that Oedipus has married
his mother and killed his father. The incompatibility of the identifying
relation grows. Therefore not only does the final state of the *fabula*
disprove the beliefs of Oedipus, but it sets up a world structure from
which it is impossible to produce the world structure of Oedipus' beliefs.
In the same way it is impossible to transform the world of Oedipus'
beliefs into the world of the *fabula*. Simply, Oedipus believed *p* and then
knows that *q* and that it is not possible that *p* and *q* hold together.

Oedipus cannot reformulate his world. He has to throw it away. A

W_{Nc}	*eMu*	*mMl*	*L*
e	[+]		(+)
l		[+]	(−)
u	[+]		(−)
m		[+]	(+)

W_N	*eMl*	*L*
e	[+]	(+)
l	[+]	(−)

Figure 8.17

good reason to go mad. Or to make himself blind. As a matter of fact, it is exactly such a story of tragic 'blindness' that our world structures have schematically displayed: how was it possible to be so blind not to see to what extent the world of one's beliefs was so inaccessible to the world of facts, and vice versa?

The two worlds would have been mutually accessible if Oedipus had approached the truth. This means (to conclude) that, when the W_{Nc} of the beliefs (or wishes, or projects) of a character has the same world structure of the world of the final state of the *fabula,* these worlds are mutually accessible. When this does not happen, these worlds are mutually incompatible. The final state of the *fabula* disproves and rejects what is structurally incompatible with itself.

To summarize the conclusions of this paragraph: as far as the S-necessary relations are concerned, when the world $W_{Nc}s_m$ is isomorphic in its world structure with the $W_N s_n$ of the state of the *fabula* checking it (where either $n > m$ or $n < m$), then $W_{Nc}s_m$ is approved by the *fabula* and the two worlds are mutually accessible. When it is not, the $W_{Nc}s_m$ is disproved and the two worlds are mutually inaccessible.

8.8.3. Relations of accessibility among the subworlds of the Model Reader and the states of the *fabula*

The worlds of the reader's forecasts seem to obey the same laws as the epistemic and doxastic worlds of the characters:

(i) the reader's world can be compared to precise states of the *fabula,* except that in this case both the approval and the disapproval always come after the forecast (a character may also ignore what the *fabula* has already said, but the Model Reader ignores only what the *fabula* still has to say);[18]

(ii) in the course of the plot, the reader may make many forecasts concerning minor sequences of events: when the possible world of his expectation is not validated by the further course of events, the modalities of accessibility between his doxastic world and the textual world are the same as those concerning characters' worlds (see 8.8.2);

(iii) when, on the contrary, the possible world of the reader concerns S-necessary properties, his world is accessible to the one of the *fabula* (and vice versa) only if the reader has imagined the same S-necessary properties. Otherwise he must get rid of his world so as to accept the state of affairs established by the *fabula* as actual in W_N.

As far as the S-necessary relations are concerned, when a given world of the reader (let it be $W_R s_1$) is isomorphic in its world structure with the

$W_{N}s_{n}$ of the *fabula* checking it (let it be $W_{N}s_{2}$), the $W_{R}s_{m}$ is approved by the *fabula* and the two worlds are mutually accessible. When it is not, $W_{R}s_{1}$ is disproved and the two worlds are mutually inaccessible.

It is enough to think of a reader who joins Oedipus in making false forecasts about the possible course of events, to discover that the situation of the reader is not different from that of Oedipus. One could object that (as maintained in 8.1.2) all the forecasts of the reader have not only been foreseen but also elicited by the text, and therefore the text should have taken them into account.

But once more one must carefully distinguish between (i) the *text* as a semantico-pragmatic process (which takes into account possible cooperation on the part of the reader), (ii) the *plot* as a strategy of semantic devices intended to elicit the pragmatic cooperation, and (iii) the *fabula* as a possible world with all its states and its structure of S-necessary properties.

The text as a multileveled structure 'knows' that the reader will probably behave in certain ways; it 'knows' that the reader will produce S-necessary properties that the *fabula* will ignore. But *the text is not a possible world*—nor is the plot. It is a piece of the furniture of the world in which the reader also lives, and it is *a machine for producing possible worlds* (of the *fabula*, of the characters within the *fabula*, and of the reader outside the *fabula*).

We can say that, in setting up a fictional text, its author formulates many hypotheses and forecasts apropos of the pragmatic behavior of his Model Reader. But this is a matter of the author's intentions. These intentions can be extrapolated from the text (as I am doing with *Drame*), but they are intentions, wishes, projects belonging to the 'actual' world and to this actual speech act which is the text.

One can say that the phrase /today it is raining/ is a speech act with a particular perlocutionary effect when uttered to convince somebody not to go out. And one can speculate about the possible world of the wishes of the utterer of such a phrase. But the phrase in itself does not outline a possible world, and the two levels of analysis must be kept independent of each other.

Therefore, between the world of the *fabula* and the world of reader's *wrong* forecasts, there is no accessibility. If they are wrong it is so because the reader has imagined individuals and properties that the world of the *fabula* could not conceive of. When the reader realizes his mistake he does not manipulate his possible (wrong) world to come back to the story. He simply throws it out.

Obviously, all this does not seem to fit the picture of *Drame*. In fact, it does and it does not. Apparently, the accident can be summarized as follows:

(i) In chapter 5 only two persons attended the ball, a Templar and a Pirogue, identified only by their symmetrical S-necessity. In chapter 6 it is said that they are different from Raoul and Marguerite. The *fabula* has never identified either a lover of Marguerite or a mistress of Raoul.

(ii) If the reader, for personal reasons, has imagined something different, it is his business. Raoul, with the S-necessary properties of being dyadically related to the Moulin Rouge and of being symmetrically related to a Pirogue, does not exist in the final state of the *fabula* and has never existed in the previous ones. The same holds for Marguerite. The same holds for those *supposed* adulterous partners, necessarily related to our two heroes. All these are S-necessary properties introduced by the reader, and his world is not accessible to the world of the *fabula*.

But beyond this apparent innocence, the *fabula* does something more and worse: by making the Templar and the Pirogue become astonished and by making, in chapter 7, Raoul and Marguerite learn something from the accident of chapter 6, it reintroduces into its final states individuals and necessary properties that belonged only to the world of reader's forecasts—and just after having proved that these forecasts were wrong.

In short, the reader has produced a world (or more worlds) inaccessible to and from the world of the *fabula*. This illicit production has been provoked by the plot. But the *fabula*, instead of ignoring it, reintroduces it into its world.

In order to understand the strategy of the plot, we have to come back to the text and follow step by step the states of the *fabula*, comprehending the W_N of the story, the various W_{Nc} of the beliefs and wishes of the characters, and the $W_R s_1$ outlined by the reader as ghost chapters. Only in this way can we understand the strategy of a plot that displays two *fabulae*, the one of the story as such and the one of the reader, so as to intertwine them at the end and to show that, though the *fabula* cannot work, the plot worked very well.

8.9   The *fabula* of *Drame* and its ghost chapters

8.9.1. Easy directions

To follow the interaction between the states of the *fabula* and the ghost chapters, let us outline a shorthand presentation of *Drame* as *fabula*. In this outline I shall consider only the events and the propositional attitudes indispensable to the development of the *fabula*.

Instead of setting up the various world structures I shall represent them, for the sake of economy, through *textual macropropositions,* where

P = the propositions describing the states of W_N,

Q = the propositions describing the various W_{Nc},

R = the propositions describing the reader's forecasts in W_R,

Z = the propositions describing propositional attitudes W_{Rc} and W_{Rcc} in W_R,

while the succession of P_1, P_2 ... and Q_1, Q_2 ... represents the univocal succession of the states of the *fabula*, R_1, R_2 ... and the depending Z_1, Z_2 ... in a given state of W_R represent alternative hypotheses as to how the *fabula* might develop.

Therefore the *fabula* of *Drame* can be represented by the following series of macropropositions:

P_1 = there are two characters identified by the S-necessary relation of being married together, of loving each other, and of being reciprocally jealous;

P_2 = in a given state there is an x who asserts Q_1;

P_3 = in a given state there is an x who asserts Q_2;

Q_1 = Marguerite will go in a further state to the ball and will be the same as the Pirogue;

Q_2 = Raoul will go in a further state to the ball and will be the same as the Templar;

P_4 = Raoul asserts that he wants Q_3, which is untrue;

P_5 = Marguerite asserts that she wants Q_4, which is untrue;

Q_3 = Raoul will go to Dunkirk;

Q_4 = Marguerite will go to Aunt Aspasia's home;

P_6 = there are two characters identified by the S-necessary relation of encountering at the ball;

P_7 = the Templar and the Pirogue cry out in surprise;

P_8 = they do not recognize each other;

P_9 = the Templar is not Raoul;

P_{10} = the Pirogue is not Marguerite;

P_{11} = Raoul learns something by knowing the above propositions P_6 ... P_{10};

P_{12} = Marguerite learns something by knowing the above propositions P_6 ... P_{10}.

Macropropositions P_7 ... P_{12} do not, however, make sense if the *fabula* does not take into account three ghost chapters written by the reader and described by the following propositions:

R_1 = there are two individuals linked to Raoul and Marguerite by the S-necessary relation of being their respective lovers;

R_2 = Raoul is planning Z_1, that is, to go to the ball as said in the letter received by Marguerite (thus the Z_1 planned by Raoul is the same as the Q_2 stated by the letter);

R_3 = Marguerite was planning Z_2, that is, to go to the ball as said in the letter received by Raoul (thus the Z_2 planned by Marguerite is the same as the Q_1 stated by the letter);

R_4 = Raoul knows the possible course of events expressed by proposition Q_2;

R_5 = Marguerite knows the possible course of events expressed by proposition Q_1;

R_6 = there are two individuals, Raoul and his mistress, linked by the S-necessary relation of encountering at the ball; Raoul is the Templar and believes Z_3, that is, that the Pirogue is Marguerite, while this proposition is untrue;

R_7 = there are two individuals, Marguerite and her lover, linked by the S-necessary relation of encountering at the ball; the Pirogue is Marguerite and she believes Z_4, that is, that the Templar is Raoul, while this proposition is untrue;

R_8 = there are two individuals, Raoul and Marguerite, linked by the S-necessary relation of encountering at the ball; they are the same as the Templar and the Pirogue; Raoul believes Z_5, that is, that Marguerite is the Pirogue and that she believes Z_6, that is, that the Templar is her lover; Marguerite believes Z_7, that is, that the Templar is Raoul and that he believes Z_8, that is, that the Pirogue is his mistress;

R_9 = if the Templar knows that the Pirogue is not Marguerite and cries out in surprise, then in a previous state he believed that the Pirogue was Marguerite;

R_{10} = if the Pirogue knows that the Templar is not Raoul and cries out in surprise, then in a previous state she believed that the Templar was Raoul;

R_{11} = R_9 is impossible because the identity of Marguerite with the Pirogue was a piece of the furniture of the W_{Rc} of the reader, while their irreducible difference is a piece of the furniture of the W_N. Since these two worlds are not mutually accessible, R_9 cannot hold;

R_{12} = R_{10} is impossible because the identity of the Templar with Raoul was a piece of the furniture of the W_{Rc} of the reader, while their irreducible difference is a piece of the furniture of the W_N. Since the two worlds are not mutually accessible, R_{10} cannot hold;

R_{13} = the ghost chapters can be rewritten by assuming that there were only two individuals, different from Raoul and Marguerite, linked by the S-necessary relation of encountering at the ball, respectively disguised as Templar and Pirogue, and the Templar believed Z_3, that is, that the Pirogue was Marguerite, while the Pirogue believed Z_4, that is, that the Templar was Raoul.

The following symbolic representation of the *fabula* will make clear the difference between various propositions outlining different possible worlds. The symbolization of the states of the *fabula* takes for granted all the results of semantic disclosures and inferences occurring at the level of the plot, or of the discoursive structures.

The following symbols will be used:

Individuals
  r = Raoul;
  m = Marguerite;
  t = Templar;
  p = Pirogue;
  b = the place where the ball takes place (Moulin Rouge);
  x_1 = the supposed lover of Marguerite;
  x_2 = the supposed mistress of Raoul.

Epistemic and doxastic operators
  B = believes   (B_rP_i = Raoul believes that P_i is the case);
  K = knows   (K_rP_i = Raoul knows that P_i is the case);
  W = wants   (W_rP_i = Raoul wants P_i to be the case);
  A = asserts   (A_rP_i = Raoul asserts that P_i is the case).

World structures
  W_NS_i = states of the fabula (the progression of states representing a progression in time);
  $W_{Nc}S_i$ = possible worlds outlined by the characters;
  W_RS_i = possible worlds outlined by the reader;
  $W_{Rc}S_i$ = possible worlds of characters' propositional attitudes imagined in the possible world of the reader;
  $W_{Rcc}S_i$ = possible worlds of characters' propositional attitudes as imagined in the possible world of another character's propositional attitudes imagined in the possible world of the reader.

S-necessary relations
  M = to be identified by a reciprocal relation of marriage;
  L = to be identified by a reciprocal relation of love;
  J = to be identified by a reciprocal relation of jealousy;
  E = to be identified by a reciprocal relation of encounter in a given place.

Nonrelational predicates
  G = to go to the ball;
  D = to go to Dunkirk;
  H = to go to aunt Aspasia's home;
  S = to show stupor;
  $\sim K$ = not to recognize.

8.9.2. **The** *fabula* **and its ghost chapters**

Chapter 1	$W_N S_1$	
	P_1: rMm, rLm, rJm	

Chapter 4	$W_N S_2$	$W_{Nc} S_2$
	P_2: $\exists x A_x Q_1$	Q_1: $Gm, s_3 \cdot m = p$
	P_3: $\exists x A_x Q_2$	Q_2: $Gr, s_3 \cdot r = t$
	$W_N S_3$	$W_{Nc} S_3$
	P_4: $A_r W_r Q_3$	Q_3: Dr
	P_5: $A_m W_m Q_4$	Q_4: Hm

Ghost chapter 1	$W_R S_3$	$W_{Rc} S_3$
	R_1: $rLx_2 \cdot mLx_1$	
	R_2: $W_r Z_1$	$Z_1 = Q_2$
	R_3: $W_m Z_2$	$Z_2 = Q_1$
	R_4: $K_r Q_2$	
	R_5: $K_m Q_1$	

Chapter 5	$W_N S_4$	
	P_6: tEp	

Ghost chapter 2	$W_R S_4$	$W_{Rc} S_4$	$W_{Rcc} S_4$
	R_6: rEx_2		
	$t = r \cdot B_r Z_3 \cdot \sim Z_3$	Z_3: $p = m$	
	R_7: mEx_1		
	$p = m \cdot B_m Z_4 \cdot \sim Z_4$	Z_4: $t = r$	
	R_8: rEm		
	$t = r \cdot B_r Z_5$	Z_5: $p = m \cdot B_m Z_6$	Z_6: $t = x_1$
	$p = m \cdot B_m Z_7$	Z_7: $t = r \cdot B_r Z_8$	Z_8: $p = x_2$

Chapter 6	$W_N S_5$
	P_7: $St \cdot Sp$
	P_8: $\sim K(t,p) \cdot \sim K(p,t)$
	P_9: $\sim(t = r)$
	P_{10} $\sim(p = m)$

Ghost chapter 3	$W_R S_5$
	R_9: $(K_t P_{10} \cdot P_7) \rightarrow B_t Z_3 S_4$
	R_{10}: $(K_p P_9 \cdot P_7) \rightarrow B_p Z_4 S_4$

but

R_{11}: $[Z \in W_{Rc} \cdot P \in W_N) \cdot \sim W_N R W_R] \rightarrow$ impossible R_9
R_{12}: $[Z \in W_{Rc} \cdot P \in W_N) \cdot \sim W_N R W_R] \rightarrow$ impossible R_{10}

Tentative *rewriting* *of ghost* *chapter 2*	$W_R S_4$	
	$R_{13}: x_1 E x_2$	
	$t = x_1 \cdot B_{x1} Z_3$	
	$p = x_2 \cdot B_{x2} Z_4$	
Chapter 7	$W_N S_6$	$W_{Nc} S_6$
	$P_{11}: K_r Q_5$	$Q_5: (P_6 \ldots P_{10}) \cdot (R_1 \ldots R_8)$
	$P_{12}: K_m Q_5$	

8.9.3. Ghost chapters

The symbolic schematization of the *fabula* shows how the ghost chapters intrude upon its states to make false forecasts and how the last states of the *fabula* ambiguously disprove and accept them at the same time, so as to lead the reader to an impossible reassessment of his ghost chapters.

Let us read the ghost chapters again to follow the desperate attempts of the cooperative reader.

Ghost chapter 1. The reader imagines that there are two imprecise individuals linked by an S-necessary relation respectively to Raoul and Marguerite. Then he attributes to Raoul and Marguerite the project of going to the ball. It remains vague whether they go because they have planned this with their respective lovers or because each of them wants to catch his or her own marital partner in the act.

In the first case the reader supposes that Raoul has really plotted with an x_2 to go to the ball (he as a Templar and she as a Pirogue) and that Marguerite has plotted with an x_1 to go to the ball (she as a Pirogue and he as a Templar). It should thus be assumed that the two adulterous couples have chosen the same disguise.

In the second case the reader is obliged (or virtually so) to assume that both Raoul and Marguerite knew the contents of the letter they did not read—that is, the reader assumes that each main character knows what is said in the letter received by the other. In doing so the reader is assuming as a matter of (fictional) fact what was referentially opaque in $W_N S_2$.

Both inferences are preposterous: the first is logically incorrect; the second, intertextually improbable.

But both have been proposed under just the pressure of intertextuality. Probably the reader shifts from one hypothesis to another, and the text has calculated this uncertainty.

Notice that in any case Raoul and Marguerite have been inserted into an S-necessary relation which gives birth to two individuals that the *fabula* does not know and that the plot has never identified, namely, the two supposed lovers. In fact, as far as S-necessary relations are concerned, in chapter 5 the furniture of W_N is actually increased by two brand-new individuals, linked by the mutual relation of meeting each other in a given place. Since the *fabula* does not say that other people with the same disguise meet at the ball, and since the *fabula* does not say that Raoul and Marguerite are at the ball, any other inference is without support.

Ghost chapter 2. However, the reader has too many intertextual clues. He is forced to believe (or to believe that it is possible to believe) four alternative possibilities:

  (i) Raoul is the Templar and believes that Marguerite is the Pirogue, while it is false.

 (ii) Marguerite is the Pirogue and believes that Raoul is the Templar, while it is false.

(iii) Raoul is the Templar and rightly believes that Marguerite is the Pirogue, but he also believes that Marguerite believes that he is her lover.

(iv) Marguerite is the Pirogue and rightly believes that Raoul is the Templar, but she also believes that Raoul believes that she is his mistress.

Provided that the suppositions of ghost chapter 1 were true, each of the suppositions of ghost chapter 2 can hold. All together they are mutually contradictory.

The reader seems to have naively trusted Hintikka (1967:42): "The fact that a character in a 'complete novel' reacts and behaves precisely in the same way as the member of another possible world is strong evidence for their identification." What he has not learned from Hintikka (1962) are all the precautions to be taken when one wants to quantify into opaque contexts governed by an epistemic operator.

In all cases the reader proceeds to a false identification by S-necessary relations: Raoul and Marguerite (either or both) are the individuals who have the property of being in that place at that moment in a specific relation of encounter with someone else. We can suppose that the reader makes one of these four forecasts, or all of them together, awaiting the further state of the *fabula* to get more clues. We could also envisage more (and maybe less organized) suppositions, but the four I have listed are enough to explain the solution of chapter 6.

Ghost chapter 3. The *fabula* says clearly that the two individuals are not Raoul and Marguerite. But it adds that the two are surprised or astonished because they do not recognize each other. The reader tries to elaborate a tentative ghost chapter 3 in which he must take into account the following argument: if the Templar knows that the Pirogue is not Marguerite and if the Templar is astonished, this means that formerly the Templar believed that the Pirogue was Marguerite (and the same holds for the other character).

But the reader also realizes that the propositions 'the Pirogue is Marguerite' and 'the Templar is Raoul' were not propositions of the W_N, but propositions outlined by the characters in a subworld of the world W_R of reader's expectations. The reader should also realize that the world of his expectations is not accessible to the world of the final state of the *fabula*. (Obviously, the naive reader of *Drame* has not at this point read 8.8.3, but the present paper has tried to present in a more rigorous form what every reader unconsciously knows very well.)

At this point the reader is obliged to recognize that in his ghost chapter 2 Raoul and Marguerite were furnished with the S-necessary property of meeting at the ball, which property is exactly denied by chapter 6. Therefore Raoul and Marguerite are absolutely nonidentifiable with the Templar and the Pirogue, since they have different S-necessary properties and since the two world structures cannot be mutually transformed.

The logic of the *fabula* follows the Leibnizian principle: "If, in the life of any person and even in the whole universe, anything went differently from what it has, nothing could prevent us from saying that it was another person or another possible universe which God had chosen. It would be indeed another individual."[19] Replace "God" with the final state of the text, and this principle will hold perfectly.

But what the reader cannot definitely understand is why, since his suppositions were wrong, the characters of chapter 6 react as if they were true.

The reader is eager to accept the revelation that he had not the right to take incorrect inferential walks. But the *fabula* seems to accept the inferential walk just after having severely disproved it. In short, were the Templar and the Pirogue Raoul and Marguerite, they would have recognized each other. Were they not, they would not have reason to be astonished.

In fact, at this point the *fabula* assumes upon itself the astonishment of the reader (the only one to have a right to amazement). Thus the *fabula* demonstrates that the only one to be structurally and pragmatically astonished was the *fabula* 'in person', since it represents the infelicitous result of an unsuccessful pragmatic cooperation.

At a second, critical reading, one is tempted to rationalize the story. There are many ways to do that. For example, the two maskers are the two lovers of our heroes, each of them expecting to meet his or her adulterous partner. But this is a kind of supposition one can make only in the world of our everyday experience, where there are many individuals at large that one still does not know. This, however, does not hold in W_N, where only the individuals explicitly named and described exist. In W_N the supposed lovers have never been singled out as such (we still do not know who the Pirogue and the Templar really are; however, there is no evidence that they are the lovers of our heroes).

Furthermore, to think this way one should imagine that two adulterous couples had devised to use the same pair of masks. This sounds repugnant to our sense of narrative etiquette (and to the most credited intertextual frames): the text should have given some previous clues to suggest this outcome, and it did not. By a sort of narrative *implicature,* we decide that no author can so blatantly violate intertextual frames and that, consequently, he wanted to suggest something else—also because every rational explanation is challenged—in any case—by chapter 7.

To learn from what happened means to be informed about everything that happened in chapter 6, including the propositional attitudes of the still mysterious Templar and Pirogue. It is true that someone could have told everything to our heroes. But this hypothesis is excluded through stylistical overcoding. To say that /*cette petite mésaventure servit de leçon à Raoul et Marguerite*/ means, according to common linguistic usages, that Allais is speaking of *their* unlucky accident and of *their* misunderstanding.

Moreover, chapter 7 is mixing up the textual world of chapter 6 more and more with the possible subworlds of the ghost chapters. Raoul and Marguerite are here behaving as if they had read all the preceding chapters, including the ghost ones. Otherwise, why the title of chapter 7— *Happy denouement for everyone except the others?* Semantic incoherence comes to support and to reinforce the fictional one. No semantic analysis of /*tout le monde*/ (everyone) can allow one to consider someone as left out. This title is really a challenge not only to semantically good intensional habits but also to commonsensical extensionality. It is a sort of epitome of the whole story, a sort of condensed allegory of incoherence and inconsistency—unless /*tout le monde*/ (everyone) were all the individuals in W_N and /*les autres*/ were the readers, unfortunately belonging to a W_0 called the 'real' world, where the laws of a wellmannered logic still hold. Which seems a nice moral to the story. Do not intrude upon a story's privacy. It is a crazy universe you can feel uneasy in. But there is also the opposite moral: *Drame* has shown how much stories request a cooperative intrusion and cannot live without it.

8.10. Conclusions

At this point we can leave the *fabula* and come back to the text in all its complexity.

The disgrace of this *fabula,* its final contradictory nature, told the reader that there are different types of fictional texts. Some ask for a maximum of intrusion, and not only at the level of the *fabula,* and are called 'open' works. Some others are mealymouthed and, while pretending to elicit our cooperation, in fact want us to think their way and are very 'closed' and repressive. *Drame* seems to stay half-way: it lures its Model Reader into an excess of cooperation and then punishes him for having overdone it.

In this sense *Drame* is neither open nor closed: it belongs to a third category of works, to an exclusive club whose chairman is probably *Tristram Shandy*. These works tell stories about the way stories are built up.[20] In doing so these texts are much less innocuous than they seem: their deep theme is the functioning of that basic cultural machinery which, through the manipulation of our beliefs (which sublimate our wishes), produces ideologies, contradictory world visions, self-delusion. Instead of describing this process from an uncontaminated critical point of view, these texts reproduce the process in their own rhetorical and logical structures (thus becoming the first victim of themselves).

But perhaps we are going too far away. *Drame* is only a metatext speaking about the cooperative principle in narrativity and at the same time challenging our yearning for cooperation by gracefully punishing our pushiness. It asks us—to prove our penitence—to extrapolate from it the rules of the textual discipline it suggests.

Which I humbly did. And so should you, and maybe further, gentle reader.

NOTES

1. The essay has been prepared through a series of seminars in which I have been variously helped by the suggestions of my students and colleagues. Alphonse Allais' story was brought to my notice by Paolo Fabbri. A first approach to the analysis of the story emerged during a seminar conducted at the University of California, San Diego, in 1975; Fredric Jameson and Alain Cohen took active parts in the discussions. A second approach developed during a seminar conducted at the University of Bologna in 1976; Ettore

Panizon, Renato Giovannoli, and Daniele Barbieri wrote a first, tentative interpretation to which I am greatly indebted (I like to refer to the title of their paper, "How to Castrate Oneself with Ockham's Razor"). A third and more substantial approach (a three-month analysis) was developed at New York University during the fall semester of 1976. Conducted for a class of graduate students in French literature, the seminar helped me to clarify many stylistic and rhetorical points of the text. Although it is impossible to mention all the participants, I want particularly to thank my colleague Christine Brooke Rose, who was one of the best auditors I have had in my academic life. Finally, the entire month of July 1977, spent with a consistent group of students and scholars at the Center of Semiotics and Linguistics in Urbino, was devoted to this analysis. Peer Age Brandt, who attended one of the seminars conducted during that period, gave an exciting personal reading of the story. An inter-mediary draft of this paper was widely discussed with Lucia Vaina, whose research on literary possible worlds has been revealing to me. Her criticism has greatly influenced the final draft—for which, however, she is not respon-sible. I have received many suggestions from my students in the course in semiotics at the University of Bologna. During the courses I taught at Yale University in 1977, Barbara Spackman wrote a paper on the second draft of this analysis, which gave me some suggestions that I have incorporated into the final draft.

2. We shall see that to postulate such a double interpretation does not mean to exhaust the cooperative possibilities of the interpreter: what is postulated is a first naive interpreter expected to commit various alternative mistakes and a second critical reader who can make different explanatory decisions (of which the one I propose at the end of this essay is only one among the possible variants). Thus to say that it is possible to recognize the *type* of reader postu-lated by the text does not mean to assume that it is possible to completely foresee his final and definitive interpretation. The two Model Readers of *Drame* are two general interpretative strategies, not two definite results of these strategies.

3. While in the course of this essay the profile of the Model Reader will be extrapolated exclusively from textual strategy, in Appendix 1 I present the results of an empirical test which validates the above extrapolation.

4. Appendix 2 comprises a faithful and witty translation expressly made by Fredric Jameson. Since the translation is faithful, one could ask why it is not used for the purpose of analysis instead of the original. Apart from any semantic discussion about the theoretical possibility of a really 'faithful' transla-tion, the difference has been maintained for reasons strictly related to the present research. Even though as 'faithful' as possible, a translation is still an *interpretation,* in Peirce's terms: it substitutes some words or groups of words with their *interpretants* in another language. In doing so it realizes the first condition of any interpretation: it fills up given expressions with their content (the content being witnessed by other expressions). In this process what was implied, presupposed, implicated, and suggested (I use these expressions non-technically) by the original expression comes to be *disclosed.* This happens with the translation of *Drame,* and the behavior of the translator will be used in some cases as a test as to what a 'model' interpretative behavior could be.

5. See Appendix 2: the translator has actualized the complete action (and intention) of Raoul by translating "hand raised to strike."

6. On fictional possible worlds see Schmidt (1976: 165–73) and Ihwe (1973: 399ff.).

7. Philosophically speaking, a more atomistic view is even possible. But let us assume the notion of property as a primitive (thus following the current literature on possible worlds).

8. See the notion of 'actual' world as a relativized semantic apparatus in relation to a single user outlined by Volli (1973). See also Van Dijk (1976c: 31ff.) and his notion of S-worlds (speaker-hearer possible worlds).

9. According to an example of Hughes and Cresswell (1968), if we suppose that W_2 contains two individuals x_1 and x_2 while W_1 contains only x_1, then W_2 is 'conceivable' from W_2 while the opposite is not possible: "We can conceive of a world without telephones . . . but if there had been no telephones, it might surely have been the case that in such a world no one would know what a telephone was, and so no one could conceive of a world (such as ours) in which there are telephones; *i.e.,* the telephoneless world would be accessible to ours but ours would not be accessible to it" (p. 78). Such an approach seems to me still exaggeratedly 'psychological'—even though probably proposed by its authors as a mere metaphor.

10. The lexical information on carriages comes from *The Encyclopedia Americana, Grand Dictionnaire Universel du XIX siècle* (Paris: Larousse, 1869), *The Encyclopedia Britannica* (1876), *The Oxford English Dictionary,* and *Webster's Dictionary* (1910).

11. See also the difference between Sigma and Pi properties in Groupe μ, 1970—a distinction which falls under the same strictures.

12. One can wonder whether there is still a point of no return where a given property cannot be judged as accidental and cannot be denied. Even in a naval museum a brigantine, to be complete, should have at least potentially the property of keeping afloat. This happens since people usually consider a brigantine as a traveling device. But a scuba diver looking for submerged treasures can still consider a sunken brigantine a brigantine even though it is no longer a fully functional ship but a piece of wreckage.

For the director of Buchenwald, a human being had the sole necessary property of being boilable to produce soap. What we have to judge is his moral right to disregard all the other properties and to blow up this sole one; what we have to object to is the ideology governing his ethics, not his formal semantics. As Allais once said, "La logique mène à tout, à condition d'en sortir." According to his frame of reference, the director of Buchenwald was semantically correct. The political problem of the free world was *only* how to destroy that frame of reference and to show its ideological partiality (see Eco, 1976, 3.9).

13. This problem has already been debated in discussions on logical analysis of knowledge and belief (see, for instance, Hintikka, 1970). Can we say that

$$\frac{p \rightarrow q}{K_a p \rightarrow K_a q} \qquad \text{or that} \qquad \frac{p \rightarrow q}{B_a p \rightarrow B_a q}$$

(whenever someone knows or believes anything he knows or also believes all
its logical consequences)? One of the 'ideal' answers is that this rule theoreti-
cally holds independently of any idiosyncratic case of ignorance or insufficient
information. But it has been persuasively shown that the correct answer depends on a given definition of what it means to understand what is known or
believed. There is a difference between what is semantically presupposed by
the encyclopedia and what is pragmatically presupposed in the process of
interpretation of a text. To ask whether knowing that a given individual is a
man also means knowing that he has two lungs depends on the *quantificational
depth* of a sentence, that is, "the maximal complexity of the configuration of
individuals considered in it at any time, measured by the numbers of individuals involved" (Hintikka,1970:170). This refers us back to the notion of
world structure of reference (see 8.4.4).

14. When Hintikka (1969b) says that if I see a man without being sure
whether he is John or Henry or somebody else and that nevertheless this man
will be the same in every possible world because he is the man I see in this
precise moment, our problem is solved. As my question is, Who is this man I
am actually perceiving? his only essential property has already been established
by my perspective on the world and by my material or empirical needs.

15. Quoted apropos of my book *A Theory of Semiotics* (1976), in Teresa
De Lauretis, "Semiosis Unlimited," *Journal for Descriptive Poetics and Theory
of Literature* 2, no. 2 (April 1977).

16. One might object that it is untrue that a W_N is accessible to W_0 only
when the essential properties in W_0 are maintained. We can imagine a fantastic
novel in which Richelieu is not French but a Spanish secret agent. As a matter
of fact, it is also possible to imagine a story in which Richelieu is not French,
not a Cardinal, did not live in the seventeenth century, and, furthermore, is
not a man but a guinea pig. If this is a joke, it represents a case of homonymy
(a friend of mine called his dog Beckett). But it can be something more serious. All things considered, Kafka imagined a situation in which Mr. Samsa
becomes a bug. But in these cases there is a strong textual topic concerning
the inner identity of the Self. In the structure of W_0 it is assumed (*under that
description*) that the unique essential properties of a human individual are
those concerning the constancy of his mental identity *under every condition*.
To have a body, to have a sex, or to have two legs becomes merely accidental. Our guinea pig would think à la Richelieu.

17. It may be objected that in fictional texts S-necessary properties can be
altered. Literary parodies are the proof of this. We can imagine a Broadway
musical in which Richelieu is a tap dancer and D'Artagnan happily marries
Lady de Winter after having sold the pendants of Anne of Austria under the
counter. There are four answers: (i) The parody is not dealing with a given
W_N but with individuals who, because of the influence of that W_N, have been
absorbed by the encyclopedia in W_0 as mythological characters. (ii) The
parody works as a piece of structural criticism showing that certain relations
were not so strictly necessary to the *fabula* or that the real *fabula* was another
one ('how to win with a blow below the belt') and can survive to a different
plot. (iii) All of the above discussion mainly concerned accessibility among

worlds, not transworlds identity. There is no difficulty in saying that in the Broadway musical d'Artagnan is another individual who differs both from the Chevalier d'Artagnan who wrote his *mémoires* in W_0 and from d'Artagnan in Dumas' W_N. The three are linked by homonymy. (iv) Even caricatures blow up certain properties of real individuals and drop out many others. Recognizability is due to the fact that they are telling us that (under a certain description) these properties were the only ones that essentially defined the individual in question.

18. There are some exceptions: (i) The reader has not attentively read the previous parts of the text (empirical accident, not to be considered). (ii) The previous parts of the text were purposely ambiguous, the events only vaguely suggested: in this case the reader must read twice and look backwards to find the previous proof or disproof of his hypothesis.

19. Letter to Arnauld, 14 July 1686.

20. This reader is thus able to focus *Drame* as message, so actualizing its poetic function (Jakobson). See also in this book the essay on Edenic language (chapter 3). *Drame* is purposely ambiguous so as to elicit the reader's attention as focused upon its textual structure; in this way, *Drame* represents an aesthetic achievement (see also Eco, 1976, 3.7).

Appendix One

The Model Reader of *Un drame bien parisien:*
An Empirical Test

In the course of Chapter 8 of this book, the profile of the Model Reader of Alphonse Allais' *Un drame bien parisien* has been extrapolated from the textual strategy itself. It is interesting, however, to see whether another, more empirical approach is able to lead to the same results.

The experiment described below supports the hypotheses made previously at a purely theoretical level and thus proves that it is possible to rely upon the notion of Model Reader as a textual construct.

A sample of readers was tested in 1977, first at the Istituto di Discipline della Communicazione e dello Spettacolo (University of Bologna) and then during the summer courses at the International Center for Semiotics and Linguistics (University of Urbino). The subjects read chapters 1–5 and were then asked to summarize them. In a second phase they read chapters 6–7 and were then asked to summarize them.

In scoring the summaries we were concerned with some basic questions such as the following: (i) Are Raoul and Marguerite remembered as husband and wife obsessed by mutual jealousy? (ii) Is the basic sense of the two letters in chapter 4 correctly understood? (iii) Are both Raoul and Marguerite (or at least one of them) supposed to have the secret purpose of going to the ball? (iv) Are either or both of them planning to assume the disguise of the supposed adversary? (v) Are either or both of them identified with the Templar or with the Pirogue attending the ball? (vi) Does anybody suspect that the characters involved in chapter 5 are more than two? (vii) Does anybody expect Raoul to discover that Marguerite is the Pirogue, or vice versa? (viii) Is Raoul expected to discover that the Pirogue is not Marguerite (and/or vice versa)? (ix) Is the solution of chapter 6 in any way anticipated by some subjects before they read it?

In the second phase we tried to detect whether the mutual nonrecognition is understood literally and whether the illogical situation is in some way realized as such; whether any subjects realize that chapter 7 is inconsistent with chapter 6; what kind of reactions the subjects display (perplexity, attempt to give rational explanations, awareness of a tricking textual strategy, total inability to catch the paradoxical aspect of the story).

The sample included both undergraduate and graduate students trained in semiotics. It has been assumed that, given the social conditions of its circulation in 1890 and its stylistic sophistication, *Drame* was directed to an audience of middling-high culture. In any case our subjects proved that even a cultivated reader gives at first reading a typically naive response. One of the subjects vaguely remembered having already read the story, but reacted as a Model Reader.

In short, a consistent majority identified rather well the two main characters (90%) and strongly believed that they plan to go to the ball or effectively go (82%). The content of the letters was correctly remembered by 72%. About 42% were convinced that Raoul and Marguerite are respectively the Templar and the Pirogue. Only 25% made a forecast as to a possible denouement, and only 15% tried to anticipate a conclusion.

In the second phase 70% recalled the scene of nonrecognition exactly and the fact that Raoul and Marguerite learn something from the episode. The sample becomes oddly fractioned as far as a critical attitude is concerned: only 4% appeared unable to grasp the basic contradictoriness of the story, 40% tried to detect a semiotic machinery, and 20% gave various sorts of rational explanations (of the following type: Probably the Templar was the one who wrote the letter to Marguerite and was convinced he would find Marguerite disguised as a Pirogue . . .). Less than 20% proved to be completely lost. All the rest of the sample gave imprecise summaries. However, if a good summary demonstrated satisfactory comprehension, the opposite is not true: one can have understood something and can have formulated expectations but not have been able to verbalize correctly, maybe because of the abrupt reaction asked for.

Interesting suggestions for this test were given by van Dijk (1975).

Appendix Two

A Most Parisian Episode

Alphonse Allais

Chapter I

In which we meet a Lady and a Gentleman who might have known happiness, had it not been for their constant misunderstandings.

At the time when this story begins, Raoul and Marguerite (a splendid name for lovers) have been married for approximately five months.

Naturally, they had married for love.

One fine night Raoul, while listening to Marguerite singing Colonel Henry d'Erville's lovely ballad:

> L'averse, chère à la grenouille,
> Parfume le bois rajeuni.
> . . . Le bois, il est comme Nini.
> Y sent bon quand y s'débarbouille.

Raoul, as I was saying, swore to himself that the divine Marguerite (*diva Margarita*) would never belong to any man but himself.

They would have been the happiest of all couples, except for their awful personalities.

At the slightest provocation, pow! a broken plate, a slap, a kick in the ass.

At such sounds, Love fled in tears, to await, in the neighborhood of a great park, the always imminent hour of reconciliation.

O then, kisses without number, infinite caresses, tender and knowing, ardors as burning as hell itself.

You would have thought the two of them—pigs that they were!—had fights only so they could make up again.

Translated by Fredric Jameson. The epigraphs have not been translated because they play upon elements of slang, phonetic analogies, and so on.

Chapter II

A short episode which, without directly relating to the action, gives the clientele some notions of our heroes' way of life.

One day, however, it was worse than usual.

Or, rather, one night.

They were at the Théâtre d'Application, where, among other things, a play by M. Porto-Riche, *The Faithless Wife,* was being given.

"Let me know," snarled Raoul, "when you're through looking at Grosclaude."

"And as for you," hissed Marguerite, "pass me the opera glasses when you've got Mademoiselle Moreno down pat."

Begun on this note, the conversation could end only in the most unfortunate reciprocal insults.

In the hansom cab that took them home, Marguerite delighted in plucking at Raoul's vanity as at an old, broken-down mandolin.

So it was that no sooner back home than the belligerents took up their respective positions.

Hand raised to strike, with a remorseless gaze, and a moustache bristling like that of a rabid cat, Raoul bore down on Marguerite, who quickly stopped showing off.

The poor thing fled, as hasty and furtive as the doe in the north woods.

Raoul was on the point of laying hands on her.

It was at that moment that the brilliant invention of the greatest anxieties flashed within her little brain.

Turning suddenly about, she threw herself into the arms of Raoul, crying, "Help, my darling Raoul, save me!"

Chapter III

In which our friends are reconciled as I would wish you also to be frequently reconciled, smart-alecks.

. . . .
. . . .

Chapter IV

As to how people who get involved in things that are none of their affair would do better to mind their own business.

One morning, Raoul received the following message:

"If you would like just once to see your wife in a good mood, go on Thursday to the Bal des Incohérents at the Moulin-Rouge. She will be there, with a mask and disguised as a Congolese Dugout. A word to the wise is sufficient!

A FRIEND."

The same morning, Marguerite received the following message:

"If you would like just once to see your husband in a good mood, go on Thursday to the Bal des Incohérents at the Moulin-Rouge. He will be there, with a mask and disguised as a *fin-de-siècle* Knight Templar. A word to the wise is sufficient!

A FRIEND."

These missives did not fall on deaf ears.

With their intentions admirably dissimulated, when the fatal day arrived:

"My dear," Raoul said with his innocent look, "I shall be forced to leave you until tomorrow. Business of the greatest urgency summons me to Dunkirk."

"Why that's perfect," said Marguerite with delightful candor, "I've just received a telegram from Aunt Aspasia, who, desperately ill, bids me to her bedside."

Chapter V

In which today's wild youth is observed in the whirl of the most illusory and transitory pleasures, instead of thinking on eternity.

The social column of the *Diable boiteux* was unanimous in proclaiming this year's Bal des Incohérents as having unaccustomed brilliance.

Lots of shoulders, no few legs, not to mention accessories.

Two of those present seemed not to take part in the general madness: a *fin-de-siècle* Knight Templar and a Congolese Dugout, both hermetically masked.

At the stroke of three A.M. exactly, the Knight Templar approached the Dugout and invited her to dine with him.

In reply the Dugout placed a tiny hand on the robust arm of the Templar, and the couple went off.

Chapter VI

In which the plot thickens.

"Leave us for a moment," said the Templar to the waiter, "we will make our choice and call you."

The waiter withdrew, and the Templar locked the door of the private room with care.

Then, with a sudden gesture, having set his own helmet aside, he snatched away the Dugout's mask.

Both at the same instant cried out in astonishment, neither one recognizing the other.

He was not Raoul.

She was not Marguerite.

They apologized to each other and were not long in making acquaintance on the occasion of an excellent supper, need I say more.

Chapter VII

Happy ending for everyone, except the others.

This little *mésaventure* was a lesson to Raoul and Marguerite.

From that moment on, they no longer quarreled and were utterly happy.

They don't have lots of children yet, but they will.

Bibliography

Austin, J. L.
  1962 *How to Do Things with Words.* Oxford: Clarendon Press.
Bar-Hillel, Yehoshua
  1968 "Communication and Argumentation in Pragmatic Languages." In
      AA VV, *Linguaggi nella società e nella tecnica.* Milan: Comunita,
      1970 (Convegno promosso della Ing. C. Olivetti & C., Spa, per il
      centenario della nascita di C. Olivetti, Milan, October 1968).
Barthes, Roland
  1966 "Introduction à l'analyse structurale des récits." *Communications* 8.
  1970 *S/Z.* Paris: Seuil.
  1973 *Le plaisir du texte.* Paris: Seuil.
Bateson, Gregory
  1955 "A Theory of Play and Fantasy." *Psychiatric Research Report* 2
      (and in *Steps to an Ecology of Mind* [New York: Ballantine, 1972],
      pp. 177–93).
Bellert, Irena
  1973 "On Various Solutions of the Problem of Presuppositions." In Petőfi
      and Rieser, eds., 1973.
Bonomi, Andrea
  1975 *Le vie del riferimento.* Milan: Bompiani.
Bonfantini, Massimo, and Grazia, Roberto
  1976a "What is the Immediate Object in Peirce?" Communication to the
      C. S. Peirce Bicentennial International Congress, Amsterdam, 16–20
      June 1976. Manuscript.
  1976b "Teoria della conoscenza e funzione dell'icona in Peirce." *VS* 15.
Bosco, Nynfa
  1959 *La filosofia pragmatica di C. S. Peirce.* Turin: Edizioni di "Filosofia."
Bremond, Claude
  1973 *Logique du récit.* Paris: Seuil.
Brooke-Rose, Christine
  1977 "Surface Structure in Narrative." *PTL* 2, no. 3.
Burke, Kenneth
  1969 *A Grammar of Motives.* Berkeley and Los Angeles: University of
      California Press.

Caprettini, Gian Paolo
    1976   "Sulla semiotica di Ch. S. Peirce e il nuovo elenco di categorie."
           VS 15.
Carnap, Rudof
    1947   *Meaning and Necessity*. Chicago: University of Chicago Press.
    1952   "Meaning Postulates." *Philosophical Studies* 3, no. 5.
Chabrol, Claude
    1973   *Sémiotique narrative et textuelle*. Paris: Larousse.
Charniak, Eugene
    1975   "A Partial Taxonomy of Knowledge about Actions." Institute for
           Semantic and Cognitive Studies, Castagnola. Working Paper 13.
Chisholm, Roderick M.
    1967   "Identity Through Possible Worlds: Some Questions." *Noûs* 1, no. 1.
Cole, Peter and Morgan, Jerry L.
    1975   *Syntax and Semantics. 3. Speech Acts*. New York: Academic Press.
Culler, Jonathan
    1975   *Structuralist Poetics*. Ithaca: Cornell University Press.
Davidson, D., and Harman, G.
    1972   *Semantics of Natural Language*. Dordrecht: Reidel.
Dijk, van, Teun A.
    1972a *Some Aspects of Text Grammars*. The Hague: Mouton.
    1972b *Beiträge zur generativen Poetik*. Munich: Bayerischer Schulbuch-
           Verlag.
    1974a "Models of Macro-Structures." Mimeograph.
    1974b "Action, Action Description and Narrative." *New Literary History* 5,
           no. 1 (1974–1975).
    1975   "Recalling and Summarizing Complex Discourses." Mimeograph.
    1976a *Complex Semantic Information Processing*. Workshop on Linguistic
           and Information Science, Stockholm, May 1976.
    1976b "Macro-Structures and Cognition." Twelfth Annual Carnegie Sym-
           posium on Cognition, Carnegie-Mellon University, Pittsburgh, May
           1976. Mimeograph.
    1976c "Pragmatics and Poetics." In van Dijk, ed., 1976.
    1977   *Text and Context*. New York: Longman.
Dijk, van, T. A., ed.
    1976   *Pragmatics of Language and Literature*. Amsterdam-Oxford: North
           Holland and American Elsevier.
Dressler, Wolfgang
    1972   *Einführung in die Textlinguistik*. Tübingen: Niemayer.
Eco, Umberto
    1962   *Opera aperta—Forma e indeterminazione nelle poetiche contem-
           poranee*. Milan: Bompiani. 4th ed., 1976 (contains the first version of
           Eco, 1966).
    1964   *Apocalittici e integrati*. Milan: Bompiani.
    1966   *Le poetiche di Joyce*. Milan: Bompiani. English tr., *The Aesthetics
           of Chaosmos*. Tulsa: Oklahoma University Press, forthcoming.
    1976   *A Theory of Semiotics*. Bloomington: Indiana University Press.

Erlich, Victor
1954   *Russian Formalism.* The Hague: Mouton.
Fillmore, Charles
1968   "The Case for Case." In *Universals in Linguistics Theory.* Edited by
       E. Bach and R. Harms. New York: Holt.
Feibleman, James K.
1946   *An Introduction to Peirce's Philosophy.* Cambridge: M.I.T. Press.
       2d ed., *An Introduction to the Philosophy of Charles S. Peirce,* 1970.
Fokkema, D. W., and Kunne-Ibsch, E.
1977   *Theories of Literature in the Twentieth Century.* London: Hurst.
Goffman, Erving
1974   *Frame Analysis.* New York: Harper.
Goudge, Thomas A.
1950   *The Thought of C. S. Peirce.* Toronto: University of Toronto Press.
Greimas, Algirdas J.
1966   *Sémantique Structurale.* Paris: Larousse.
1970   *Du Sens.* Paris: Seuil.
1973   "Les actants, les acteurs et les figures." In Chabrol, ed., 1973.
1975   "Des accidents dans les sciences dites humaines. *VS* 12.
1976   *Maupassant—La sémiotique du texte: exercices pratiques.* Paris:
       Seuil.
Greimas, A. J., and Rastier, François
1968   "The Interaction of Semiotic Constraints." *Yale French Studies* 41.
Grenlee, Douglas
1973   *Peirce's Concept of Sign.* The Hague: Mouton.
Grice, H. P.
1967   "Logic and Conversation." William James Lectures, Harvard Uni-
       versity (and in Cole and Morgan, eds., 1975).
Groupe d'Entrevernes
1977   *Signes et paraboles: sémiotique et texte évangélique.* Paris: Seuil.
Groupe μ
1970   *Rhétorique Générale.* Paris: Larousse.
Hawkes, Terence
1977   *Structuralism and Semiotics.* Berkeley and Los Angeles: University
       of California Press.
Hintikka, Jaakko
1962   *Knowledge and Belief.* Ithaca: Cornell University Press.
1967   "Individuals, Possible Worlds, and Epistemic Logic." *Noûs* 1,
       no. 1.
1969a "Semantics for Propositional Attitudes." In *Philosophical Logic.*
       Edited by J. Davis et al. Dordrecht: Reidel.
1969b "On the Logic of Perception." In *Models for Modalities.* Dordrecht:
       Reidel.
1970   "Knowledge, Belief and Logical Consequence." *Ajatus* 32 (revised
       version in J. M. E. Moravesik, ed., *Logic and Philosophy for Lin-
       guists.* The Hague: Mouton-Atlantic Highlands, Humanities Press,
       1974).

1973   *Logic, Language-Games and Information*. London: Oxford University Press.
Hirsch, Eric D., Jr.
1967   *Validity in Interpretation*. New Haven: Yale University Press.
Hjelmslev, Louis
1943   *Prolegomena to A Theory of Language*. Reprint ed. Madison: University of Wisconsin Press, 1961.
Hughes, G. E., and Cresswell, M. J.
1968   *An Introduction to Modal Logic*. London: Methuen.
Ihwe, Jens
1973   "Text-Grammars in the 'Study of Literature.' " In Petőfi and Rieser, eds., 1973.
Jakobson, Roman
1957   *Shifters, Verbal Categories, and the Russian Verb*. Russian Language Project, Department of Slavic Languages and Literatures, Harvard University.
1958   "Closing Statements: Linguistics and Poetics." In *Style in Language*. Edited by T. A. Sebeok. Cambridge: M.I.T. Press, 1960.
1970   *Main Trends in the Science of Language*. Reprint. New York: Harper, 1974.
Karttunen, Lauri
1969   "Discourse Referents." Preprint 70. International Conference on Computational Linguistics (COLING), Sånga—Säbry/Stockholm, 1969.
Kempson, Ruth M.
1975   *Presupposition and the Delimitation of Semantics*. Cambridge: Cambridge University Press.
Kerbrat-Orecchioni, C.
1976   "Problematique de l'isotopie." *Linguistique et sémiologie* 1.
Koch, Walter A.
1969   *Vom Morphem zum Textem*. Hildesheim: Olms.
1973   *Das Textem*. Hildesheim: Olms.
Koch, Walter A., ed.
1976   *Textsemiotik und strukturelle Rezptionstheorie*. Hildesheim: Olms.
Kripke, Saul
1971a   "Identity and Necessity." In *Identity and Individuation*. Edited by M. K. Munitz. New York: New York University Press.
1971b   "Semantical Considerations in Modal Logic," In Linsky, ed., 1971.
1972   "Naming and Necessity." In Davidson and Harman, eds., 1972.
Kristeva, Julia
1969   Σημειωτική—*Recherches pour une sémanalyse*. Paris: Seuil.
1970   *Le texte du roman*. The Hague: Mouton.
Lausberg, H.
1960   *Handbuch der literarischen Rhetorik*. Munich: Hueber.
Leech, Geoffrey
1974   *Semantics*. Harmondsworth: Penguin.

Lewis, David K.
  1968   "Counterpart Theory and Quantified Modal Logic." *The Journal of Philosophy* 65, no. 5.
  1970   "General Semantics." *Synthèse* 22 (and in Davidson and Harman, eds., 1972).
Linsky, Leonard, ed.
  1971   *Reference and Modality*. London: Oxford University Press.
Lotman, Ju. M.
  1970   *Struktura chudozestvennogo teksta*. Moscow.
Lyons, John
  1977   *Semantics*. Cambridge: Cambridge University Press.
Minsky, Marvin M.
  1974   "A Framework for Representing Knowledge." MIT Artificial Intelligence Laboratory. AI Memo 306.
Montague, Richard
  1968   "Pragmatics." In *Contemporary Philosophy: A Survey*. Edited by Raymond Klibansky. Florence: Nuova Italia.
  1974   *Formal Philosophy*. New Haven: Yale University Press.
Nida, Eugene A.
  1975   *Componential Analysis of Meaning*. The Hague: Mouton.
Pavel, Thomas G.
  1975   " 'Possible Worlds' in Literary Semantics." *Journal of Aesthetics and Art Criticism* 34, no. 2.
Peirce, Charles S.
  1931–1958   *Collected Papers*. Cambridge: Harvard University Press.
Petőfi, Janos S.
  1974   *Semantics, Pragmatics, Text Theory*. Urbino, Centro Internazionale di semiotica e linguistics. Working Papers, A, 36.
  1975   *Vers une théorie partielle du texte*. Hamburg: Helmut Buske.
  1976a "Lexicology, Encyclopaedic Knowledge, Theory of Text." *Cahiers de Lexicologie* (special issue edited by A. Zampolli) 22, no. 2.
  1976b "A Frame for Frames." *Proceedings of the Second Annual Meeting of the Berkeley Linguistic Society*, Berkeley, University of California.
  1976c "Structure and Function of the Grammatical Component of the Text-Structure World-Structure Theory." Workshop on the Formal Analysis of Natural Languages, Bad Homburg. Mimeograph.
  1976d *Some Remarks on the Grammatical Component of an Integrated Semiotic Theory of Texts*. University of Bielefeld. Mimeograph.
  s.d.   "A Formal Semiotic Text-Theory as an Integrated Theory of Natural Language." Mimeograph.
Petőfi, J. S., and Rieser, H. eds.
  1973   *Studies in Text-Grammar*. Dordrecht: Reidel.
Pike, Kenneth
  1964   "Discourse Analysis and Tagmeme Matrices." *Oceanic Linguistics* 3.
Plantinga, Alvin
  1974   *The Nature of Necessity*. London: Oxford University Press.

Prior, A. N.
    1962   "Possible worlds." *Philosophical Quarterly* 12, no. 46.
Putnam, Hillary
    1970   "Is Semantics Possible?" In *Language, Beliefs, and Metaphysics.*
            Edited by H. E. Kiefer and M. K. Munitz. Albany: State University
            of New York Press.
Quillian, Ross M.
    1968   "Semantic Memory." In *Semantic Information Processing.* Edited
            by Marvin Minsky. Cambridge: M.I.T. Press.
Quine, W. V. O.
    1951   "Two Dogmas of Empiricism." *Philosophical Review* 60 (and in
            From a Logical Point of View. Cambridge: Harvard University
            Press, 1953).
Rescher, Nicholas
    1973   "Possible Individuals, Trans-World Identity, and Quantified Modal
            Logic." *Noûs* 7, no. 4.
    1974   "Leibniz and the Evaluation of Possible Worlds." *Studies in Modality
            —American Philosophical Quarterly.* Monograph Series, 8.
Riffaterre, Michael
    1971   *Essais de stylistique structurale.* Paris: Flammarion.
    1973   "The Self-Sufficient Text." *Diacritics* (fall 1973).
    1974   "The Poetic Function of Intertextual Humour." *Romanic Review*
            65, no. 4.
Salanitro, Niccolò
    1969   *Peirce e i problemi dell'interpretazione.* Rome: Silva.
Sceglov, Yu. K., and Zolkovskij, A. K.
    1971   "Kopisaniyu smisla svyaznogo teksta" (Institut russkogo yazyka
            ANNSSSR, predvaritel'nye publikatsii). Vypusk 22. English tr.,
            "Towards a 'Theme-(Expression Devices)-Text' Model of Literary
            Structure." *Russian Poetics in Translation* 1, 1975. ("Generating the
            Literary Text")
Schank, Roger C.
    1975   *Conceptual Information Processing.* Amsterdam-New York: North-
            Holland and American Elsevier.
Schmidt, Siegfred J.
    1973   "Texttheorie/Pragmalinguistik." In *Lexicon der germanistischen
            Linguistik.* Edited by H. P. Althaus, H. Heune and H. E. Wiegand.
            Tübingen: Niemayer.
    1976   "Towards a Pragmatic Interpretation of Fictionality." In van Dijk,
            ed., 1976.
Scholes, Robert, and Kellogg, Robert
    1966   *The Nature of Narrative.* New York: Oxford University Press.
Searle, John
    1958   "Proper Names." *Mind* 67.
    1969   *Speech Acts.* London-New York: Cambridge University Press.
Segre, Cesare
    1974   "Analisi del racconto, logica narrativa e tempo." In *Le strutture e il
            tempo.* Turin: Einaudi.

Sini, Carlo
    1976   "Le relazioni triadiche dei segni e le categorie faneroscopiche di
            Peirce." *VS* 15.
Stalnaker, Robert C.
    1970   "Pragmatics." *Synthèse* 22.
    1976   "Possible Worlds." *Noûs* 10.
Thomason, Richmond
    1974   "Introduction" to Montague, 1974.
Titzmann, Manfred
    1977   *Strukturale Textanalyse*. Munich: Fink.
Todorov, Tzvetan
    1966   "Les catégories du récit littéraire." *Communications* 8.
    1969   *Grammaire du Décameron*. The Hague: Mouton.
Vaina, Lucia
    1976   *Lecture logico-mathematique de la narration*. Institut de Recherches
            Ethnologiques et Dialectales, Bucuresti. Ph.D. dissertation, Sorbonne
            IV.
    1977   "Les mondes possibles du texte." *VS* 17.
Valesio, Paolo
    1977   *Novantiqua: Rhetorics as a Contemporary Theory*. Manuscript.
Volli, Ugo
    1973   "Referential Semantics and Pragmatics of Natural Language." *VS* 4.
    1978   "Mondi possibili, logica, semiotica." *VS* 19.
Winston, Patrick H.
    1977   *Artificial Intelligence*. Reading, Mass.: Addison-Wesley.
Wykoff, William
    1970   "Semiosis and Infinite Regressus." *Semiotica* 2, no. 1.